LIFE OF GUSTAVE DORÈ

Illustrated Enlarged

SPECIAL EDITION

Life of Gustave Dorè
Illustrated Enlarged Special Edition

Written by Blanchard Jerrold
Cover design by Mark Bussler

Copyright © 2021 Inecom, LLC.
All Rights Reserved

No parts of this book may be reproduced or broadcast in any
way without written permission from Inecom, LLC.

www.CGRpublishing.com

Best of Gustave Doré Volume 1:
Illustrations from History's Most
Versatile Artist

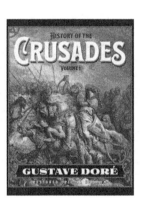

History of the Crusades
Volumes 1 & 2: Gustave Doré
Restored Special Edition

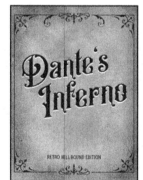

Dante's Inferno
Retro Hell-Bound Edition

GUSTAVE DORÉ.

TABLE OF CONTENTS

Part I

Chapter 1 – Strasburg 10
Chapter 2 – Doré's Early Success 41
Chapter 3 – The Labours of Hercules 58
Chapter 4 – La Sainte Russie – Rabelais 67
Chapter 5 - The Wandering Jew and Balzac's
"Contes Drolatiques" 88
Chapter 6 – The Boy of Genius 106
Chapter 7 – Dante 126
Chapter 8 – From "The Inferno" to "Don Quixote" 141
Chapter 9 – The Bible, Paradise Lost, Fontaine's Fables . . 154
Chapter 10 – "London: A Pilgrimage" 169
Chapter 11 – Gustave Doré in London 209
Chapter 12 - Doré's Shakespeare 235

Part II

Chapter 13 – Doré the Painter 250
Chapter 14 – Early Paintings 260
Chapter 15 – 1860 to 1870 277
Chapter 16 – "Christ Leaving the Prætorium " 300
Chapter 17 – The Siege of Paris 316
Chapter 18 – The Completion of "Christ
Leaving the Prætorium " 325
Chapter 19 – 1870 to 1880 339
Chapter 20 – Doré the Friend and Companion 354
Chapter 21 – The Death of Madame Doré 381
Chapter 22 – Gustave Doré the Sculptor 392
Chapter 23 – Death 401
Chapter 24 – The Funeral 419
Chapter 25 – The Crowning Work 435
Chapter 26 - Appendix 449

LIFE OF GUSTAVE DORÉ.

WITH ONE HUNDRED AND THIRTY-EIGHT ILLUSTRATIONS

FROM ORIGINAL DRAWINGS BY DORÉ.

BY THE LATE

BLANCHARD JERROLD

(*Officier de l'Instruction Publique, de France*).

LONDON:

W. H. ALLEN & CO., Ltd., 13 WATERLOO PLACE. S.W.

PUBLISHERS TO THE INDIA OFFICE.

1891.

(*All rights reserved.*)

PREFACE.

I have divided the Life of Gustave Doré into two parts, because, as an artist, he lived two distinct, separate, and, indeed, antagonistic lives. The illustrator, or the draughtsman, and the painter were separate warring individualities. From his earliest years Doré's ambition was to be a painter. His first plaything was a pencil; but he was still a very little child when he got his first brush and box of colours, and painted a hen Veronese green. As a boy the extravagance of his fancy expressed itself, as the reader will find, in caricatures, and grotesque pictures of observations of his home-surroundings. But as he approached manhood, the power he felt to be within him took a bolder and a loftier flight.

He had not left college when he began to paint in downright earnest. It was at first the pastime of the illustrator; but as the years went by, and when he found that his contemporaries who applauded the productions of his pencil almost refused to look at the results of his brush, the painter became the imperious master, and the illustrator was lowered to the servant who supplied his wants. Doré was obstinate. People smiled upon his drawings and tossed their heads at his canvases. He only became the more sternly resolved that they should not favour the illustrator at the expense of the painter.

In the following pages will be found a chronicle of the struggle between the blithe and free-minded Doré of early manhood, and the morbidly sensitive and sad painter of the great pictures which are to be found chiefly in the Doré Gallery in Bond Street.

The first and the happier man is presented to the reader in the first Part; the greater but the gloomier being figures throughout the second.

The life of the steady worker has, as a rule, few vicissitudes. The striking personal incidents of Doré's career might be briefly told in a few pages. He was not an actor in any public event. His days were passed in walks from home to the studio, and from the studio home again, with occasional holidays in London, the Alps, the Vosges, or the Pyrennees. A golden chain of unbroken labour, a temperate, uneventful life of dreams, few but warm friends who lay near his heart, a little society and much music—here is the life of the gracious man of genius whom it was my privilege to know and love. I have only filled in the simple design, in the hope that a closer

PREFACE. vii

knowledge of the man as he lived day by day may help to keep his personal memory green. In my task I have been assisted by many who were close comrades or fast friends. M. Taine, Colonel Ernest Doré, his beloved brother and heir, Dr. Joseph Michel, his nephew, Colonel Teesdale, the Rev. Canon F. K. Harford, whom he loved as a brother, M. Paul Balloz, editor of the " Moniteur," M. Templier, of the firm of Hachette & Co., Miss Amelia B. Edwards, Messrs. Fairless and Beeforth, the enterprising proprietors of the Doré Gallery, MM. Quantin, M. Pisan, his friend and most skilful engraver, M. Octave Uzanne, the editor of " Le Livre"; and humbler folk, as his good servant Françoise, who assisted at his birth and at his death, Jean, his faithful studio assistant, and Jean's honest successor: to these, one and all, I am indebted for traits, notes and anecdotes, letters and sketches, tendered generously in aid of my task, and I here tender them my sincere and cordial thanks.

The illustrations which accompany the text are chiefly unpublished sketches from my own collection, and those of Dr. Michel and the Rev. Canon F. K. Harford. They are not presented as samples of Gustave Doré's finished work. They illustrate his progress as a draughtsman even from his nursery, his methods of working, the manner in which he made pictorial notes of ideas as they arose in his mind. I believe that his rough outlines of pictures, his studies of groups, his trials of effects, and various compositions for the telling of the idea he wanted to present, will be found interesting. These illustrations may, in short, be regarded in the light of a scrap-book raisonné.

[NOTE.—This Preface was written by the late Blanchard Jerrold, in 1884. It is published as he wrote it, because it explains the sources whence the information was derived and the spirit in which the book is written.]

THE LIFE OF GUSTAVE DORÉ.

CHAPTER I.

L'OURS ET SON PETIT. (*Drawn by Doré in his Tenth Year—1842.*)

THE life of Gustave Doré was, on the whole, a very happy one; for his day-dreams never ceased, and he never lost the power of working them out, until he lay cold in death. To the end he had all his faculties at his command. The eye was never dimmed, the hand never failed in cunning. From his early infancy to the eve of his dissolution, the rich gifts of nature that lay within him were his obedient servants, albeit he tasked them to the utmost. To work was his delight. He was impelled, as a child, by a blind, irresistible impulse—what he called an "éblouissement d'enfant"—to give form to his dreams, to his humour, to his fancy, even to his most extravagant passing whims. It was perhaps his misfortune that he was never able to discipline his forces; but, wild as they remained to the end, they did such service as cannot be got out of academies.

They were wild because they were over-crowded; they were luxuriant to excess; as the tangled primæval forest is wild, one beauty overlapping the other, the flowers covering the stalwart trunk, the feathery ground-growths masking and overpowering the blossoms of many tints, and then overhead, masses of matted creepers wrestling with sinewy arms of kingly forest-trees. Such variety and confusion of natural power had Doré. He had the vision of a poet, the tongue of a wit and humorist, the heart of a woman, and the courage of a hero. These qualities were expressed in his manly bearing, his commanding presence when he was earnest, his flashing and pensive eyes, and in the sweetness of the smooth, regular face.

In the main the life of Gustave Doré was, I repeat, happy; but he had his sorrows, and his disappointments. As time wore on he felt with increasing bitterness the injustice of his countrymen towards him; and even the generous enthusiasm of his welcome in England, and the extraordinary success his gallery in Bond Street commanded, could not chase away the shadows that stretched over the atelier in the Rue Bayard from the Salon opposite. The affection and good-will of strangers may soothe the spirit that has been bruised at home; but it cannot heal the wound.

We begin with the happy days; with the fair, bright-eyed gamin (Paul Gustave Doré), who was born "coiffé" (with a caul), as his nurse related. The event took place in the Rue Bleue, at Strasburg, within the shadows of the Cathedral, on the 6th of January in the year 1832. While still a little child—about the year 1841—young Doré went with the family to Bourg, in the Department of l'Ain, whither his father, as Chief Government Engineer for the Department of the Ain, had

1 *

LIFE OF GUSTAVE DORÉ.

been transferred. These two residences of his earliest youth gave a distinct direction and colour to Doré's imagination. The weird old cathedral, with its fantastic lines and gloomy corners, was the cradle of those visions which sank into his mind, and formed a storehouse whence his inexhaustible imagination drew scores of pictures of the Middle Ages, that had in them the very soul and spirit of the past. Afterwards, at Bourg, he became the daily observer of mountain and pine forest, of those rugged and sublime scenes in which his genius revelled to the end. It may be said that in the mountainous part of Alsace, called the Dreystein, his earliest impressions of Nature were made. The deep gloom of a pine forest, and the suggestive lights and shadows of an ancient cathedral, were the studies of his infancy. In some notes of his life, in the possession of his nephew Dr. Michel, Doré has acknowledged the importance of these first visions: "These spectacles were my first vivid impressions. They were those *éblouissements d'enfant* which determine a taste." He revelled in the forest, over such ruins as the Convent of Sainte-Odile, by Barr, and all the weird scenes he came upon as he followed the footsteps of his father, who was charged with the construction of the line between Lyons and Geneva. He became familiar with the valley of the

Rhone and with the Jura mountains. He even accompanied his father to the bleak, rocky regions of Savoy and to the Oberland, with his pencil cut at both ends in his pocket. He was not stirred by such soft sylvan byeways as Corot loved. He was "cribbed, cabined, and confined" in leafy lanes, and by wayside episodes of rural life. He was inspired by *la grande nature*; and in quest of the mighty aspects of the wilderness, the dark ravine, the towering hills, "hearsed" with pines, the play-places of the Titans, where tumbled rock and roaring waters made mighty solitudes over which the lonely eagle soared. He would climb, a solitary traveller with pencil and paper, to the most daring heights, a song upon his lip, and his quick, searching, dreaming eyes, gathering in effects and details—the sweep of the clouds and their shadows, as well as the tints of the moss at his feet. The boy was father of the man. The child's eyes opened, I repeat, upon the grandeur of Strasburg Cathedral, and they were fed in infancy on the congenial beauties of the Vosges and the Alps. To his latest days these early impressions remained strong in him, and his last excursions out of Paris were to the Righi Vaudois and the Pyrennees.

He could not tell you when he began to draw. His old nurse, Françoise, has described him as never without a pencil after his fourth year. As an infant he would crawl out of his crib into his mother's room, and cry, "*Maman, je ne sais ce que j'ai.*" He could not sleep. "*Je veux crayonner*," he would add, and then go back to bed with a pencil in his hand. Abd-el-Kadr was the hero of his childhood. In his fifth year he made drawings of the taking of Constantine, and the Battle of Mazagran, the vigour and movement in which struck all who saw them with amazement. Pencil and paper came naturally to his baby hands. He would beg his father's friends to cut his pencil for him, and to cut it at both ends, because it would last longer. The desire to give form to his thoughts and observations was irresistible. Here is a specimen of his baby pencillings, treasured by his mother. It is in a child's copy-book, crumpled and dog's-eared. Doré was only eleven years old when he borrowed lithographic stones at Ceyzeriat, a little town near Bourg, and executed several drawings. The interior of a school is one of the earliest. There were also humorous representations of the statue to Bichat, and of a famous slide dear to the boys of Bourg. The early tendency of the young artist towards the grotesque is apparent in these boyish works. The first drawings he sent

to the Salon were studies made of the romantic scenery and the peasants near his home.

His father watched his artistic proclivities with anger and alarm. He wanted the boy to go to the Polytechnic school, and become an engineer like himself, or an artillery officer. In the hope of diverting the child from art, he surrounded him with ingenious toys; but instead of playing with them, Gustave sketched them in his copy-books. In despair the father bought a violin; but this only revealed another artistic faculty. Young Gustave soon astonished his friends and neighbours by the verve and fidelity with which he caught the airs the military bands played in the public gardens at Strasburg. He was not only a born painter but a born musician. The father despaired of the precocious genius, who covered the walls, shutters, and windows with his scrawls, and whose fiddling could be heard all over the house. Even the child's grey blouse was used as canvas to paint upon!

Gustave was a tiresome and wilful boy, full of tricks and espiègleries. His first exploit was with a *montgolfière*, a fire-balloon. He constructed one himself, and, having lighted under it some cotton steeped in spirits, let it go. It fell in a barn full of hay, which it fired, and caused a dangerous con-

LIFE OF GUSTAVE DORÉ.

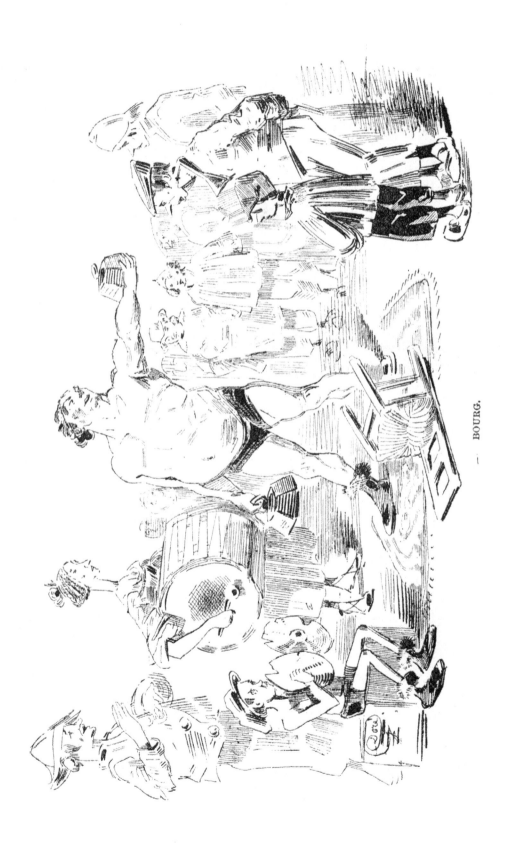

— BOURG.

flagration. Doré used to say that the severe scolding his father administered so impressed him, that he could never after look without aversion at a balloon. He was a great kite-flyer also; and it was the remembrance of his child's passion for this amusement that made his mother love the drawing he made, as a man, (and which hung in her bed-room,) of a host of upturned faces looking at a kite. But it was as a gymnast that Gustave at play was most remarkable. His leap-frog and his jumps and climbings attracted the notice of his professor of gymnastics before he left Strasburg for Bourg. His daring at rope-climbing, the giant's stride, at wrestling and swimming, and even as a rider, was remarkable. He used to fix a book between the toes of his feet, and by a jerk throw it over his head. He would take a piece of cane, about a foot in length, and, holding it between his hands, jump through the ring made by it and his body. He could lie upon his back, with his arms across his chest, and rise to his feet without the use of his hands. He was fond of walking through marshy districts, on stilts, in the fashion of the Landes; and he would indulge in humorous imitations of the stork and heron. He was a good skater, and an intrepid swimmer. Both at Strasburg and Bourg colleges he was a ringleader of mischievous tricks and practical jokes; and his power of caricature made him a little person to be feared by all. His nurse and governess had many difficulties with the strange, bright-witted, self-willed youngster, who would insist upon being conducted outside the Strasburg fortifications that he might observe the changing features of the country. In his sixth year he would rise with the first flush of dawn, and watch the light steal from spire to spire of his native city. He was a great observer of the clouds; and drew and coloured them with his baby fingers. He would dream and watch in the meadows for the hour together; and the "Prairie" is a picture which is but a reminiscence of the days when he lay close to the tall gentian, the white narcissus, and the abounding grasses of his beloved Alsatian fields. He revelled in the thickets of wild raspberry and rose, and lay enraptured upon the brown banks of moss. The broad brow, and the searching, pensive eye, were the only physical infantile indications of the great artist, who was developing mind and body in the wayward manner of genius. He could not get his fill of pleasure out of the natural beauties which encompassed his nursery. If he revelled in the gracious flowers of the meadow, he had kindly glances for the stone-crop and wolf's-claw moss of the moun-

STRASBURG—BOURG.

BOURG.

tain. He would often talk to himself, as he walked and observed; and his old friends bear in mind how, after surveying scenes intently, he would suddenly clasp his forehead with his hands, as though the emotion were too much for him.

Thus in his child-life he betrayed, in every act and thought, the precocity of his intelligence, and the acuteness and avidity of his power of observation. Before he could write he could copy the letters of any book he read. He could sketch accurately what he had seen; he could play on his little fiddle any air he had heard. When he was only six years old he talked to his father of his resolution to be an artist; and the opposition of his parent, albeit he was compelled for a time to bow to it, and even to give a solemn promise that he would cease from sketching and give himself wholly up to his lessons, only whetted his appetite to use the faculty which he felt to be supreme within him. He could not choose but study Nature, and strive to reproduce her grandeur and her solemn beauties.

He has related in the few biographical notes he left behind him how that, when he was only seven years of age, he stole away from his father's country-house at Barr, one sunny and balmy evening in early summer, in order that he might revel in a sunset, from the lovely and impressive heights where the shrine of Sainte Odile is situated. The dreaming little wayfarer walked on and on, from beauty to beauty. The glow of the sunset deepened; the stars twinkled, the moon rose, the peasants looked at him as they closed their cottage-doors for the night. Still enraptured, the lad trudged on, gazing towards the ruins crowning the Hochfeld plateau. From the height before him he would see the most splendid view of the Vosges, and Strasburg in the distance! But, in the dark forest of St. Odile, fairly worn-out, the unbreeched wanderer lay down, beneath the ruins called the Trois Pierres, and fell asleep. He soon awoke with a start, and thought of his mother, and the distress she would be in at his absence. The moaning of the trees seemed to reproach him; he read ominous signs in the trooping clouds; and then the roar of the wind in the valley sounded to him like a pack of wolves approaching.

Convinced that the pack was gaining upon him, he leapt to his feet, and ran homewards as fast as his short legs would carry him. He had not gone far when the notes of horns, the barking of dogs, and the sound of familiar voices reached him. There were neighbours and servants of the family in search of him. His father scolded him severely; but his

LIFE OF GUSTAVE DORÉ.

BOURG

mother took him to her heart, and covered him with kisses.

Doré used to relate the episodes of this truant expedition with real enjoyment. It was fixed, to the minutest detail, in his memory. It was followed by a family council, at which Gustave was sternly lectured by his father, on the evils to which his propensity for sketching and picture-making had already led him. He had neglected his lessons, and had incurred the displeasure of his parents, his governess, and all who were in authority over him. Finally he was asked to promise that he would never transgress again with his pencil. He promised, and then asked leave to withdraw. He returned in half an hour with a spirited sketch, executed on the fly-leaf of a Latin dictionary, of his family, servants, and neighbours, as they appeared when in search of him.

His father said, "But this is no proof that you will keep your promise."

"It's the only proof I can give," Gustave boldly answered.

The father insisted, however, that his son should prepare to enter the Polytechnic school, that he might be able to earn his living. Doré senior loved both literature and art, but he would not hear of art as a bread-winner. The consequence to Gustave Doré was a series of stormy scenes at home, throughout his school-days, at his lack of zeal over his mathematical and classical studies. His mother, however, soothed him, and her rare intelligence enabled her to see that there was nothing for it but to give freedom to Gustave's genius; even while she obeyed her husband's commands, and kept pencils and colours out of the boy's hands. He fretted under the restraint; and it was only when it became evident his health was suffering, that his art-tools were returned to him. His mother even went the length of allowing him to attend a drawing academy, held by a Mademoiselle Jeannot. Doré was set to copy a Niobe. Instead of proceeding with his task, he preferred studying from the life, and drew the countenances of the young ladies of the academy. When reproved he sketched the Niobe, but he surrounded the figure with fantastic illustrations of her adventures. He wrote also and illustrated, about this time, a "Voyage Infernal" in one of his copy-books.

At the Strasburg and Bourg colleges, Gustave was by no means considered a tractable collegian. He was wayward, mischievous, and insubordinate. The caricature of the interior of a class-room, executed at this time, is an instance at once of his skill as a

SCHOOL INTERIORS. (DRAWN BY DORÉ WHILE A SCHOOL-BOY AT BOURG.)

STRASBURG.—BOURG.

LA NOCE. AN EARLY CARICATURE BY DORÉ PRINTED AT CEYZERIAT.

boy-artist and of his idleness as a student. He chafed under discipline. He boldly argued with his masters. His school-fellows soon looked up to him as the champion of independence; and the weak adored him as one who was always ready to fight for his comrades. The elder boys, at Bourg I presume, jealous of his popularity, once organised a coalition against him. A thrashing was decided upon by a band of the upper forms. Doré stood up alone, before his assailants, and very soon sent them flying. From that hour his sway was undisputed. His word became law, and his mandates were punctually obeyed, not only in consequence of his muscular strength and his athletic science, but because of the superiority of his judgment and the unswerving truthfulness of his nature. Matches at foot-ball, and the construction of snow-giants, were his favourite winter games. His delight was to roll huge masses of snow to the spot where the giant was to be erected. To him, naturally, fell the part of sculptor of the monster, who generally had coals for eyes, and assumed a rakish aspect, with the help of an old hat and a clay pipe. In the end the monster was pelted with snow-balls until he fell.

Doré delighted, as a boy, in the malicious snowballing of inoffensive people in the streets of Strasburg. He was the leader of the snow-fights at the college; and in one of these, when he led the attack, he received a wound in the forehead (the scar of which never passed away) from a treacherous foe who had loaded his snow-ball with a stone. Doré had caricatured the young rascal, and offended him.

His love of caricature, at this period, was spiced with more than a pinch of malice, as he fully admitted afterwards. The young are cruel. He would draw laughter from men's foibles, follies, and misfortunes. It was want of thought, and not want of heart. And when he remembered his early ill-nature, he looked back with distress and sorrow upon it. As a man he disliked satirical designs; and he was glad to be quit of them when he left the *Journal Amusant*.

Having one day met one of his teachers, fishing, he detected him buying a fine trout of a poor labourer. This teacher was in the habit of boasting of his successes with his rod. Doré saw the whole history of it at a glance, and made a sketch of the incident, and passed it about among his comrades. The master caught sight of it, and punished the delinquent by sending him to the college-prison—an attic, littered with reams of paper.

The prisoner set to work, and tore the entire store

LIFE OF GUSTAVE DORÉ.

EARLY STUDIES OF HEADS.

into small scraps. When he had made an immense pile, he threw the bits like snow-flakes in showers into the street. The wind was blowing, and in a short time the passers-by thought the roofs were covered with snow. Thus the streets far and wide became horribly littered. When the author of this freak was discovered, he was laughing in his delight; while, below, the head-master was endeavouring to pacify the indignant crowd at the college-gates.

Doré was summoned by the master who had locked him up, to explain his fresh misconduct. He answered: "You said I should never be good till it snowed in June. I merely wished to prove to you, this being the month of June, that I was willing to be good, by causing a fall of snow."

The tender chord in the gamin's nature was struck now and again in his school-days. He loved, as I have remarked, to wander in the old cathedral, and even to look at the poor pictures in it.* While he was a boy in Strasburg a poor old artist, M. Meikle, presented the cathedral with a large picture ("St. Paul before the Areopagus"), which became the laughing-stock of

---

* "They are detestable," he used to say afterwards, "yet each time I return to my native town I pay a visit to these croûtes."

LIFE OF GUSTAVE DORÉ.

CALYPSO INCONSOLABLE.

the townsfolk. Even the young collegians scoffed. Doré was only nine years of age, but he felt a strong sympathy for the aged artist, albeit he was unknown to him. He resolved to pay him a visit. He called, and he talked about the picture so cleverly that the old man burst into tears. Terrified at the effect he had produced on so venerable a person, the boy fairly took to his heels; and it was with difficulty he could be comforted with the assurance that he had not hurt the artist, but, on the contrary, had pleased him.

As we have seen, Doré had already acquired a reputation among his friends and neighbours as a designer and draughtsman, when, in his ninth year, his father sent him to the Bourg Lyceum. He began by a travesty of Telemachus in his copy-book, which lies before me. His masters understood the force and bent of his mind, and they humoured the little student who could not fix his attention on the curriculum of the school; but whose vivid intelligence flew to the heart of things, and gathered in knowledge in its own original way. It is related of him that, on one occasion, in the place of the lesson which had been set him, he handed in his translation of the murder of Clitus in the shape of a drawing of the murder, true in all its

"VULCAN TERRASSA CLYTUS." (A grotesque drawing in one of Doré's school books.)

accessories. The professor gave Doré the first place in his class. It was by promises that, if he obtained certain prizes at the Lyceum, he should go with his father to Paris, that the impetuous young artist was at length induced to apply himself to his lessons. He took his prizes, and claimed his reward.

We have an account of his arrival in Paris in his own words:— *

"In September 1847, my parents, being called to Paris by serious affairs, took me with them. Our stay was not to exceed three weeks. The idea of returning to the country after seeing this centre of light and learning troubled me much. I thought over the means of remaining; for I had already resolved, in spite of the stout resistance of my parents, on being an artist. They destined me, like my two brothers, for the Polytechnic School.

"One day I had passed the shop-window of Aubert and Philippon, on the Place de la Bourse; and, on returning to the hotel, I made some caricatures in the style of those I had seen in the window. While my parents were out, I went to the publishers, and showed them my sketches. M. Philippon looked kindly and attentively at these beginnings, questioned

---

* Biographical notes in the possession of Dr. Michel.

me as to my position, and sent me back to my parents with a letter inviting them to call upon him. They went; and M. Philippon, using all his persuasive eloquence, prevailed upon them to leave me in Paris,

telling them that he could at once make use of my talent, and pay me for my work.

"From that day it was decided that I might devote myself to my drawing. Had it not been for

STRASBURG.—BOURG.

THE VENDOR OF ASS'S MILK, BOURG

the good nature of M. Philippon (I say good nature, for what I could do then was very childish and incorrect), I should have gone back to the depths of my province, and lost several years there."

And so, a child in years, his pockets full of quaint bits of humour rendered with an original facile touch, destined to be known half over the world before he was twenty, Gustave Doré turned his back upon the little country town where he had dreamt his first dream of glory, and took his mother's hand and entered Paris with his brothers, Ernest and Emile, the latter of whom was about to be placed in the Polytechnic school.*

A few months later Paris was in the throes of the Revolution of 1848; and the young artist watched the tumult, the fighting, the barricades, the grim processions—not as a partisan, but as a student. He attributed his early mastery of crowds to the careful observation of Paris streets in that year; as well as to his boyish enthusiasm over the exploits of Abd-el-Kadr.

* He is now lieutenant-colonel of artillery. The eldest brother, Ernest, has made considerable reputation as a composer.

CHAPTER II.

BOURG.

DORÉ'S EARLY SUCCESSES.

According to Colonel Doré, his brother Gustave was introduced to M. Philippon by the landlord of the house in the Rue Neuve St. Paul, where the Doré family took up their quarters, on their arrival in Paris after the death of the father in 1848. The fact appears to be, that Doré was in Paris some months before his family settled there; and that he was under the roof of his mother's friend, Madame Herouville, when he was entered at the Charlemagne. Philippon, manager of the *Journal pour Rire*, knew what he was about. The caricatures submitted to him by the young artist were remarkable, especially a series on the Labours of Hercules. The result was that Philippon undertook to give work to Gustave to the extent of 5,000 francs per annum.*

At the Charlemagne, Doré had for companion, among others, M. Edmond About, whom he was to illustrate a few years later. We may dismiss his career at his college in a few words. He continued his Bourg method. He demonstrated that he had mastered his lessons, with his pencil. His professor of history would say:

"Doré, step up to the board, and draw a portrait of Nero, that these gentlemen may fully understand what I have been saying."

---

* Doré remained the grateful friend of his early patron until his death (Jan. 26, 1862).

DORÉ'S EARLY SUCCESSES.

BOURG PEASANT WOMAN

When he had completed his "rhetorique," the artist withdrew from college life, without waiting to receive his diploma of bachelor of letters; for by this time he was besieged by the publishers, and he set to work with Bertall and Philippon upon illustrated papers, Pierre Bry's cheap romances, indeed, upon all kinds of popular literature, and, in his teens, became one of the illustrators of the day. In his teens he ranked with Grandville, Bertall, Gavarni, and Daumier, and we see traces of all these in his early work. His "Labours of Hercules," the legend of Polydore

Marasquin, and other ideas of his own—as the *Ménagerie Parisienne*—cast prodigally over the pages of the *Journal pour Rire*, the *Journal pour Tous*, the *Musée Franco-Anglais*, established by him in

DORÉ'S EARLY SUCCESSES.

conjunction with M. Philippon, the *Monde Illustré*, spread his name and fame far and wide.

It has been remarked that French caricaturists generally are utterly destitute of truth, good taste, and moderation, and that their pleasantries have no point. This, like nearly all sweeping assertions, is incorrect. Take Cham as an instance. He was true to nature, and his faculty as a caricaturist and a humorist who reviewed the passing hour with a running pencil, was inexhaustible. In the main he was moderate and in good taste, that is, in good French taste, for we must not estimate taste by the narrow British standard. He had twenty ideas for every one Leech put forth. He had not Leech's delicacy, nor his grace, nor his sense of beauty. But the ideas crowded into Cham's pictorial weekly reviews are extraordinary for their brightness and their infinite variety.

Doré, however, was a caricaturist who seldom raised a laugh. Indescribable grimness and hardness appear in his comic drawings. Perhaps his earliest, with which he entered Paris—the "Labours of Hercules"—have more genuine fun in them, both in idea and execution, than any he drew afterwards. He was whimsically suggestive and extravagant, and he was a wit on paper, as well as in conversation; but a hearty laugh was rarely raised by his pencil.

When we were together at Boulogne in 1855, a person of suspicious aspect would press his attentions upon us, offering us advantageous places to see the Queen land, and seats in the Imperial train. While he talked, Doré, who was at his table, drew the picture which appears on the opposite page, and tossed it to me. It was a portrait of our bore, as a satyr—a brute to be avoided. Doré was a pictorial satirist rather than a caricaturist. In his extravagant drawings, as in his conversation, happy and striking ideas turned up plentifully. His pictorial commentaries and interpretations often resemble, in the ideas which they embody, the suggestiveness of Kenny Meadows, whose feeble and faulty drawing could never do justice to his conceptions. In Meadows's Shakspeare, and in his contributions to *Punch*, there are scores of dainty thoughts and poetic interpretations of his text, quite in the vein of Doré. But Doré had the artistic power, the habit of systematic observation; in short, all that poor Meadows lacked to make an artist. If Doré kept clear of academic training, he was severe master to himself.

He remarked to Mr. Hamerton, for instance, that he had systematically educated his memory. He

DORÉ'S EARLY SUCCESSES.

observed things, as he walked, with the intention of remembering all he could of them. "He told me," says Mr. Hamerton, "how he had discovered a way by dissecting a subject, by division and subdivision, so as to lay it all by in good order, and find the details, when he wanted them, in their right places. By long practice of this kind he can carry away with him a wonderful quantity of facts, and has even tested his memory by a contest with a photographic apparatus, a friend of his photographing a cathedral, Doré *looking* at it, and drawing it afterwards at home whilst his friend developed the photograph. On comparing the two, drawing and photograph, it appeared (much to the astonishment of the photographer) that Doré had omitted no detail of importance, a few minor inaccuracies being alone discoverable."

Doré remarked that the cultivation of the artistic memory might be carried to any extent, provided the artist observed methodically. He measured and learned the relative proportions of great masses; then he divided and subdivided them, and then filled in each subdivision, thus fixing the minutest details in his memory. To the cultivation of artistic memory, it should be observed, the learner must bring ripe knowledge of nature, and of men and things. We have seen that Doré obtained his profound and never-

DORE'S EARLY SUCCESSES.

BOURG

failing command of the mountain and the pine forest, and of Gothic architecture, in his child-

BOURG MARKET WOMEN

hood; and its light was a potent aid to the cultivation of his memory. By his familiarity with every detail of one Gothic cathedral, he was able to apply his memory with unerring effect to all Gothic work; and when he entered a pine forest or a ravine, he came with a full mastery of the forms of the tree and mountain, the sweep of the valley, the dark recesses of the wooded wilderness, the mighty Alpine wreckage of the storm. By his unflagging observation and his trained memory, he got within his skull the secrets of grand effects, and the food on which his imagination could journey into the vast Unknown. He was familiar with the swell and twist and whirl of the thunder-cloud. He was master of the weird vagaries of the moonlight. His genius rode the storm, and snatched with his pencil the many awful mysteries of the deep—"le grand vague," as he called it.

I was riding through Windsor forest one day. I begged him to stop the carriage and make some studies of the venerable trees which rear their historic heads in that ancient place.

"No, no," he answered, without taking his eyes from the landscape. "I have plenty of collodion in my head."

He proved it afterwards by several *tours de force*

when we were on our travels through the streets of London.

It was the physical and intellectual impetuosity of Doré's organization that enabled him to produce at a high speed. Mr. Hamerton remarks on this quality of the artist, that in his review of the Salon of 1863, he had said that Doré's published designs might already be " counted by thousands," and then somewhat hesitatingly added, " perhaps even by tens of thousands." Later, being in Doré's studio, he asked him how many drawings he had published—a question that was never a pleasant one to the artist, who believed that he had suffered by exaggerations of his fecundity. But he answered, on being pressed, that in the month of May, 1862, a friend had made an estimate, and had counted up to forty-four thousand. This, of course, was an exaggeration.

Thousands of these illustrations were crude pen and pencil scratches of his boyhood. He produced upwards of four hundred during his first year on the *Journal pour Rire*. They were cast forth without a second thought. They were replies to publishers who crowded his doorway, cast out in the pursuit of gain by a young man who had suddenly found a fortune at the point of his pencil; but if we

go over the mass in cold blood, and with every disposition to be sharply critical, we shall find in them—as I have already endeavoured to show by a few examples scattered through these pages—hosts of brilliant ideas, fantastic, extravagant, coarse, cruelly sarcastic, grimly humorous, horrible by turns, but still revealing a poet and a humorist, who, if not a master of the springs of laughter, often touched the source of tears.

M. Emile de Girardin, with his one idea a day, was intellectually a very slow coach in comparison with the beardless artist in the Rue Saint-Dominique, who bounded along his table from subject to subject, with an idea for any one of the rows of wood blocks before him. His outlines were often inaccurate; he had no time for the niceties of perspective; there were innumerable points of ignorance, incongruities, and disproportions in these drawings made while the publishers' messengers were waiting, but in them there were thoughts enough to fill the lives of twenty artists moving at the ordinary speed. Between Doré and Ingres, or Meissonnier, or Gérome, comparison is impossible. One perfect outline engaged the intellect of the creator of *La Source* for years; but the impatient imagination of Doré hastened to realise ideas, passing over correctness of details with something like disdain.

The rate of production is no test of the merit of the artist. The sluggish, mediocre man delights in endeavouring to discredit the famous creator, whose heat and strength leave him no rest, but who is tortured with the perpetual desire to put out all that he feels within him. Doré was mercilessly attacked because he pretended to paint as well as to illustrate, to etch as well as to mould his conceptions in clay. He was the universal artist, who laid all methods and materials under contribution. "Universality," Hegel teaches us, "is readily confused with emptiness, because it is a freedom from all that is particular." The painters said Doré could not paint, and this in the presence of his "Family of Acrobats," his "Neophyte," his "Rizzio," his "Francesca," his powerful poetic landscapes and his series of grand Biblical scenes. The sculptors admitted that he had ideas in his groups, but he was not "sculpturesque;" and the wielders of the dry point denied him the gifts of an etcher, even when contemplating the plate of his "Neophyte" and his portrait of his friend Rossini. I called upon him in the Rue Saint-Dominique, and found him up in one of the garrets, where

DORÉ'S EARLY SUCCESSES.

he had hidden himself to give his mind wholly up to his etching. He had discarded several plates as not wholly satisfactory, and was at work upon another.

"*Bon jour, mon ami*," he said, without raising his eyes from his plate. "You see, I have the patience of the ox." It was only the seventh plate that he let pass. So far as his countrymen were concerned, it was in vain. They would have him keep to his illustrations.

DRAWING IN ONE OF DORÉ'S FIRST SCHOOL-BOOKS, OF "LE GRAND CHAR D'ENFER," ILLUSTRATING HIS "VOYAGE INFERNAL."

CHAPTER III.

THE LABOURS OF HERCULES.

Gustave Doré made his first formal appearance before the world in a small album (one of the Jabot series),

THE LABOURS OF HERCULES.

published by Aubert & Co., of the Place de la Bourse.* The publishers introduced the artist in a brief preface:—

" 'The Labours of Hercules,' have been designed, drawn, and lithographed by an artist fifteen years of age, who has taught himself drawing without a master, and without classical studies. It has appeared to us that this is not the least curious fact about this original album, and we have desired to cite it here, not only in order to specially interest the public in the works of this young draughtsman, but also to mark the point of departure of M. Doré, whom we believe to be destined to take distinguished rank in art.

"M. Doré's second album will be executed in pencil, and will appear in the course of February.

"AUBERT & CIE."

If his countrymen, in after years, declined to give Gustave Doré a hearty welcome and high place as a painter, at least they acknowledged him at once when he presented his earliest designs to them. He was frankly accepted, before he was out of his boyhood,

* *Les Travaux d'Hercule.* Par G. Doré. Paris: Chez Aubert et Cie, Place de la Bourse, 29.

both as a caricaturist and an illustrator of marked and surprising originality. He was put in a line with Cham and Topfer, who were the stars of the Jabot series, and he at once vindicated his right to the honour.

The subject of the "Labours of Hercules" came naturally to the schoolboy, who had just been crammed with Greek myths. This, the most popular of the myths of the Æolian race, remains the most interesting of them in our modern schools. Doré's caricatures of the "Twelve Labours" are full of genuine fun. The album is a pictorial burlesque. Eurystheus is a monarch of the type which the late Frank Matthews made familiar to the British stage. Hercules is such a strong man as we have seen in a booth at a country fair. The myth is travestied to the taste of the French public of 1848.

The muscular monster starts on his expedition against the Nemean lion. The kingly beast springs at Hercules, but Hercules, "uniting skill with strength," catches him by the tail and swings him above his head with the swiftness of a teetotum. The freedom and spirit of this drawing are astonishing, as the work of a boy of fifteen. So tremendous is the force of Hercules, that he flings the lion a distance of two leagues, and he is driven into the ground like

THE LABOURS OF HERCULES.

a thunderbolt. The pace of the lion's gyrations, under the impetus of the arm of Hercules, is described thus:

Then Hercules carries the lion off in triumph to a tanner, that his skin may be dressed, and that he may wear it " as a winter paletot." He receives the mayor of the commune of Nemea by the way. Hercules, in a chair of state, and the rustic mayor and his son, are admirable bits of the pure grotesque. In the interminable *queue* of country folk flocking to the tanner's yard to see the Nemean lion's skin, there is another early indication of that power of drawing crowds reaching from the foreground to the uttermost distance, in which Doré was afterwards unsurpassed. Hercules, in his new paletot, makes his bow to his tyrannical cousin Eurystheus. The King, who has a bet with Hercules, fearing he may lose it, commands him to go forth and destroy the Lernæan Hydra, a great water-serpent, which was ravaging the country of Lerna, in Argolis, destroying both men and cattle. He finds, by the jumping of innumerable frogs, that he is in marshy land. Then he sinks into a bog, and as he scrambles out of it, soaked and covered with weeds, he comes upon the hydra. His fight with the monster, the heads flying in the air, the terrified rustics mounted on stilts, as in the Landes, when he shows the headless hydra to them; and, finally, their rejoicings over their deliverer, are full of a free and frank humour not apparent in Doré's later grotesque work. The country folk pouring out wine in honour of Hercules, and the majestic pose of the mighty slayer, are capital bits of extravagance. Throughout the album the rustics are full of character. The boy-artist had studied them in his provincial home at Bourg. The learned men discoursing on the body of the slain hydra are also capital. They are subtly conceived, freely and firmly pencilled.

THE LABOURS OF HERCULES.

Eurystheus is in abject fear about his wager with his cousin. Laying his trembling hand upon the shoulder of Hercules, he points to the Erymanthian boar, wasting the corn-fields. Hercules goes forth, drags the animal by the tail, and then bears him in his arms into the presence of his cousin, who faints with fright.

The race after the hind of Cerynea, the destruction of the Centaurs, the scattering of the Stymphalian birds—the latter being brought home to Eurystheus to make a rich fricassée (which disagrees with him), the securing of the girdle of Hippolyte, including her muff and cashmere shawl, the driving of the oxen of Geryones to Mycenæ, and the carrying off the golden apples of the Hesperides, lead up to the cleansing of the stables of Augeas, and the marriage of the hero to Hebe,

marchande de limonade, and goddess of youth. With the apples of Hesperides Madame Eurystheus makes marmalade. Hercules, who returns penniless from one of his labours, sits to a painter as he appeared

THE LABOURS OF HERCULES.

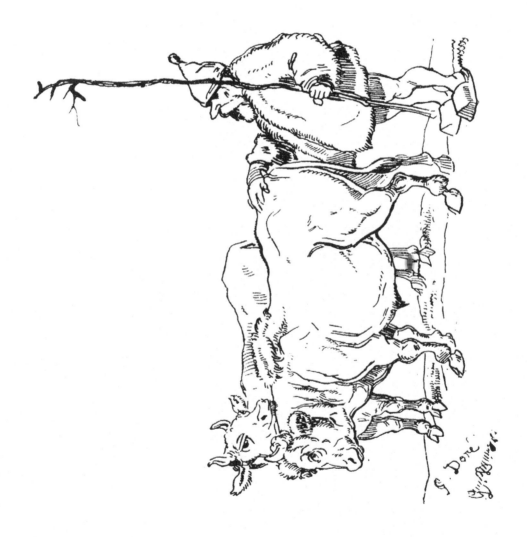

slaying the Nemean lion. In the end, Eurystheus admits that he has lost his bet, and pays for a bottle of beer, like a man.

CHAPTER IV.

LA SAINTE RUSSIE.—RABELAIS.

Domestically, Doré's lines were cast in pleasant places. Before he was a man he was settled in the old and spacious house in the Rue Saint Dominique, in the St. Germain quarter, which had been built by his maternal grandfather. His mother, as we shall see, watched over him with an all-engrossing love and pride till she died; and the faithful Françoise, who had received him in her lap when he was born, was by his bedside when he breathed his last.*

In the Rue St. Dominique, and in a small studio in the Rue Monsieur le Prince, Doré spent the early years of his life as an artist. He was methodical in the distribution of his time. His friend and fellow-

---

* This faithful servant has been in the Doré family fifty-four years. Her portrait, by her master, is in the Doré Gallery in Bond Street.

LIFE OF GUSTAVE DORÉ.

traveller in Spain, Italy, and the Tyrol, Paul Dalloz, writes of him: "His life was one of extreme simplicity, like that of men who are jealous of all invasions of their working hours. *Il se claquemurait* in his work, shutting out any avenue to his mind by which other pre-occupations might have entered it. But he kept a way open for friendship, and I shall always remember as an honour the affection he bore me."* He was up betimes, and he would be found at home, working at the long table where he executed his drawings, before six on summer mornings. He went into the fashionable world, to the first nights at the theatres, to musical parties, and to official receptions and balls; but these diversions—even the wild gaieties of the Caveau—were never permitted to interfere with his art. A glass of water before leaving was his refreshment at rout or ball. He retired early, that he might be at his wood blocks under the sweet morning light. His afternoons he gave to painting in his studio. He produced amazing numbers of drawings, never neglecting to make his appearance in the Salon, first with pen-and-ink sketches, and then with ambitious canvasses. It was not that he was impatient

* Letter to B. J. Paris, July 10th, 1883.

to gain wealth and fortune, but that he could not choose but give form to the crowded images and ideas of his impulsive imagination. Like the poet who lisped in numbers for the numbers came, Doré drew, as I have shown, from his babyhood, because pictures came, and would come, to the point of his pencil. His impatience to express his ideas in pictorial forms cannot be better illustrated than by the observation of his nurse Françoise, that, as a child, he would have his pencil cut at both ends.

We have seen that he arrived in Paris, on the death of his father, just in time to see the Revolution of February. He observed the tumult of the streets; hosts of men moving under strong excitement; the picturesque attitudes and groupings of street-corner politicians, and the processions of revolutionary bands bearing dead men, through the wintry night, and all the grim picturesqueness of barricades. The scenes left indelible impressions on his mind. He was of no party. He would not suffer political questions to get a hold on him. But his early experiences of the violent days of 1848 left in him a hatred of extreme politicians, which would burst out again and again when a political discussion arose in his presence. He chafed under any influence that tended to draw him, even for an hour, from his art.

LA SAINTE RUSSIE.

But Gustave Doré was an ardent patriot. He may have been the most German of French painters; he was assuredly a Frenchman to the backbone in sentiment and in love of country. His appearance was Alsatian: his heart was as French as Hugo's. We find him deeply moved by the excesses of the revolutionists of 1848, in the first place; and by the Crimean war, in the second. His "Battle of the Alma" in the Salon first gave him prominence as a painter; and a scathing pictorial satire, conceived and wholly executed by himself in his twenty-first year, in the midst of confusing masses of weekly work for the illustrated papers, showed the measure of his scorn for the enemy of France.

This pictorial satire consists of 500 drawings,* which describe grotesquely the dark and cruel history

of Russia. The title consists of figures wielding the

---

* *Histoire Dramatique, Pittoresque, et Caricaturale de la Sainte Russie.* Commentée et illustrée de 500 magnifiques gravures par Gustave Doré, gravées sur bois par toute la nouvelle École sous la direction generale de Sotain. Prix 4 francs. Paris: I. Bry Ainé, 27, Rue Guénégaud. 1854.

knout, and victims dropping red-hot tears. A black smudge describes the origin of the history of Russia, lost in the darkness of antiquity. Then we learn thus—

that the first era of this history presents nothing of interest. But, the chroniclers report, about the year 11 or 11½, the beautiful bear Polnor was seduced by the charms of a young walrus, and their offspring was the first Russian. Other chroniclers pretend that the female was a penguin and not a walrus. The consequence is a free fight among the learned opponents, during which the air is thick with books, pens, and inkstands. A blank page represents the absolute barrenness of the next century.

The Russians adored Peroun, god of peace, of the harvest, of armies, of friendship, of commerce, of war, of honour, of glory, of falsehood, of orthodoxy, and other virtues and vices. He was, in short, a thorough god-of-all-work, and his priests invented the knout and other invigorating and persuasive instruments. Peroun is drawn, seated upon a rock, with an iron mask covering his face, and Russians wildly dancing round him.

The ancient Russians made much of their women, and permitted themselves to be led about by them. We find two lazy and hairy ruffians lounging in a heavy cart, drawn by their wives. Then the nation becomes tired of being governed merely by its brutal instincts, and proceeds to elect a chief. After the fight which ensues, and in which heads and limbs fly about in every direction, it is discovered that there is not a whole man left to undertake the office of governor. They have to beg two or three men of a neighbouring state. Three brothers are sent, on approval, in a closed cart. On opening it, the Russians find that Rurik has managed to despatch his two brothers *en route*. He is, therefore, just the man to be autocrat of sacred Russia!

Rurik is no sooner placed on the throne than he marches on Constantinople. He returns to die of colic. His successor, Igor, marches on Constantinople, and returns to Novgorod to die like his predecessor. Oleg, the third monarch, also marches on Constantinople, and goes home to perish like Igor and

Oleg, of " Czarina colica." In this vein the history continues; the caricatures of Muscovite heads, the grotesque duels, the battle-pieces being full of humour. Matters come to a state of horrible perplexity. Four usurpers succeed one another upon one battle-field. The branches of the " Czarial families " get intermixed, lost, and annihilated, and anarchy succeeds. It is described in one of Doré's matchless hosts of fighting men.

After the storm a calm ensues. Jaroslaw reigns, until his subjects become tired of peace and goodwill. They divert themselves by cutting at one

LA SAINTE RUSSIE.

another, under a "tariff of mutilations." A rich Boyard can allow himself the luxury of decapitating a couple of his fellow-countrymen now and then; but the economical have to calculate to a leg or a finger. On the death of Jaroslaw, five pretenders fight for the throne, until five helmets are all that remain of them.

The throne passes from one occupant to another much in the same way. Crime, violence, brutality, run their course through the history, interspersed with extravagant incidents. The burlesque story is kept up with unflagging verve, and the most biting satire, and with touches of pure humour. Valdimir reviewing the candidates for his hand (p. 57) is a perfect burlesque monarch. The invasion of the Tartar hordes is worthy of Richard Doyle. There are horrible episodes in the history, which serve their purpose in it as a fierce satire, but which are revolting to look upon as the bloody deeds of Ivan the Terrible. A man hacked open from chin to bowels with a copious stream of blood pouring from him, victims impaled upon lances, like larks upon a spit, Ivan's dinner, with tortured men or the hanging a baby by way of amusement, are not within our range of the humorous.

We turn away, with the historians of Ivan, in disgust. We are bidden to take off our hats and cast our eyes in the direction of Peter the Great. The tell-tale variety of head-gear is capital:—

Peter, mending shoes, sawing, and performing other kinds of manual labour, is presented to us. These occupations prepare him to rule, and he issues a ukase by which he suppresses all his predecessors, and the history of Russia. Before him, Russia is a blank. In order to show that his ideas are liberal, and that men should rise by merit, he mounts guard at his own palace gate.

The drawing of Peter, in his dream, hidden behind the North Pole, scraping out the map of Europe, with a night-light placed upon the globe to guide him, is a fantastic form of humour that was congenial to Doré. Then the artist's pencil stops, refusing to enter upon the coarseness and the horrors of the history of Russia after Peter the Great; in spite of the remonstrances of M. Bry, the publisher. It is at length agreed that an immense vine-leaf shall cover the reign of Catherine. At her funeral, her coffin is borne to the grave by walking crosses, inscribed "Ci git l'Amitié," "Ci git l'Honneur," "Ci git la Conscience," &c.

We pass on to the reign of Nicholas. The figure of Nicholas is the master-stroke of the book. The man is majestic, imposing; but his head is that of a mannikin. At a reception on a gala-night at the theatre, on looking out upon the broad expanse of Europe, the figure of the Czar is superb. The survey of Europe, through the wrong end of the telescope, Nicholas insisting that it is the right end since he wills it so, is a grim and cutting caricature.

The satire closes with the Crimean War, all to the disadvantage of the Russians, and to the glory of France, who is represented thrusting 1812 down Muscovite throats. The drawing of two French troopers, reading the news of the latest victory,* is full of spirit and observation.

The studies of the heads of sycophantic historians of the reign of Joan the Terrible are good.

* See page 54.

LIFE OF GUSTAVE DORÉ.

Mr. Hamerton remarks, with truth, that Doré, as a designer on wood, had at least half-a-dozen styles of his own—styles adapted to the varieties of subjects and of treatment he had in hand. For instance, his manner in the head and tail pieces to his *Don Quixote*, and, again, in his *Contes Drôlatiques*, is quite apart from that of the *Wandering Jew*, *Dante*, and the *Ancient Mariner*, and all the foregoing are distinct from those of his *Rabelais*, and his fine and delicate illustrations to Tennyson and Ariosto. It is, moreover, true that he discovered several new resources in wood-engraving, and formed a school in Paris of which he was justly proud, and which he cultivated with great care, going the round of his engravers' workshops in the afternoons, in the interval between his *déjeuner* and his return to his painting. In his earlier work on wood, the lights and shadows are violent. When he departed from his strong effects, he was apt to be feeble or *fade*. He appeared in his early time to have no sense of many gradations in light and shade. Whether this was due to the immense quantity of rough designs he was called upon to do for Bry, Philippon, Aubert, and others, and much of it at night, whereby delicacy was sacrificed and the eye became sensitive only to sharp contrasts, it is difficult to determine. But it is indisputable that, after a time, he was on his guard against the abuse of his sense of the supernatural in its sombre aspects; and that he came, relieved, out of his black shadows into the sun and under the stars, as Dante issued from his Inferno, through his Purgatory, to the white light of his Paradise.*

In the *Contes Drôlatiques*, as in the *Rabelais*, there is what has been called the true old Middle-Age spirit. It is difficult to believe that these 425 designs were by the hand of a young man, living in Paris in our own time, and taking his pleasure among the Bohemians of the Rue des Martyrs. But here, as in *Rabelais*, and afterwards in the *Inferno*, Doré caught the spirit of his author, and identified himself with it. He was Rabelaisian with Rabelais and Balzac, Dantesque with Dante, and he laughed and revelled with children in the tales of Perrault. From the grim visions of the great Florentine he passed with joyful relief to Little Red Riding Hood.

The works of François Rabelais,† edited by the

---

* M. Pisan was perhaps his most distinguished interpreter on wood.

† *Œuvres de François Rabelais, Precédées d'une Notice Historique sur la Vie et les Ouvrages de Rabelais, augmentée de Nouveaux Documents,* par P. L. Jacob, Bibliophile. *Nouvelle édition, revue sur les meilleurs textes et particulièrement sur les travaux de J. Le Duchat et de S. De L'Aulnaye, éclaircie quant à l'Orthographe et la Ponctuation, et accompagnée de Notes succinctes et d'un Glossaire,* par Louis Barré,

"bibliophile Jacob" and Louis Barré, and illustrated by Gustave Doré, was first published in 1854—in Doré's twenty-second year. Doré, tired of the *pot-au-feu* labours to which he had been restricted by the pressing demands of the proprietors of illustrated papers, found in the pages of Rabelais a work entirely suited to his mood and to his power. It was to him a wholly congenial labour, in which he revelled; and in which he was encouraged by the "bibliophile Jacob." But the publishers would none of it. In the artist's extravagant humour they could not perceive a spirit profoundly Rabelaisian. The wild imagination was shapeless, inarticulate confusion to them. But the "bibliophile" estimated at their right value the wealth of humour, of thought, and creative force in the enthusiastic young artist who had thoroughly saturated his mind with his author, and presented him pictorially as no artist had presented him before. At length M. J. Bry was persuaded by the book-worm to give the volume a trial in the cheapest possible form; and it was brought out in the roughest manner upon something very like tea-paper, by the publisher, who dedicated it "à mon ami, Gustave Doré."

Ancien Professeur de Philosophie. Illustrations par Gustave Doré. Paris: J. Bry aimé, 27 Rue Guénégaud.

LA SAINTE RUSSIE.—RABELAIS.

The "gentil et ingénieux Rabelais," the beggar monk whom Jean du Bellay called to his table, commanding his servants to respect him as "le plus gentil esprit et le plus docte personnage de la république des lettres," the roystering, humorous, and learned bon-vivant, with his Middle-Age surroundings, and above all, with his marvellous Middle-Age romances of Gargantua and Pantagruel, set Doré's imagination aflame. He felt that he held the rich and rare subject on which he might embroider immortal work. He fell to with ardour that left him no rest, until he had given the final touch to *la dive Bouteille*.* The frontispiece presents to the reader Rabelais—the head modelled with fine touches—holding the open page of the life of the great Gargantua father of Pantagruel, with Montaigne, Molière, Scarron, Voltaire, Lesage, and a host of smaller literary fry down to the Romanticists of 1830, pressing round to copy it. Montaigne is writing an essay, Molière is showing Tartufe and Scapin, and Lesage presents Gil Blas. When we open the book we find Doré's brightest work. His imagination is fresh, his spirit is jocund, there is the breath of youth in the lively scenes. It is sensuous and ribald even to the level of the author. Nothing

* He published three editions of *Rabelais*, the first, with only a few illustrations, and lastly his splendid folio edition.

is toned down nor avoided. The young Bohemian revels in the wit, the humour, the irony, and in the rough and Middle-Age flavours these have from the hand of the learned Hellenist, the omnivorous student, and the riotous boon companion rolled into one. Doré appears to miss the philosophic depths of Rabelais; he has hardly, to use Rabelais' phrase, broken the bone and sucked the marrow; but his piercing imagination, aided by his familiarity with the externals of the Middle Ages, his high spirits and his sharp enjoyment of the humorous, the fantastic, the weird and grotesque scenes and figures unfolded in the story of Pantagruel and Panurge, in Grangousier and Gargamelle, to the Sonnante and Frère Jean des Entommeures, has enabled him to revive, to fortify, and to explain the marvellous imagination and variety of the great Tourangin. Doré's command over a confused multitude is nowhere more striking than in Panurge's victory over the army of the Dipsodes, the revels interrupted by the birth of Gargantua, Gargantua in his bath and at nurse, the Inn of the Cave-Peinte, and Gargantua going to mass. The studies of heads are of extraordinary power and variety. Trippa, Messire Oudart, Homenaz, Albian Camar "maistre éditue" of the Isle Sonnante, Grippeminaud, Gagne-beaucoup, Panurge and Frère Jean are rare studies of character; indeed, the series of heads in Doré's *Rabelais* dispose, once and for all, of the remark of one of his serious critics, that his creations were mere shadows.

THE INFANT GARGANTUA.

His gothic piles, his old streets, and the crowds with which he peopled them, are the creation of a mind that had observed much and deeply. His visions have their roots in the earth. Panurge and Frère Jean, Grippeminaud and Gagne-beaucoup are grotesque presentments of human character. They are freshest in the original edition of *Rabelais*; but they are elaborated to the utmost, and are masterly studies, in the later edition which Doré issued on a costlier plan when his fame could command publishers for his most ambitious and costly creations. In this first rough edition we have the charm of the sketch— the idea thrown down in the true, *insouciant* Rabelaisian spirit of the *gamin de génie*, as Theophile Gautier loved to call his young friend. In the more ambitious and laboured work we have patience, with craftsmanship, and a soberer and discreeter spirit. On the whole I prefer the inspired work of the *gamin*, with its daring, its riot, and its reckless abuses of undisciplined strength. It is an orgy of the imagination where battles and executions, dancings and hangings, bloodshed and banquetting, love-making and terrors of the night, the wilderness and the storm, make one confounding hurly-burly; but it is such pictorial thinking, jesting, and rollicking as the eye of the curé of Meudon would have twinkled over, and for which he would have called the artist to his side to make merry in very gratitude and gladness.

BOURG.

CHAPTER V.

"THE WANDERING JEW."—BALZAC'S "CONTES DRÔLATIQUES." *

THE public had been struck by the remarkable illustrations of *Rabelais* drawn by a boy, almost unknown, save to one or two proprietors of illustrated papers. There was thought in every line of his pencil. Crude and harsh, and often grotesque to the utmost verge of extravagance, his figures had a meaning and a duty to perform in illustration of

* *La Légende du Juif Errant.* Compositions et Dessins par GUSTAVE DORÉ, gravés au bois par F. Rouget, O. Jahrer, et I. Gauchard. Imprimés par J. Best. Poème avec prologue et epilogue par PAUL DUPONT. Préface et notice bibliographique par Paul Lacroix (Bibliophile Jacob), avec Ballade de Béranger mise en musique par Ernest Doré. Paris: Michel Levy Frères. 1856.

LIFE OF GUSTAVE DORÉ.

the text, nevertheless. Fond of violent motion; of trees bent low by the hurricane; of dark gable ends; of strongly-marked features and well-defined muscles; given to the humorous in the drawing rather than in the idea—Gustave Doré at once commanded attention. He was puffed and abused in one breath. The followers of the masters in vogue—all men, in fact, tied to well-known *ateliers*—laughed at him. Of no school, he could not be of any worth. Such was the immediate verdict of the Paris critics; but the public recorded a very different decision. Loiterers along the quays might be seen poring over the pages of Doré's *Rabelais*—for it is before the book-boxes of the Quai Voltaire that the true Parisian critics are to be found. He became accepted—outside and away from the Academy—as an original artist, destined to prove to the French people that there may be true and noble interpretations of nature in minds ignorant of acadamic severities—strangers to the *École des Beaux Arts*—unconscious of the necessity of a journey to Rome.

The Wandering Jew was the second ambitious work Doré gave to the world. He had paintings stored in his studio, but of these the public knew nothing. If this legend of the Wandering Jew, as told by Doré, had not substantial claims to our attention as a work of art, it would still command notice as the most pretentious specimen of wood-engraving that has been put forth by French engravers for many years. Indeed, the "bibliophile Jacob" deigned to introduce the plates—not only with a survey of the "Legend of the Wandering Jew," but also with a sketch of wood-engraving from the block of Saint Christopher, dated 1423, down to the completion of the engraving of Doré's great drawings. Nor are the bibliophile's remarks on the value of wood-engravings, as faithfully reproducing the free strokes of the artist's pencil, without value. MM. Rouget, Jahrer, Gauchard, and others, who engraved the drawings, strove to produce effects that were to exhibit the utmost capability of the material. Here was an attempt to create a revolution in Art, by proof that all the fine gradations of colour shown in engraving on metal and lithograph, might be equally well rendered on boxwood. The subject was well chosen. It was one in which the young illustrator of Rabelais might find a broad field for his bold conceptions—his startling effects of light and shade—his intrepid dealings with form—his close studies of the human figure.

The legend of the Wandering Jew has retained its hold wherever superstition has lingered, or still lingers, in Europe. It was the great legend of the

Middle Ages. Its origin is lost in the mists that close upon the past beyond the thirteenth century. Still it presses through, here and there, in the history of superstitions, but more especially in those of Germany, as a story worthy of all respect. The "bibliophile" surmises that this majestic allegory was originally imagined by some preacher or poet, who put forth the Wandering Jew as the type of his scattered nation—scattered, but indestructible!

The Jews had crucified the Son of God (says the "bibliophile")—had insulted Him in His last hour. Their punishment was told by Christ Himself, who wept over doomed Jerusalem. They were expelled from their country after the destruction of the city of Titus, and dispersed over the Roman Empire. Since that time we have watched the strange destinies of a scattered people—surviving their dispersion, and preserving, in the midst of other nations, their nationality, the characteristics of their race, their laws, and their religion, in the teeth of persecutions to which they have been universally subjected. Outraged, despoiled, driven from place to place, they have never wholly lost heart. They change their refuge with resignation; they obstinately return to former resorts; they brave anew dangers from which they have just escaped; they affect poverty in order to become rich

"THE WANDERING JEW."

with impunity; they hide themselves to escape outrage and punishment; they will not, however, put off their costume nor alter their peculiar aspects, because they persist in remaining Jews till the coming of the Messiah. Such has been the fate of the Jews, according to the "bibliophile"; and such is the condition of the Wandering Jew, according to the legend.

It is the Wandering Jew, as this great type, with whom Doré dealt, leaving to the "bibliophile" the task of tracing back the legend—of noticing the disputes of theologians on the identity of the Jew with Malchus, whose ear was cut off by St. Peter in the Garden of Olives, or of his confusion with the impenitent thief. The artist took the broad and obvious signification of the story as it has come down to us. His view may be compared rather with that of Béranger, in the poem accompanying the plates—and in the modern and graceful epilogue of Pierre Dupont—than with the cold classical precision and the love of fact for which the "bibliophile's" preface is chiefly remarkable. Thus, the first plate presents the Crucifixion; and here the daring of the artist's imagination becomes at once apparent. The central figure is that of the Saviour bearing the Cross, and bearing it with superhuman might. Crowded about this grand figure are men, women, and children—all wondrously human by contrast. They stretch in unbroken crowds up the dim hill. Some are lying about the awful spot, others are idling by the way. And then the mob winds from the distance into the foreground. Here a chubby little Israelite is perched upon the parental shoulders; there brawny guards, all laughing, elbow their way past, Jewesses looking carelessly on. In the left-hand corner is the gable-end of a house in deep gloom. A rough, dirty, uncombed man, with a crisp beard, a boot in one hand and a shoemaker's tool in the other, has come out to see the procession go by. He stares defyingly at the Saviour, who turns towards him, and, it is evident, would speed him on his awful pilgrimage. Above the Jew's head is the sign, "*A la Botte Judaïque.*" The power with which the scene is grouped—the impressive reality given to it by trivial realities—even the cur barking at the Saviour's feet—are the emanations of a rich and reverential imagination. They are part of the secret of the success which is coming to the artist. Here speaks one who thinks for himself. He puts down a scene as it presents itself to his mind's eye, not as he imagines Titian or Vandyke would have rendered it.

The second plate discovers the Wandering Jew already far on his journey. His hair is white; his blanched beard flows to his waist. Heavily leaning

"THE WANDERING JEW."

upon his staff, and clutching his bag of gold, with a storm beating upon his head, on a lonely road, hemmed in with rocks, he pauses at a wayside cross, about which the trees bend low before the tempest. The distance, with the faintly-seen steeple, is a masterly effort of light and shade, that has all the force of Rembrandt's etchings. The third scene shows the humour of the artist. The Wandering Jew, passing through the streets of Brabant (and how picturesque are the old, angular wooden houses!) is surrounded by a crowd of citizens and citizens' children.

> Jamais ils n'avaient vu
> Un homme si barbu.

The group of fat old citizens, with their quaint, dimpled children, and the company of soldiers penetrating an awfully dark street on the right, but all turning back to look at the wondrous old man, are ideas most happily rendered. Then there are weird thoughts here and there. For instance, one *bourgeois*, riding by upon his ass, has stopped close to the Jew to examine him attentively, while his animal, taking advantage of his proximity to the old man's beard, has caught a clump of it between his jaws. Even the strolling geese have waddled from the gutter, and are

LIFE OF GUSTAVE DORÉ.

cackling at the strange sight. But perhaps the finest conception in the series is the scene (and it is grand for its half-defined, its mystic meanings) where the Jew, walking upon the waters, sees the reflection of the Crucifixion in the waves. His eyes are riveted upon the revelation. He hurries forward, but the picture dances before him, an unutterable horror. The church-yard scene has the same power; but here the Crucifixion, half made out, floats over the old man's head in majestic masses of cloud. The Jew wanders, unharmed, through battle-fields; and in one of these experiences Doré took up the legend. The battle going forward in the distance is a very remarkable tangle of fighting men, excellent for the variety of its animation; but the foreground where the Jew stands almost paddling in blood is one of Doré's unfortunate exaggerations. It is a nightmare: a bit of realism which degrades instead of enforcing the story. A man, with both arms cut off, is fighting still, by holding his sword-hilt in his mouth. Legs, arms, and trunks lie bleeding on all sides. Two amputated arms are actually fencing in the air. The trunk of a man sitting in a pool of blood is aiming a last arrow at the foe, and two bleeding hearts smoke in the central point of the picture, through which, with staff and money-bag firmly clutched, the very

"THE WANDERING JEW."

old Wanderer goes on his way unharmed. These horrors are redeemed only by two or three touches. For instance, the plump old monk kneeling in the midst of the wounded on the Jew's path, and holding up a crucifix to a dying soldier, is a happy thought.

Let us pass to where the Jew traverses a vast wilderness. An anaconda hangs from a tree overhead, and dangles its fangs close to the Wanderer's ears. He steps between the coils of a boa; crocodiles open their jaws before him; the hippotamus sniffs at him; and the lion, afar off upon a high rock, looks disdainfully down like a king upon him. This is the last experience of the Wanderer which Doré treated—except the closing scene.

I can compare this scene—for its terrors, for the extraordinary power of invention manifested in it, and for its audacity—only to some of those old Flemish pictures, teeming with figures, that have startled many a tourist in the gallery at Antwerp. From the right comes a flood of light, bearing angels upon its rays: not plump, draped angels, but creatures something thinner than skeletons—the next thing to immaterial essences—blowing trumpets. The gloom is deep over the earth, yet in the darkness you can perceive countless hosts of shrouded forms rising from the grave. A mother's hand reaches down for her rising child.

LIFE OF GUSTAVE DORÉ.

In the foreground bones are flying together, and the Jew sits solitary—an awfully old man—with the last trump sounding in his ear. Look steadfastly through the gloom, and you will see packed hosts ascending from the earth: examine the foreground, and you will find it peopled with devils. There is a gap in the earth from which flames are spurting, and demons are dragging forward the wicked to tumble them into it. So tough is the contest, that one imp has stretched a sinner's leg out to twice its natural length. Then there are all kinds of costumes peeping from under the shrouds that are in the half-distance only; it is, in short, a strange and confusing scene—very powerful, very daring in conception, and full of ideas.

The skill and artistic feeling with which the engravers realised Doré's original pencilling was remarkable. The work was a revelation of the highest power of wood-engraving; it was also another revelation of the young artist's original, but untamed and impatient spirit.

The *Légende* was subsequently reprinted in the *Magasin Pittoresque*; and two editions of it have appeared in England.

Doré's drawings of this period, wherein he was said to have created a Middle Age of his own, were in many respects his most original and imaginative creations.

BALZAC'S "CONTES DRÔLATIQUES."

The method adopted by the young artist in Balzac's *Contes Drôlatiques*,* was that best adapted for swift and striking execution. The drawings are picked out of a black ground with touches of white. There are few, if any, half tints. There is no delicacy. The effects are dazzling; for instance, in the Fair Imperia,

BALZAC WRITING THE "CONTES DRÔLATIQUES."

where the figure is picked out of the black with pure strokes and dots of white. Here the method is adapted excellently to the result sought—that of bewitching the young priest; but in many of the designs

* *Les Contes Drôlatiques*, etc. Par le Sieur de Balzac. Illustrée de 425 dessins par Gustave Doré. Paris: Garnier Frères, 6 Rue des Saints Pères.

THE PHYSICIANS AND SURGEONS.

the hard effect is that of light upon metal. It tells, however, with the happiest results when fantastic Gothic architecture is to be realised, as in the Château d'Azay. There is, however, more drawing here than in many of the designs; there is, indeed, in most of the weird, Middle-Age architecture, out of which Doré's imagination twisted so many essentially true, if exaggerated scenes. Le Chastel du Bonhomme Bruyn is an example. In spirit, it is true, as we find it in the leaning tourelles, the confused piles of buildings, the sharp spires and crestings of open metal-work, which abound in the *Contes Drôlatiques*.

Then the studies of heads, the grotesquely stately High Constable, the cunning face of Avenelles the advocate, the monks scampering down the hill, and even jumping from the windows to see what their brother Amador has brought from the castle, Guillaume Tournebouche, le Vieux par-Chemins (a face that strongly resembles Cruikshank's Fagin); these and others might be cited as imaginative heads and scenes, based on keen observation. The men are not every-day men, they are of the land of dreams; but the dreamer is one who has observed deeply and keenly among his fellows. Take Monseigneur Hugon de Sennecterre, aged 93, as an example; or the group of physicians and master surgeons—the latter being a

LIFE OF GUSTAVE DORÉ.

MONSEIGNEUR HUGON DE SENNECTERRE, AGED 93

good example of Doré's rough, free manner, and of the play of his imagination in its most grotesque mood.

Never was an artist provided with text more entirely adapted to his genius than Doré, when, in his earliest manhood, his eye wandered over the pages of *Rabelais*, *The Legend of the Wandering Jew*, and the *Contes Drôlatiques*; and he never more happily nor completely manifested his various powers than in

THE FAIR IMPERIA.

these works. They were extraordinary successes, which, in a few years, made him famous throughout Europe, as the most suggestive illustrator of his time. He illuminated his text, he added humour to the author, and threw fresh light upon his meaning, and this with all the spirit of youth. As he worked, he improved. Compare the *Rabelais* with the *Wandering Jew*; the advance, albeit they were produced in rapid succession, is marked. The workmanship in the latter is varied, skilful, careful, and, above all, original throughout. Doré had discovered a new method of producing effects upon wood. In the *Wandering Jew* his blocks have the fine lines and the depth of tone of Rembrandt etchings. In the *Contes Drôlatiques* we perceive the power which is apparent in rough forms in the *Rabelais*, intensified and disciplined unconsciously by practice. Balzac's *esprit gaulois* is caught, and tossed about in a hundred audacious drawings. The subjects are sensual, coarse,

even brutal here and there; but they are all true to the time. The orgies of a scholar, humorist, and wit, who could interpret the life of the Middle Ages by the light of that of the nineteenth century, found a congenial reveller in the illustrator of *Rabelais*. It has been remarked that "in this debauch of genius, this full-blooded and full-flavoured expression of romanticism as its strongest and most reckless, Doré, the last of the romantics, found his happiest and greatest chance." He is cruel and horrible in his pictures of slaughter, not because he delighted, as Mr. Hamerton alleges, in the cruel and the coarse, but because his piercing imagination realized the details of bloodshed

and torture, and he identified himself with his author. The horrors, the decapitations, the blood-lettings, are overdone in many cases. The imagination appears to be inflamed by its food. The celebrated drawing of the lover cut in twain by the tremendous sword of the jealous husband is ghastly; but the power in it is extraordinary. When there is a fight, the arrows are as thick in the air as gnat-swarms on a summer evening. Heads fly about; blood spurts; writhing limbs lie in all directions. But these cruel revels emanate from the text. The artist is one with the author.

Mark him in his quieter moods. The moonlight effects upon the mountains, the dark pine-woods, the cavalcades riding bravely along the road through splendid scenery, the serenade in the quaint old street, the stately halls where ladies and gallants make love, the silent and solitary cloisters of the monks, relieve the orgies of wine and blood.

We shall see, as we proceed, how Doré could be impressive and tender at the same time, in his *Croquemitaine*, his *Perrault*, his *Don Quixote*, his *Ariosto*, and finally in his illustrations to Tennyson.

CHAPTER VI.

THE BOY OF GENIUS.

IT was Theophile Gautier who called Gustave Doré *un gamin de génie*. They had travelled together, with M. Paul Dalloz, when he was in the hey-day of his youth; and Doré had been the life and soul of the party. He ran, he sang, he played the fiddle, he was full of practical jokes, and he delighted in feats of skill and strength. He was like a school-boy let loose. There was more than a pinch of malice in him. The majestic, oriental calm of Gautier was a foil to Gustave's high spirits. The life in him brimmed and bubbled over in many directions. The wilder the joke the more it was to his liking. He would challenge some ploughmen in a field to lift a heavy stone with him, or run a race against him; and Gautier looked quietly on

LIFE OF GUSTAVE DORÉ.

enjoying the fun. They travelled to the Pyrenees, and over the border into the north of Spain. They had hired an old coach.

Putting up one night at a rough roadside inn, they found an old harpsichord in the corner of the sitting-room. Doré heard that a *curé*, about three miles off, possessed a fiddle. He sent a polite note to the holy man, begging the loan of it; and when it was brought, one of the party led on the harpsichord, while Doré played the fiddle, and the country-folk were invited to dance. The ball was kept up till morning dawned; the fiddler from his elevated position studying the uncouth attitudes, the countenances, and the love-making of the villagers, while Gautier looked solemnly down on the scene. At another resting-place, Doré and Dalloz mounted behind their own coach and acted as servants, to the bewilderment of the by-standers, who thought some grand personage was in their midst, until Doré jumped upon the roof of the vehicle and executed a fantastic *pas seul* before them. In Verona, Dalloz was taking a photographic view of one of the picturesque streets, Doré trying to keep the crowd off. It was a difficult task. The more he gesticulated and threatened, the greater the throng became. "Wait a minute," Doré called out to Dalloz; "I'll disperse them."

THE BOY OF GENIUS.

He took off his coat and threw it upon the ground; and then, putting on a pitiful expression, he went round, with his cap in his hand, to beg for a few soldi. As he advanced, the crowd retreated, and Dalloz obtained his negative.

The young men loved to break the Olympian serenity of their powerful critic; especially when they were leaving their night quarters. They would carry off his waistcoat, or his cravat, or some of his linen, and then call impatiently for him to come forth and start. He would be seen presently, issuing with ruffled dignity from the inn, with his unclosed bag and his belongings hanging through the aperture. He bore their boisterous laughter with the gravity of an Arab.

In the evening the travellers often got into heated and even angry discussions. Gautier and Doré disagreed fundamentally on the aims and methods of art. Gautier loved correctness, perfect form, the technique, in short, of art; whereas Doré contended that art which said nothing, which conveyed no idea, albeit perfect in form and colour, missed the highest quality and *raison d'être* of art. Doré was a brilliant talker, and had original and happy, sarcastic, and even biting ways of expressing and defending himself; nor was he slow to attack, so that the word-bouts were very fierce occasionally. M. Dalloz remembers one occasion—art was the subject, and generally an irritating one to Doré and Gautier—when the great Théo., maddened by the thrusts of the *gamin de génie*, raised the soup tureen in the air, and threatened to break it upon his head. On another, when the dispute (on a literary question) was between Doré and Dalloz, they went forth into the open, still vehemently talking. It was in the mountains, and Doré took a stone and emphasized a remark by casting it in the direction of Dalloz. They were both getting angry. Dalloz replied sharply with another stone. And thus began a furious pelting, each combatant dodging behind a rock. One of their companions rushed forward to put at end to the fight; whereupon the two turned upon the peace-maker. But, in a minute, they both perceived the absurdity of this; and the battle ended with general shouts of laughter.

In 1855 I suggested to Mr. Herbert Ingram, the proprietor of the *Illustrated London News*, that he should ask Doré to illustrate the Queen's journey to Paris. Ingram agreed, and we travelled to Boulogne to meet him. Doré sang, talked, and laughed all the way, being exhilarated by the journey, and the excitement of the event to which we were tending. At Boulogne we met Mr. Ingram, had a merry dinner with him and some friends he had invited to meet us;

THE BOY OF GENIUS.

and then, in the twilight, sauntered to the shore to enjoy our cigars. Doré surprised the grave persons of the party by taking off his coat and rolling and turning surprising somersaults in the sand. In the evening, at the hotel, while Ingram and his friends took their grog, Doré, smoking in a corner, covered a broad sheet of paper with sketches and caricatures full of obser-

vation and fancy. Ingram was astonished, and, being up before us, and leaving for Paris, carried off the broadsheet, to show to his friends on his return to London. We followed in the imperial train, travelling with one of the Prince of Wales' tutors; with a dainty lunch spread for us in the centre of the carriage. Doré talked of his art schemes, looking dreamily out of the windows, and forgot Emperor and Queen and all the solemn ceremonial of the day. He passed swiftly from gay to grave moods; but in his early time, when he painted in the Rue Monsieur le Prince, and drew for Philippon, and was at work upon his Russian pictorial pamphlet, his *Wandering Jew*, his *Rabelais*, and his *Contes Drôlatiques*, the natural buoyancy of his youth, and the turmoil of his tempestuous imagination, made him exactly what Gautier called him, a *gamin de génie*.

He was the pet of the intellectual coteries of the time, most welcome in literary Bohemia.

Victorine, a courtesan, of a certain age, established, at the lower part of the Rue des Martyrs, in the Bréda quarter, a *table d'hôte* for the lively but immoral frequenters of the neighbourhood. It became famous as the "Cavern." It was a cheap ordinary, at three francs a head. The dinner consisted invariably of the pot-au-feu, bouillon and bouilli, fowl, salad, a sweet dish, and plenty of dessert, over which Victorine, from the head of the table, cried to her guests, "Who stands champagne?" The company consisted of little actresses, artists, journalists, and lively strangers who gathered about this gay company to hear the jokes and see the fun, which often became fast and furious. The high spirits of youth gave all the charm the place could boast. After dinner the noisy company passed into Victorine's drawing-room, where they danced, played jokes—sometimes very rough ones—and occa-

sionally got up a little baccarat. Lespès (the Timothée Trimm of after years), Charles Monselet, and many others who have since become known and serious men, were frequenters of the Cavern. Here, the story runs, a diner, now the grave director of one of the principal Paris theatres, was the subject of a wonderful practical joke; viz. the reduction of his costume to that of Cupid at the hands of the ladies. On another occasion one of the convives asked a provincial if he would do him the honour of dining with his family. The provincial accepted, and presented himself in evening dress, at the dinner hour, in Victorine's drawing-room. Victorine and the ladies present received him with great dignity; and at the table he was placed between two young beauties whom he understood to be the cousins of his friend, Victorine being the aunt. While the dinner went on, first the lady to the right, then the lady to the left, winked at him. Then one squeezed his hand under the table, while the other pinched his leg—each casting amorous glances at him. Finally one kissed him, and the other was about to repulse her, when, in utter dismay, the bumpkin rose from the table, threw down his *serviette*, and rushed out of the house.

In this *milieu* Doré played many pranks, and was

known as "le petit Gustave." But none of his gambols in Bohemia interfered with his dreams and his labours as an artist. In such places as the Cavern he studied the grotesque work he produced in the *Journal pour Rire* and other places; but in his studio and in his quiet house, where his mother sate while he pored over blocks and plates, he read his Dante, his Rabelais, his Bible, and his Shakespeare, and drew from them the richest stores of his imagination. So deep and incessant was the mastery of this imaginative force in him, that it would arrest him at the height of his wildest pranks; and the laughing face of the gamin would become calm and full of reverie as that of Wordsworth or Shelley.

It is pleasant, however, to dwell on the extraordinary faculty of enjoyment which Doré possessed in his early manhood, before the harsh criticism of his fellow-countrymen had embittered his lofty and generous nature. In the early time he had always a laugh for a joke, and was ready to indulge in any humorous whim. He had invited a naval captain to dinner, and was perplexed how he should entertain him. He consulted some friends, asking them what they did when they had a post-captain to dine with them? Getting no hint, he bought nautical things, anchors, compasses, and models of all kinds—among them that of a full-rigged frigate; and he was amused when his guest arrived and congratulated him on his nautical tastes—Doré, who took a fortnight to summon courage enough to cross the channel!

In some reminiscences of him for which I am indebted to our mutual friend M. H. Taine, the reader will find a picture of the artist and the man, rendered in a few paragraphs.

"During three or four years," says M. Taine,* "about 1858 I saw him often and had many conversations with him. Since that time we have lived in different worlds, but I went now and then to see him in his studio, and we were always pleased to meet. . . . We never made a journey to the Pyrenees together. When he illustrated my little book† he had nothing more, I believe, than photographs of the country. It was M. Hachette who brought us together, and who acted as the plastic medium between the pen and the pencil. Doré had already illustrated *Rabelais* and Balzac's *Contes Drôlatiques*.

"I was not at college with him. I had been at Bourbon when he was at Charlemagne. I was much older than he. About this time mutual friends had taken me to his studio in the Rue Monsieur le Prince.

---

* Letter from M. H. Taine to B. J., dated August 10, 1883.
† *The Pyrenees.*

LIFE OF GUSTAVE DORÉ.

There were immense pictures in it, with twenty life-size figures — among others the murder of Rizzio under the eyes of Mary Stuart,* and big landscapes by the score, representing the mountains and the Vosges where he was born. These frameless canvasses were heaped up against the walls. He drew them out, like the slides of a magic lantern, and showed them to us. Marcelin, Emile Lami, and other friends were, like me, astonished at this overflow of imagination and of productive power.

"At his mother's house in the Rue St. Dominique, in the house where he died, he received once a week. His brother (Ernest), an excellent musician and composer, improvised abstracts of operas in a corner. I have often passed evenings with him discussing *Fidelio*, the *Prophète*, &c. Madame Doré, in black silk, her head folded in black lace, with most striking countenance and eyes of extraordinary brightness, sat at the fireside, receiving the visitors, who were, for the most part, engineers—colleagues of her late husband. As for Gustave Doré, he would be at a table drawing. At the time I am describing, I think he was working on his *Wandering Jew*. One saw the figures take life under his pencil. The power and freshness

* M. Taine is in error as to the size of the Rizzio. The reader may see it in the Doré Gallery.

of his invention were astonishing. He would often pause and go to the piano to listen, or to improvise; but modestly, for he played only indifferently well. Sometimes, at midnight, when he accompanied us to the street, he would execute feats of strength on the horizontal iron bar that held the gates. Even in the salon I have seen him, in a burst of animal spirits, cast his violin or his pencil aside, and stand upon his head upon the sofa, to the stupefaction of any grave visitors who might be present. His mother, half cross and half-laughing, would go to him and pull him down by his coat.

"At this time his dreams of success were prodigious. But they were amiable, lively, accompanied by good nature, and, above all, justified; for every imagination appeared languid in comparison with his. For energy, force, superabundance, originality, sparkle, and gloomy grandeur, I know only one equal to his—that of Tintoretto. All that Doré wanted was to have been born in a good atmosphere, and to have drawn from twelve to twenty years in a thorough studio, or academy. Our only regret in regard to him was to see him producing too rapidly, and appearing before the public too soon. It was said that at fifteen years of age, while a student at Charlemagne, he was drawing caricatures for Philippon. These caricatures, violent and harsh in form, but full of admirable spirit, have been reprinted in rolls and sold by the mètre to paper walls. Afterwards he himself regretted that he had begun so early and produced so much. He said to me one day (I think it was after the appearance of Dante's 'Hell'): 'My adversary, at this moment, is myself. I must efface and kill the illustrator, and be spoken of only as the painter.' But the illustrator had yet to accomplish much famous work, that was destined to bear his name

> Quite round about the globe.

And the painter was destined to die, before he had won the place he coveted."

Jules Claretie has alone described him as he appeared about this time* in his studio. "He paints, he lunches, he gossips, he comes and goes, pauses, runs from one picture to another, laughs and plays tricks, and then, at a bound, goes from jokes to æsthetics: just now Gavroche, and now Camille Desmoulins. Gustave Doré is very young, and yet nearly fifteen years have passed since he suddenly won fame. He had all the qualities neces-

---

* *Peintres et Sculpteurs Contemporains, &c.* Notices par J. Claretie. Cinquième Livraison, Gustave Doré. Paris: Libraire des Bibliophiles, Rue Saint Honoré, 338. 1883.

THE BOY OF GENIUS.

GUSTAVE DORE   (*Drawn by Himself.*)

sary to success: gaiety, energy, the sacred fire, also—must I say it?—a prepossessing face, for there are fortunate faces. Doré was small, thin, lively, elegant. If it be possible, reckon up his drawings, paintings, and sketches, and before the prodigious total you will imagine that the creator of so many battles, landscapes, fancies, and caricatures, must be a colossus built expressly to labour day and night. Not at all. Look! he is thin, almost delicate. But there is so much activity in his sparkling eye, so much humour on his lips—the lower of which projects, giving a mocking expression—the hair is so rich and fine, that you recognize a bold temperament full of sap and strength, and apt at improvisation. If the eye sparkles, it dreams also. Its expression is compounded of southern petulance and the dreamy melancholy of the north.

"To much wit and repartee, Doré added a certain Rhenish grace, which he drew, no doubt, from the memories of his infancy, within the shadows of that immense Strasburg cathedral which darts towards heaven its spire* charged with gnomes and sprites. The dreamy and somewhat mysterious character

* Doré, as we have already noticed, has twisted the most fantastic spires out of these memories of infancy, in the *Contes Drôlatiques*, and other Middle-Age illustrations.

THE BOY OF GENIUS.

of Doré's drawings, attracted one to them. The *Legend of the Wandering Jew* and the *Dante*, include, in this sense, veritable masterpieces. . . . In his designs the light plays vividly, and the colour comes out as in an etching by Rembrandt. Since Callot, perhaps, we have not had so rich and rare a draughtsman, innovator, and creator. For he would have effaced the illustrator—he whose life-long dream was to illustrate Shakespeare!—to be accepted as a painter."

Some of Doré's most delicate and finished pencil studies of scenery are to be found in M. H. Taine's *Tour in the Pyrenees*.* Sunset on the river at Bordeaux, with the serried masts of the shipping, carried to the farthest distance, and the views of the Landes; a head-piece of Saint Jean de Luz; Orthez, including an exquisitely and truthfully pencilled woodland corner where the dreamer may, as M. Taine says, "forget the useful and think only of the beautiful"; the Pic du Midi of Ossan, a rare combination of harmonious effects; Eaux Bonnes, a noble series of studies of mountain peaks and gorges and pine-forests, some shivered by the lightning and broken and scattered by the hurricane: these are but a few of the close

* *Voyage aux Pyrénées.* Par H. Taine. Illustré par Gustave Doré. L. Hachette et Cie. 1re Édition, 1855. 8me Édition, 1880.

LIFE OF GUSTAVE DORÉ.

studies of nature to be found in M. Taine's book. The illustrations to the Legends are in the vein of those which vivify Balzac's *Contes Drôlatiques*. The studies of bears, goats, pigs, dogs, turkeys, and other local animated nature are charged with life and grace. The humorous episodes are unexaggerated. Above all, the craftsmanship is of a quality rarely seen in Doré's earlier work. It is, as I have remarked, extremely delicate; and it is at the same time notable for breadth and brightness. It has the qualities we discern later in the little head-and-tail-pieces of the *Don Quixote*, brought to perfection. Some of the landscape pencilling is as finished as any etching; it might be examined with a microscope. Doré's contributions to his old friend's charming descriptions and observations may, in short, be held up as an answer to those careless detractors, who have denied that he had correct skill in the craft of picture-making. Here the craftsmanship is masterly and in many styles. Compare the portrait of Froissart (page 67) with the beggars of Bagnerre de Bigorre (page 419), or the performing bear (page 397), or the Park at Pau (page 116). The surprising part of this vivid art-work is, that it was inspired by photographs of the places represented.

CHAPTER VII.

DANTE.

Doré's *Inferno** appeared in 1862. The poet who "passed through all the circles of the kingdom of sorrow," struck deep into the heart of Gustave Doré, as he has struck to the core of the lives of generations of imaginative men. Macaulay, whose mind was thoroughly penetrated with the great Florentine, said of him that he took his execution to be beyond that of any other artist who has operated on the

* *L'Enfer de Dante Alighieri.* Avec les dessins de Gustave Doré. Traduction Française de P. Angelo Fiorentino. Accompagnée du texte Italien. Paris: L. Hachette et Cie., Rue Pierre Sarrazin, 14. 1861. Fifth Edition, 1877.

imagination by means of words. He stirred that of Doré to its depths. Mr. Gladstone has found lifelong solace in him, loving in him the ardent Italian politician as well as the supreme poet. To him the author of the *Divine Comedy* is the Italian patriot who first raised his voice for a free and united Italy, and who is a master of the highest forms of oratory. His sharply-cut luminous phrases make the truth and beauty they embody sparkle to the eye.

But it was not for rest from the busy scene of the world that Gustave Doré penetrated to the core of Dante's genius. He found in it kinship with his own.

Mr. Hamerton is of opinion that, "when at last, weary of scattering himself in ephemeral newspaper illustrations, and sketches of all manner of subjects in cheap novels, travels, and histories," for money, he felt that the time had come to assert his power, and to let the world see him at his best; he naturally chose the *Inferno* of Dante, because he had a great passion for the horrible, "being as ferocious as a healthy boy five years old (which, except a tiger, is by his instincts the most cruel of all animals)." We are told that his imagination revelled in every possible sort of horror and pain, adding to it whatever augmentation his ingenuity could devise. "In his combats, several heads and limbs fly about in the air like tennis-balls. Skulls and skeletons are as plentiful as in a charnel-house, disease as common and familiar as in a hospital. His puppets do mad work. They thrust with lances, they hew with swords, they hang and are hanged, they poison and are poisoned, they burn, they put to torture, they fight furiously in battle, driving whole squadrons over precipices, crushing massed battalions under rolling rocks and falling walls. They impale, they transfix, man and horse, lover and mistress, with mighty thrusts of spear. They stab in secret, they throw themselves on rapier-points. They live in bloodshed, and they die in agony."

Here Mr. Hamerton piles up the agony, selecting his illustrations from the immense masses of Doré's work to support his argument. He picks out sword-thrusts, impalements, poisonings, heads flying about like tennis-balls, and limbs darkening the air, from many works, from the *Contes Drôlatiques* to the *Crusades*, in support of a charge that Doré's imagination revelled in the horrible. It would be nearer the truth to say that the impetuosity and thoroughness with which he seized his author's conceptions, and identified his imagination with theirs, led him to the fearless realization of the most horrible incidents and scenes. He felt the fascination of terrors, and gave his imagination up to it. He had gained that composure in the presence of the horrible and the painful which the accomplished surgeon has.

Having become master of his feelings, and being impelled by a passion as intense as that with which Dante betook himself to the *Inferno*—viz. that of fame—Doré valiantly prepared for a task in which he was to spend not only many anxious days and nights, but a heavy sum set aside from his earnings, to serve his ambition.* He has himself described the difficulties which met him when he approached publishers with his idea of the illustrated classics of various countries. "The publishers," he says, "to whom I submitted my plans, were of opinion that my proposition was not a practical one. They argued that it was not at a time when the fashion was to produce at the lowest possible price they could venture upon volumes at a hundred francs. They believed there was no hope of being able to stem the current which was towards excessive cheapness.

"On my side, I contended that at a time when

* M. Pisan, the distinguished engraver, who engraved some of Doré's best work, especially in the *Dante*, informs me that the artist made five or six finished designs which he had engraved at his own expense. Then he submitted his idea to MM. Hachette & Co., who undertook the work.

an art or an industry was degenerating, there were always a few hundreds of people who protested against the deluge of common things, and who were ready to buy at its fair value the first careful work that was submitted to them."

Doré was right, but he could not persuade publishers to adopt his view.

"Doré selected a famous poem," says Mr. Hamerton, "immortal by reason of its intensely genuine imaginative character as a true *vision*, a narrative of things actually *seen* by the mortal eye of the narrator, but a poem which is at the same time the most cruel, the most ferocious, the most diabolical in the whole range of the world's literature." He selected it, not to revel in its horrors and its cruelties, but because he felt and saw with Dante, and his imagination could master and interpret the mystical vision without flinching. Besides, the *Inferno* was essentially a pictorial poem. It presented a series of grand and awful scenes, capable of the highest artistic treatment. Doré had no idea of freezing the blood of "the gentle dames of Paris," but a very distinct determination to offer to the world a signal proof of his power as a poetic artist. Beyond question Doré looked at the *Inferno* as he had looked at the *Contes Drôlatiques* and the *Wandering Jew*, from a Frenchman's stand-point.

LIFE OF GUSTAVE DORÉ.

The Frenchman is not so easily shocked as we are. We have suppressed the *Contes Drôlatiques* for their coarseness and licentiousness ; but they are neither coarse nor licentious in the eyes of respectable and well-educated French people. In the same way the *Inferno* does not make our neighbours shudder. The art in Doré's designs, the imaginative power, the command of light and shade, and of weird and fantastic grouping, strike the Gallic mind and justify and even commend the horrible.

"We see," as Mr. Hamerton says, " Francesca of Rimini floating naked with her lover in the gloom of hell's foul atmosphere, her limbs drawn or stretched in pain, her sad face weary with its unending anguish, dark drops oozing still from the unhealed wound between her breasts. We see the lovers of good living, a naked crowd, chilled and shivering under cold, perpetual rain. And if any Protestants care to know what sort of punishment hell has in store for them, Dante has described and Doré pictured it." This is the highest praise to the artist. He is on a level with the poet ; and he follows him as Dante followed Virgil—even where fiends bear sinners at the end of their forks and "dip them in molten pitch as a chandler dips candles in tallow." Nay, it is the artist's duty where the man is nailed to the earth through his hands and feet (a superb conception as realized by Doré), and where hosts of men contend with the strength of frenzy against serpents. "Then," says Mr. Hamerton, "comes the merciful passage already alluded to, when Dante pulls the hair from the head of the man he has just hit in the face. This last bit, the most abominable in the book (except one), Gustave Doré illustrates with much satisfaction. Nor could he omit the well-known Ugolino incident, where he perpetually gnaws the head of the archbishop. Indeed the story of Ugolino, being altogether revolting, is dwelt upon with especial favour, and gets no less than four illustrations."

It is not more fully treated than other, and these the purest and grandest, passages of the *Inferno*.

> That forest, how robust and rough its growth,
> Which to remember only, my dismay
> Renews, in bitterness not far off from death. *

This rough and robust forest, with its cavernous depths of shadow, and tangled undergrowth in which the feet of Dante are engaged, is one of Doré's fine imaginative landscapes; and so is the awful wilderness in which the poet is confronted by the lion that bars his way, with a she-wolf at his heels. The meeting

* Cary's translation.

LIFE OF GUSTAVE DORÉ.

with Virgil, and the early scenes of their journey, are told in a series of pictures full of various imaginative power. The starlight night, the appearance of Beatrice in a grove, and then the rock-bound portal of the city of woe—past which all hope must be abandoned, were fresh revelations of creative resources in the artist. Charon on the livid lake; his "demoniac form, with eyes of burning coal," driving "Adam's evil brood" into his boat; the meeting with Homer, Horace and Naso, when the scenery becomes serene, and nature is in gracious mood; then, again, to the dread judgment-seat of Minos—to the dark height whence Dante sees how

> The stormy blast of hell,
> With restless fury drives the spirits on
> Whirl'd round and dash'd amain with sore annoy,—

and so on to what Mr. Hamerton would call the creations of Doré's genius in its cruel and licentious mood, and thence into the daylight, a sweet and peaceful scene, and into the placid starlight night, at the end; make up a powerful manifestation of the vision and the faculty divine at Doré's command when he was stirred by a kindred creator or dreamer. As an example of Doré's most careful and powerful drawing on wood, the frontispiece portrait of Dante is the best I can call to mind. The workmanship is equal to the idea of the great Florentine's features. The figures of Dante and Virgil, throughout the poem, are true in conception, and this of the highest order. Dante goes on his way throughout, affrighted, disgusted, and here and there dazed; while Virgil, familiar with the awful scene, leads and guides him, confident and cool as a sexton in a charnel house. Indeed, as Claretie has remarked, Doré saw greatly, strangely, surprisingly.*

In November 1868 Doré announced to me the approaching publication of his *Paradise and Purgatory* of Dante, and I received an early copy of it from him. Six years had passed since the publication of the *Inferno*—six years of hard work with pencil and brush, darkened with disappointments, but also brightened with many new conceptions and plans, that were the salt and strength of Doré's life. From the *Inferno* and its gloom and horror he had turned to sunnier subjects—to the *Contes de Perrault*, and now to the " Purgatory " and " Paradise " of his poet. In the " Purgatory " we have traces of the savage crea-

---

* Doré planned the form of his *Inferno*. The illustrations which fill pages separate from the text, are printed upon toned paper with a broad white border, and the explanatory extract is upon the fly-leaf which protects the design.

tions, the fierce realization of pain and terror; but through it we perceive the dawning light of Paradise. We have glimpses of the heavenly host—till

> . . . suddenly upon the day appear'd
> A day new ris'n, as He, who hath the power,
> Had with another sun bedeck'd the sky.

The visions of angels bathed in sunbeams, the enchanting effects of light and shade, the dainty bits of laughing landscape, the silvery mists veiling the glory of heavenly mysteries, and the final processions and circles of the angels — all peace and harmony and celestial light, prove to the observer that the genius of the artist was not essentially cruel nor licentious, but that it was many-sided.

The illustrator of Dante, and particularly of his *Inferno*, at once took foremost rank among the illustrators of his day. Doré enjoyed to the utmost the glory of his great success. In his delight he turned for refreshment, after the gloom of the *Inferno*, to the bright pages of *Perrault*, and to his college friend About's *Roi des Montagnes*. Mary Ann, in the *Roi des Montagnes*, is one of the best drawings of an English girl Doré has left; but her mother, Mrs. Simons, of the firm of Bailey and Co., London bankers, is a caricature—based on the old *Charivari* and *Journal pour Rire* models of Englishwomen. We find the same figures in *Le Chemin des Écoliers*. William Lobster and Harris the American were no more studied from the life than M. About's models. Doré's Germans in the *Chemin des Écoliers* were good, because he had known them from his infancy. Author and artist are wide of the mark, as a rule; albeit there are, here and there, touches of truth both in the text and the drawings. Yet there are charming sketches in the illustrations to *Roi des Montagnes*. The brigands are full of character. The drawing is free and vigorous. There are admirable conceits scattered by the inexhaustible artist over M. About's pages; as, for instance, the Loves nestling fledglings in a heart that is a nest. Of course, there are headless figures—two girls, their heads severed from their bodies by order of Hadgi-Stavros—a scene as ghastly as the head of the dead drunkard Vasile—the latter, a wonderful rendering of death.

Among the *étrennes* of New Year's Day 1862, we find *Les Contes de Perrault, dessins par Gustave Doré*, with a preface by Hetzel, the publisher, describing the pleasure the artist had taken in the work, as a relief from his studies of Dante.

When Sainte Beuve* saw Doré's edition of the

* *Nouveaux Lundis*. Par C. A. Sainte Beuve. Tome I. Paris.

Contes de Perrault upon his table, he exclaimed that it put all other editions in the shade: it was a gift-book for a king. Had every child become a Dauphin of France? He could hardly tell where he should begin to praise it—it was so far beyond all other editions, and would probably remain so. The print was a delight to the eye. Doré's illustrations renewed these stories even for those readers who knew them best. The fruitful and untiring artist who began with Rabelais, who had revived and added to Dante, had now given his pencil to the illustration of children's stories. Saint Beuve protested that he had not Théophile Gautier's power of art analysis; he could only say that the drawings appeared to him very beautiful, opulent in form and grace, and with a grandiose air which raised the humble stories. They had a German air about them. The castles reminded him of Heidelberg; the woods, of the Black Forest. He thought of the brothers Grimm, and asked whether the artist did not hail from the German frontier, and incline to the scenery of Lorraine? He was enchanted with the superb dark forests to which Doré led the family of Petit-Poucet. The landscapes were admirable transcripts from nature. The surroundings of the Sleeping Beauty were really enchanting. He risked the prophecy, in short, that Perrault would never find so brilliant and tender an interpreter again. The only way to rest from the contemplation of all this luxury of art was, according to a friend of Sainte Beuve, to buy the four sous copy of Perrault in the *Bibliothèque bleue.* " I know," said the distinguished critic, " the child of a vendor of costly toys who is tired of sumptuous dolls and their houses, and who cares only for playthings at one sou each. Doré's Perrault may possibly have a similar effect upon book amateurs."

What would Boileau have said to see the gentle and gracious Perrault, the object of his scorn, dressed in all this artistic glory, with his Little Red Riding Hood, his Bluebeard, his Cinderella and Petit-Poucet and other company tricked out for immortality by the romantic genius of Doré? Perrault's fairy world was collected from the traditions of the Germans, Italians, Scandinavians, and even from the wilds of Scotland; but it was his genius that brought them together and presented them to the children of France. The service was an immortal one. He caught floating stories as delicately as the Indian gathers the attar of roses from the bosom of the stream with the blade of a sword-lily.

Sainte Beuve remarked that the print—the letterpress of the 17th century—was so fine and spacious

LIFE OF GUSTAVE DORÉ.

that the air seemed to circulate about the letters. It was easy to the sight of the infant and the old man. "How M. Doré excels," he exclaims, "in these forest depths and windings, these masses of giant fir and oak! How skilful he is in losing us in the hollows and gloom of ravines, in the wake of Tom Thumb." *

Following up the vein of Perrault, Doré, in 1862,

---

* L'édition des contes à laquelle ces notes vont servir de préface, cette extraordinaire édition, va coûter beaucoup d'argent.... Aussi cher que la représentation d'un ballet de l'Opéra, qu'un joujou moyen de chez Giroux ou de chez Tempier, qu'une boîte de bonbons de chez Boissier, qu'une fleur artificielle d'un prix modéré, que la fumée, enfin, de quelques cigares de choix..... Je le veux bien : ce qui est trop d'argent pour une chose qui reste, ne serait rien pour la chose qui passe ; mais avouez qu'elle est hors de comparaison avec toutes celles qui l'ont précédée, cette édition de Perrault, et qu'on a bien fait de donner à ce premier de nos livres, à ce premier de nos classiques, cette forme magnifique et magistrale..... Si ce monument, élevé à la gloire de Perrault et au profit de ses admirateurs de tous les âges, voit le jour, prenez-vous-en au plus jeune, au plus vaillant de nos génies contemporains. Tout en composant intrépidement à ses frais, à ses risques et perils, sa grande et sombre illustration de Dante, Gustave Doré désirait que dans le même moment et que dans le même format splendide parussent, comme pendant et comme contraste, les *Contes des Fées* de Perrault. D'un côté, le merveilleux dans ce qu'il y a de plus funèbre, de plus tragique et de plus ardu ; de l'autre, le merveilleux divertissant, spirituel, émouvant jusque dans le comique et comique jusque dans l'émouvant, le merveilleux à son berceau. Il voulait ainsi, tout à la fois, rasséréner son crayon, au sortir des épouvantes un peu monocordes de l'enfer, et prouver la variété de ses moyens.—*Contes de Perrault; Introduction par P. I. Stahl.*

gave to children his sumptuous legend of *Croquemitaine*,* as well as his picturesque studies of the Rhineland.†

THE APOSTLE JOHN.—"ORLANDO FURIOSO."

* *La Légende de Croquemitaine*. 1 vol. 4to. Illustré de 175 Vignettes sur bois. MM. Hachette et Cie. 2nd Edition. 1874.
† *La Mythologie du Rhin*, in 8vo., 29 gravures. MM. Hachette et Cie.

CHAPTER VIII.

FROM THE "INFERNO" TO "DON QUIXOTE."

THE feverish rate at which Doré produced both illustrations for books, contributions to the *Journal pour Tous* and the *Journal Amusant* (the new title of the *Journal pour Rire*), and pictures, in the short interval between the appearance of the *Inferno* and that of *Don Quixote* and Chateaubriand's *Atala*, both of which appeared in 1863, surpassed even that of his earliest years. He scattered his shot in his haste to rid his ardent imagination of its crowding creations. The year that gave his *Don Quixote* and *Atala* to the light, was that in which he exhibited in the Salon his "Paolo and Francesca da Rimini," perhaps, for poetic beauty and careful and masterly finish, the most perfect work in oil that he has left behind him. We find his hand in page after page of the *Journal pour Tous*. Views in Colorado, and a series of illustrations based on M. De Trévise's sketches for M. Moges' *Voyage en Chine et au Japon*, 1857-8, a number of drawings of African subjects, Choctaw Indians, a prairie on fire, a distribution of decorations in the camp at Chalons, ruins in the Tyrol, an opera ball, and fifty other subjects, employed the feverish hand of the unresting artist in the Rue St. Dominique, who worked, as M. Taine has told us, even when his mother was receiving company in the room where his table stood.

Doré's daily life with his mother was much that of the Primrose family, to whom the seasons brought, by way of incident, only migrations from the blue room to the brown; but, now and again, his engagements as illustrator drew him away from Paris. Even when he travelled, however, he worked. He had not been in an hotel twenty-four hours before his sketches were scattered about his rooms, and throughout his letters to his friends. When, in 1862, he was drawn away by his friend, Charles Davillier, to Spain, he went because he had *Don Quixote* in his mind, and had resolved to improve his acquaintance with the country the frontiers of which he had glanced at in the joyous company of Théophile Gautier and Paul Dalloz.

In a few prefatory words to his *Spain*, the Baron Charles Davillier has described the origin of his journey with Doré, early in 1862:—

"For a long time past my old friend Doré had talked to me of his desire to see Spain. At first it was only a vague project, cast out between two puffs of a cigarette. But it soon became a fixed idea, one of those dreams which will not leave the mind at rest. I never saw him that he did not ask me point blank—

"'When do we start for Spain?'

"'But, my dear friend,' I answered, 'you forget that I have wandered over the classic land of the castagnette and the bolero at least twenty times.'

"'The better reason,' he said. 'If you have seen Spain so often, there is no reason why you should stop now.'

FROM THE "INFERNO" TO "DON QUIXOTE."

"I could find no argument to rebut such reasoning, and a few days later we took our tickets for Perpignan."*

The tour in Spain was that in which Doré had opportunities of thoroughly mastering the many picturesque varieties of Spanish life, the striking phases of Spanish scenery, and the characteristics of the various cities. The series of Spanish landscapes, of Spanish groups, of ruins, of streets and buildings, together with pictures of processions, village dances, bullfights, funerals, street musicians, churches and cathedrals, smugglers, the Alhambra, exquisitely pencilled interiors, the balconies of Granada, the groups of peasantry of the various provinces, the orange groves, the torreros, Spanish boatmen, the prison of the Inquisition at Barcelona, and other subjects, may be taken as notes executed by the artist, who had resolved to fix Spanish life and scenery in his mind, that he might have a rich fund to draw upon in aid of his imagination when he turned to the pages of Cervantes.

"What facility!" Théophile Gautier exclaimed,

---

* According to Monsieur E. Templier, of the great firm of Hachette & Co., Doré went to Spain to study for his *Don Quixote*, which appeared in the following year. His illustrations to Davillier's text appeared first in the *Tour du Monde*. Davillier's work was published in a separate form only in 1874.

LIFE OF GUSTAVE DORÉ.

looking over Doré's work. "What richness, what strength, what intuitive depth, what penetration to the heart of the most diverse subjects! What sense of the real, and, at the same time, what insight into the visionary and the chimerical! The to be or not to be, the body and the spectre, the sun and the night—Gustave Doré can interpret anything. It is to him the world will owe the first illustrated *Dante*, since that of Michael Angelo is lost."

It is to him that the world is indebted for the first illustrated *Don Quixote*. Cervantes' incomparable study of human character, from its good-natured side, was exactly in harmony with the essentially romantic genius of Doré. He revelled in it; and this is obvious as well, perhaps more, in the delightful bits of study and suggestion—the head-pieces and the tail-pieces—as in the more elaborate designs. Mr. Russell Lowell, in the course of a lecture he delivered at the Working Men's College of London, on *Don Quixote*, said, that the book was full of thoroughly good humour, and that this was the more remarkable because it showed that the optimism of its author had survived more misfortunes than had fallen to the lot of many. It was in this optimism, and all-pervading good-humour, that Doré found his congenial subjects. It gave him a deeper pleasure than he had felt in the gloom of Balzac's *Contes*, or the mystery of the legend of the Wandering Jew,—albeit all these attracted him, by their direct appeal to his power to bury himself in the Middle Ages, and create a new world of his own out of them. *Don Quixote* is the most sprightly, the most ambitious, and the completest emanation of this phase or section of Doré's genius.

When he returned from Spain, he arranged with his friend and engraver, Pisan, to make, at his ease and at his own cost, some forty drawings to illustrate the exploits of Cervantes' most whimsical hero. But, as the subject fastened itself upon him, he became impatient to realize all his conceptions; and he burst one morning, in the early summer, into M. Pisan's atelier, to announce that he had made arrangements with a publisher to have his *Don Quixote* out before the end of the year, and in two volumes. Then artist and engraver fell to; and, as M. Pisan has remarked to me, they were both worked to death. But it was always so. Yet, with all his haste, Doré never became careless. At the last moment he would have a drawing engraved two or three times. It must be, to his eye, as good as he could make it. He respected the public, and he respected himself.

He who would form a just estimate of the varieties

in Doré's humour and sarcasm, should take him from his *Labours of Hercules* and his *Sainte Russie*, straight through his *Rabelais*, his *Contes Drôlatiques*, his *Munchausen*, his *Croquemitaine*, to his *Don Quixote*. The gradations of the humour, and the differences in style, in treatment, and in workmanship, will repay the discerning critic. The *Munchausen*, for instance, and L'Epine's *Histoire du Capitaine Castagnette*, are, in the highest degree, fantastic, rough, and sketchy—it may even be said, coarse—in execution, like the artist's first pen and ink drawings of a subject. These observations apply to *Croquemitaine*. In *Don Quixote* will be found the perfection of Doré's free pencilling, and the outflow of his imagination in its liveliest moods. Mr. Russell Lowell has said that Cervantes' characters are not so much taken from actual life as the conception of life. The remark applies to nearly all Doré's illustrations. "*C'est un type*," was constantly on his lips when we were travelling about London, or elsewhere, together. He often mistook something monstrous or extravagantly eccentric for a type; and his imagination dealing with types, gave an unreality, or a grotesqueness, to his pictures of every-day life;* but these

* The outpost of owls is weird as well as humorous, and the spare bedroom at the "Crocodile" is a horrible chamber.

qualities in the artist, which weakened his objective work, his *London* for instance, gave incomparable richness to his illustrations of works of the imagination. They shone in *Don Quixote*. His romantic dreaming mingled with that of Cervantes. He apprehended the very heart and soul of the romancist's conceptions, and, by the help of his store of types, his life-long analytical studies of the human countenance, and the play of human foibles and passions, could embody them. The fantastic, the quaint, the heroic, the romantic, the purely humorous and the picturesque, are assembled, in an extraordinary degree. From the highly-fanciful picture of Don Quixote in his study, to a tail-piece describing a corner of a Spanish farm-yard, with a few children and chickens in the foreground, Doré's illustrations not only embellish, but interpret, and give fresh meanings to the text. The power and tone are steadily maintained throughout. The atmosphere is Spanish from the beginning to the end, and the period is the old romantic. If we are borne to the land of dreams with the hero, we touch *terra firma* in the familiar scenes. Herein we perceive distinctly that we have in Doré an accomplished and a poetic landscape painter. The dreamer sits on a bank at the way-side, and puts us in direct com-

LIFE OF GUSTAVE DORÉ.

DON QUIXOTE IN HIS STUDY

munication with the Spain he saw, and which was the framework of Cervantes' romance; the land over which Cervantes' knight bore his trusty Durandal, with fat Sancho Panza in his wake. We have him, weird and worn and hollow-eyed, musing over the crowd and hurly-burly of chivalry; and then, on his adventures, giving battle, doing penance, avenging the wrongs of a spotless lady; the victim of a noble faith, the simple gentleman, the knight-errant, fallen among the scoffers and rogues of a degenerate day.

In all respects Doré's *Don Quixote* is a noble performance; the full and sustained expression, I repeat, of the artist's various powers at their best.

Atala, albeit not equal to *Don Quixote*, gave the critical public further evidence that in Doré Nature had a sympathetic and poetic interpreter. He approached Nature in the spirit of Turner. He could select and reject. His memory carried passing effects of light and shade. He could remember the limbs of an oak, as he could retain the features and expression of a face. He could never work off all he had stored up in Spain, although he never tired of Spanish scenes to the end of his life. He was seldom at a loss how to fill in his designs. The forests and savannahs, and the mighty sweeps of landscape, to be found in his *Atala*, are true to Nature as the poet sees her; albeit Doré had never beheld the scene of Chateaubriand's romance. But he could represent the Titanic growths of the virgin forest, the matted tropical vegetation, the gloom of the cypress, the light laughing in the swaying flowers of the undergrowth, the scene prepared for the death of Chactas, by [the Indians, in the "wood of blood." He had wooed Nature lying on the grass, and taking the lowly flowers of the meadow for his theme, as well as in her grander aspects. The first finished studies from Nature, by Doré, when I was in his studio in 1855, were breadths of herbage and field-flowers painted lying upon the ground, that were a perpetual feast to the eye. One of these, " The Prairie," was exhibited many years afterwards in the Bond Street Gallery; and was accepted with pleasure as a new aspect of a genius that had already shown many facets. He must have loved Nature with his whole heart, who lay at full length in the grass for many days, studying the haunts of the daisy and the violet.

"Amongst Doré's various claims to distinction is the fact that he possesses beyond all other Frenchmen the sense of sublimity in landscape. Had he chosen to give the time necessary to the full expression of this faculty, he might have been by this time (1864) the greatest of all French landscape painters; as it is, he fails only from want of information, not from want of sympathy. The rocks, all through the *Inferno*, are in this age of geology simply ridiculous, but this is sheer ignorance, or deference to ignorant old masters. And although Gustave Doré has not that knowledge of Nature which would be necessary to entitle him to rank with the real masters of landscape, he possesses the landscape instinct in a more intense degree than any Frenchman who ever touched canvas."

Mr. Hamerton's reference to the geology of the rocks of the *Inferno*, is a bit of hyper-criticism of the most extravagant kind. Doré, as a landscape-painter, was not objectively correct. He had little, if any, scientific knowledge of trees, grasses, flowers, of shrubs and crops. He was an imaginative student of Nature in her grand forms and combinations, but he could see beauty in the flowers of the field. He was, as Mr. Hamerton admits, capable of feeling interest in natural scenery for itself and in itself, without any help of human interest. He was not a minute student. He had none of the botanist's nor geologist's enthusiasm. It was Nature in the mass that most easily set him dreaming and drawing in savage solitudes, amid the mountains, the emerald lakes cradled in their cold bosoms, the overshadowed valleys, and amid the moaning pines, "fallen flakes and fragments of the night," as Mr. Ruskin* calls them, sloping down to villages, perched like birds'-nests in the "forest hair" of the hills.

* It is to be deeply regretted that Mr. Ruskin has never made the *amende* to Doré's genius, since he so cruelly and blindly attacked it.

SKETCH FROM A LETTER WRITTEN *en voyage*.

CHAPTER IX.

THE BIBLE.—PARADISE LOST.—FONTAINE'S FABLES.

In M. Paul Dalloz, Gustave Doré had a zealous friend and a cordial, even an intrepid, admirer. Many were the bouts he had with the artist's detractors, who were mostly mediocre and disappointed draughtsmen or painters, and who fastened mercilessly upon him when they found that he winced under their treatment. Few of the leaders of the French school of his time, moreover, comforted Doré with a word of encouragement when his pictures figured in the Salon. A many-sided man is hateful to the man of one idea, one subject, one mode of treatment.

He saw himself passed over again and again when lesser men were added to the Legion of Honour; and he could not take the slight with composure. It chafed and worried him. M. Dalloz put an end to the injustice. In 1861 he went straight to M. Walewski, then Minister, and pointed out the impropriety of neglecting an artist whom all Europe had acclaimed as a man of genius. M. Walewski replied that Doré was young enough to wait.

"Do you know all he has done?" M. Dalloz asked.

The Minister was puzzled to answer. Whereupon Dalloz left him, called a cab, drove to Doré's studio, and half filled the vehicle with the volumes and journals the artist had illustrated. He laid the ponderous heap before the Minister, who confessed that, in the presence of such arguments, he could not resist; and Gustave Doré figured in the next list of Knights of the Legion of Honour.* When

---

* A similar effort on the part of M. Dalloz obtained justice for Doré after the Exhibition of 1878, at which he had exhibited his colossal vase. He had been passed over by the authorities

THE BIBLE AND "PARADISE LOST."

Dalloz remarked to him that he was surprised to see that he attached so much value to a bit of ribbon:

"It is not the decoration of a button-hole," he answered, "that gives me pleasure. It is the official answer to the men who have tried to put me down and crush me." It was his country's reply to the critics who had attacked his "Battle of the Alma," his landscapes, his "Francesca," and, indeed, all his labours at his easel. It sent him rejoicing on his way; it was most fortunate in this, that it reconciled him to his fame as the great illustrator of his epoch who could enter into the heart and spirit of his author, and enrich his page by adding thought and light to it. In 1864 he gave to the world his *Bible*; in the following year, his *Milton*; in 1866, he began to illustrate *Montaigne*; he produced a pictorial edition of his friend Gautier's *Capitaine Fracasse*; in 1867 his *Fontaine* was published; and in 1868 his illustrations to *Tennyson*, and the conclusion of his studies of Dante—*Purgatory and Paradise*. This work of four years was prodigious. It was an unprecedented outpouring, not only of mechanical labour, but of emotional thought,

whose function it was to recommend rewards. The faithful friend repaired to the Minister of the day, expostulated, and Doré was raised to the rank of officer.

and it told upon the worker. It aggravated his irritable moods. His fame was at its zenith; men of mark from all quarters of the globe found their way to his new studio in the Rue Bayard—to behold the living Bayard of art; he was sought by the publishers at his own price; even his pictures were beginning to find their way into good collections; and the settled injustice of his countrymen was in part compensated by his growing glory as a painter abroad, especially in England and the United States. His French critics shrugged their shoulders, and said, in their ignorance, that the English (classing the unlettered with the lettered—Ruskin with a country bumpkin looking heavily over his mug of ale at the *Illustrated Police News*) knew nothing of art. Doré felt this stab. He was told that, as a painter, he must go where art was not understood in order to find admirers—in short, that he was good enough for the English, but not for the countrymen of Ingres and Gerome.* It was not until he was sent to

---

* Une œuvre seule comme ces poèmes de Tennyson, ou comme *Londres*, ou le *Roland Furieux*, sût rende un artiste à jamais célèbre. Mais quoi! on discutait Doré parceque ce charmant bon garçon était prodigue de son génie, parcequ'il donnait des œuvres, et souvent des chefs d'œuvre, à poignées. Ah! s'il eut été étranger, Anglais ou Allemand, ce Doré, avec quelle passion nous aurions *inventé* sa gloire! " Vous ne vous imaginez pas; il y a,

THE BIBLE AND "PARADISE LOST."

London, in 1862, to report to the Imperial Government for the *Moniteur*, that Théophile Gautier discovered that England had a distinct and notable school of art; his compeers who never crossed the Channel remained in darkness on the subject, but they wrote criticisms on our blind art instincts nevertheless.

We return to Doré as an illustrator; and, first of all, to his *Bible** and Milton's *Paradise Lost*.

In these works the dreamer takes some of his grandest flights into that unsubstantial, vague, supernatural world which it was the highest faculty of his genius to people. In both the *Bible* and the *Paradise Lost*, the quality of the crafts-

---

quelque part, en Italie ou en Autriche, un certain Doré qui fait des *illustrations* comme personne au monde et qui est un artiste . . . un artiste! Ah! quel artiste!" Hélas, Gustave Doré ajoutait au tort d'être fécond, ardent et généreux, le vice d'être Français. Venu d'Espagne, son *Don Quichotte* eût fait pousser ici des cris d'enthousiasme. Il venait de cet atelier de la rue François 1er (M. Claretie should have said Rue Bayard) qui avait jadis été le Gymnase Amoros; ce n'était pas assez loin. Et alors en discutait on niait Doré, qui, à la fin, en *faisait trop!*—*Peintres et Sculpteurs Contemporains.*

* When at the end of 1865 the *Bible* was published, MM. Mame & Son, of Tours, had embarked close upon £20,000 in the enterprise. It created, as the publishers admit, an unprecedented enthusiasm. It was published at 200 francs (£8) the copy; and in a month an edition of 3,000 copies was sold. The second edition appeared in the following year; the third in 1873; and the fourth in 1882.

manship varies. Occasionally the imaginative interpreter of the sacred page, and of the greatest poem in the English language, misses the spirit of the text, or strains or falsifies it; but in both there are creations of perfect beauty, and of impressive grandeur. In these two books we may discern the first inclination of Doré's mind to sacred subjects, wherein he found at last his highest inspiration, and by which he climbed to heights where the malignant mediocrities who had tormented him so long, failed to reach him. It has been objected to his illustrations to the *Bible* that they are too theatrical. M. Claretie is never tired of likening Doré's canvases to drop-scenes. The objection is a fair one in many instances. The effect of the whole of the *Bible* and *Paradise Lost* illustrations is that of the domination of an unresting genius. The lack of repose affects the feeling of dignity, of solemnity, of awe that should be the consequence of a painstaking survey of two such works. They are in short, too dramatic; we may even say that some of the illustrations are melodramatic, and suggest blue-fire and stage carpentry. "Death on the Pale Horse" is powerfully conceived. It is one of Doré's scenes of vague and shadowy terrors; but Death, who should be looking down to the earth with his scythe folded in his arms, sits his steed like a circus-rider, and appears to be looking defiantly at a crowd of spectators. "The Deluge" is more satisfactory, more Biblical. A tigress with her cub, and some children, have taken refuge upon a rock from the rising waters, under the ebon sky. The drowning parents in the water push their babe to the last place of safety; and the lioness holds her cub aloft from the waves.

There are 230 page illustrations to the *Bible*; and in these pictorial commentaries or sermons on the text poetic and devotional ideas abound. They might become subjects of original and impressive discourses, and it is surprising that they have not been turned to account in schools.

In *Paradise Lost*, Satan's

> steep flight in many an aëry wheel

to the earth is the subject of a design of solemn beauty. The fiend's downward flight through the firmament towards the cloud-encompassed orb, with a break of light revealing a section of the round, the dark star-studded blue above, and sombre sweeps of vapour drifting below, is an effort of pure imagination without a blemish. Doré said that the passage it illustrated was that which had most deeply impressed him. It is the creation of a poet out of a poet's lines. It is a break of light upon a grand passage of Milton. Subsequently Doré exhibited the "Victor Angels," a painting of broad effects and of powerful design. Michael and his heavenly hosts had vanquished the rebel legions of Satan. The white-winged victors crown the hill in the evening light, and mount guard under the shadows of the night, while the beaten foe crouches and slinks away. It is an impressive scene that stirs the heart, albeit it is open in several parts to the censure of the critic who stipulates for correctness and fulness of detail.

Doré's few illustrations to *Montaigne* and his *Capitaine Fracasse* followed his Biblical and Miltonic studies.* These subjects were a relief from the severer work.

Among the sixty illustrations to Théophile Gautier's romance there are few which are entirely worthy of Doré. The "Castle of Misery," the path to which was choked with tangle-wood, moss, and stagnant pools made musical only by the croaking of the frogs, was a subject made for the illustrator of *Croquemitaine*. It is, however, a tame drawing of an ordinary castle.

* They appeared in 1865.

The best of the compositions are "The Pedant," "The Burial of Matamore," "Maître Bilot and his Dog," "The Baron de Sigognac and the Marquis de Bruyères"; the "Tavern of the Crowned Radish"—an animated cabaret scene, alive with incident and variety of character; and a landscape as deep in tone, and skilfully disposed as to light and shade, as a Rembrandt etching—"The crumbling Chateau of the ruined Sigognac." There are also some groups of picturesque beggars, and some dramatic incidents dramatically told; but, as in *Croquemitaine*, there are repetitions of old effects and figures and groups— as, indeed, there are even in the *Bible* and *Milton*. The consequences of over-production are evident.

There is weariness in the labour, even in that of Doré's illustrated *La Fontaine*.* Since the appearance of *La Fontaine's Contes* in 1726, in the sumptuous edition known as that of the Fermiers Généraux, he had not worn so luxurious a dress. What charming village and forest scenes and landscapes there are in Doré's quarto, touched with an infinitely delicate pencil! These are reminiscences of his travels— instances of the faithfulness with which his eye

---

* *Fables de La Fontaine*. In folio, avec 80 grandes compositions et 250 têtes de page. Par Gustave Doré, 1866–7. Cheaper Edition, 1868. Paris: MM. Hachette et Cie., Boulevard Saint Germain, 77.

carried scenes for years. In the heading to "The Two Mules" we have a reminiscence of Spain; in another, a glimpse of Alsatian village life. The animals are often weak and conventional; but now and again they tell the fable admirably, as in "The Wolf and the Lamb." Again, "Death and the Woodcutter" is a happy study of nature by an imaginative artist. Doré's lions are very poor beasts indeed. His foxes and wolves are better. His troops of sheep are good. "The Shepherd and the Sea" is illustrated by a beautiful sweep of land and sea. "The Town Rat and the Country Rat" gives the artist an opportunity of producing a delicate, highly-finished study of still life. The flagons and dishes are worthy of Desgoffes. In the fables we have evidence that, if the artist had not made birds and beasts his special study, he had a strong sympathy for them. He was fond of animals, and had two pet owls in his studio, which he brought home from one of his visits to Scotland. I have found him in his studio, more than once, lying upon his back, with his four or five pugs running over and playing with him. When he rang at the bell in the morning, the whole pack rushed to the door to meet him.

From *La Fontaine*, Doré passed to Tennyson's

TENNYSON.

Idylls of the King.* According to M. Claretie, the thirty-six compositions illustrating the *Idylls* rank with his best inspirations, and are enough to make the lasting fame of an artist. Doré was at home in Tennyson's exquisite dreamland. He revelled in the succession of pictures, Merlin resting against an old oak, the exploits of Lancelot, the heroic deeds of the Knights of the Round Table, the black shadows of the forest, the enchanting lakes. Poet never had daintier dressing than the Laureate had in the *Idylls of the King*, as produced by Messrs. Moxon. It was said of them, "Their issue has given wings to the muse of Mr. Tennyson." These wings bore them to foreign lands and gave them new homes.

The illustrations were engraved on steel. Elaine was the least satisfactory. The girl is not a British maiden. There are discrepancies between text and illustration. There are lovely bits, but the romantic landscapes are the chief beauties. "The Moonlight Ride," "The Dawn of Love," and the "Joyous Sprites," are the gems of the twenty-seven plates. "The Dawn of Love" is, perhaps, the loveliest. In all this work we recognise the student of the

---

* *Les Idylles du Roy.* Traduction de L'Anglais. 1 Vol. in folio ; 36 Dessins sur acier. 1869. Paris : MM. Hachette et Cie. Boulevard Saint Germain, 77.

little inn at Barr with a hand grown firm and delicate.

The series of *Tennyson* drawings, from which the steel-plates were engraved, may be seen in the Doré Gallery in Bond Street: Enid and the countess, Geraint charging the bandits, Geraint and Enid riding away, Vivien and Merlin entering the woods, the cave scene, Vivien enclosing Merlin in the tree, King Arthur discovering the skeletons of the brothers, Lancelot approaching the castle of Astolat, Elaine on the road to the castle of Lancelot, the body of Elaine on its way to King Arthur's palace; and then, from *Guinevere*, the moonlight ride, the cloister scene, the fairy circle, and the finding of King Arthur. The fancy and the "faculty divine" of the artist dallied heartily with these themes, albeit he could not approach the poet save through the medium of the translator. In his pictorial poems called into being by Tennyson's *Idyll*, there are glaring faults from the drawing-master's point of view. These are to be found in any of Doré's illustrations, in spite of his methodical observation. The proportions of trees and buildings and figures are puzzling and annoying; and they might have been set right so easily.

The truth is, not that Doré committed these

faults through ignorance, but that they passed unnoticed under his eye, which was fixed on the whole effect—the realisation of the idea within him, which imperatively commanded him. Once liberated through his pencil, other ideas crowded to the front, out of the fertile and vivid brain. It was thus that he was able to produce at a speed never before attained by an artist, because no predecessor had ever started with such a fund of original invention. None before him could have taken up *Rabelais*, *Dante*, the *Bible*, or *Don Quixote*, and delivered the work wholly out of his own creative mind straightway to the public.

It has been said that Doré, in the twenty years during which he was chiefly employed illustrating classics for the publishers and rough drawings for the press, produced more designs than all his countrymen put together. We have heard that when he was thirty, viz. in 1863, he had delivered upwards of forty thousand drawings. In 1853 he was only twenty-one years of age. In 1848 his *Labours of Hercules* were executed, as we have seen, and were his introduction to the public. Consequently he must have executed upwards of forty thousand drawings in fifteen years, or some two thousand six hundred a year, including such works as

LIFE OF GUSTAVE DORÉ.

Sainte Russie, Rabelais, Taine's *Journey to the Pyrenees,* the *Wandering Jew,* the *Contes Drôlatiques,* the *Inferno* and the *Purgatorio, Croquemitaine,* the *Contes de Perrault, Atala,* and *Don Quixote.* This estimate of production rates Doré's fertility at upwards of fifty drawings a week, all the year round and every year; with a part of each day given up to painting! If the estimate were reduced by one-half, it would be an extravagant over-estimate. Hundreds of the designs put forth by Doré, within this period, could not be executed, even by his nimble pencil and driven by his rapid invention, in a single day. Take the *Wandering Jew.* The labour expended on these scenes was immense, and lasted over months, to my own personal knowledge. Then there were the artist's rounds of visits to his engravers. I have been with him on these rounds; seen him examine the blocks in progress; heard his discussions with the art-workmen whom he had schooled to render his touch faithfully, as Leech drilled his engraver; and have admired the energy, sustained by unfailing earnestness and respect for his art, manifested in these drives from workshop to workshop. It was thus he created a new school of art-craftsmen, who caught something of his enthusiasm, and laboured in the light of his genius, and learned to love him for his gracious ways and his generous heart.

OUTCASTS: LONDON BRIDGE.

CHAPTER X.

"LONDON: A PILGRIMAGE."

THE work on London, which was the joint production of Gustave Doré and the present writer, was under-

* Macaulay's New Zealander contemplating the Ruins of St. Paul's.—See also p. 160.

taken at the suggestion of the latter, when the artist was staying with him in Jermyn Street, and was busy establishing his gallery of paintings in Bond Street. The idea as described to Doré, was of far greater importance than that which was realised. The writer sketched a comprehensive work embracing every phase and aspect of London life. [See Appendix I.] It was to have filled twenty, or even thirty parts. As the plan was unfolded one morning, while Doré was smoking, and dreamily covering paper with sketches, it gradually engrossed him. It would make a great work; and we would begin by a series of pilgrimages to the "eccentric" quarters. He would, by way of experiment, execute a set of finished drawings, that should be bound in a colossal album; and that would give in half an hour a broad outline of our conception. "Then," Doré said, "we can treat for it from a commanding position."

In pursuance of this plan we spent many days and nights visiting and carefully examining the more striking scenes and phases of London life. We had one or two nights in Whitechapel, duly attended by police in plain clothes; we explored the docks*; we visited the night refuges; we journeyed up and down

---

* His London Docks have the aspect of Nineveh. —Claretie.

the river; we traversed Westminster, and had a morning or two in Drury Lane; we saw the sun rise over Billingsgate, and were betimes at the opening of Covent Garden market; we spent a morning in Newgate; we attended the boat-race, and went in a *char-a-banc* to the Derby, and made acquaintance with all the riotous incidents of a day on a race-course;

we dined with the Oxford and Cambridge crews; we spent an afternoon at one of the Primate's gatherings at Lambeth Palace; we entered thieves' public-houses; in short, I led Doré through the shadows and the sunlight of the great world of London.* His constant

---

* The writer of the obituary article on Doré in the *Times* (Jan. 25, 1883) relates this story of him: "One evening he was roaming near the Farringdon market, when an appalling object, one mass of rags on a gaunt frame of bones, rose up before him, croaking, 'I am a gentleman; I am a clergyman!' Doré was so much struck that he put the man into a cab and took him to his hotel, where the hall-porter, as was only natural, evinced some surprise. As Doré was fond of joking, he said coolly, 'Give your arm to this gentleman up the stairs, please; he is my uncle'; and

"LONDON: A PILGRIMAGE."

remark was that London was not ugly; that there were grand and solemn scenes by the score in it. We went, once, at midnight to London Bridge, and remained there an hour, while he meditated over the two wonderful views—that above, and that below, bridge. His heart was touched by some forlorn creatures huddled together, asleep, on the stone-seats. (See p. 149.) He has reproduced it, again

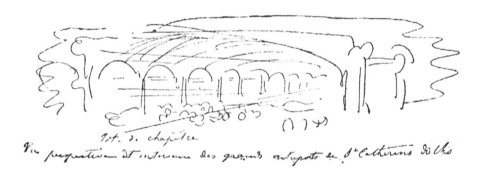

and again, with pencil and with brush. He never appeared to tire of it. I could seldom prevail upon him to make a sketch on the spot. The notes of scenes to be found scattered through this chapter and the next, were the utmost he would take on the scene. He made his old answer: "J'ai beaucoup de collodion dans la tête." But he was shy. The approach of a stranger made him shut up his book

when he had got his 'uncle' up-stairs he drew a ghastly sketch of him preaching from a pulpit to a congregation of other drunkards. The picture might have served as a companion to that of Cruikshank on 'Drink.'"

LIFE OF GUSTAVE DORÉ.

at once. In the docks, when I had insisted he ought to fortify himself with some notes of the shipping, he complied only on the condition that I would stand before him to shield him. The conse-

Epsom — Le triomphateur

quence of this reliance on his memory was that there were many blunders, in detail, in his work. Besides giving Norman arches to London Bridge, he made at least fifty horses run for the Derby!

"LONDON: A PILGRIMAGE."

When the album was completed he had a dinner in the Rue St. Dominique to exhibit it to his friends. "The effect of it," he wrote to me, "will be striking—I am certain. Arranged as it is, it has *très grand air*. I reckon thus, my dear friend, on your coming. It would be *hors de toute logique* if you were absent from this little inauguration."

At the dinner, over which Madame Doré presided, a quarrel arose between Gustave and his eldest brother, Ernest, and high words ensued. Madame Doré turned towards Doré, as though he were a boy of ten, and said, "Hold your tongue, Gustave; I am ashamed of you."

Doré, who had worked himself, regardless of the presence of his guests, into a fierce passion, became suddenly calm and silent at the command of his mother, and, bowing to her, resumed his dinner.

But the incident did not end here. When we had retired to the great salon, the brothers Doré disappeared, to re-appear in a few minutes, each holding an end of the colossal album that was to be submitted to the company. Madame Doré followed her little boys, who had both passed their fortieth year, smiling. I never saw Doré happier than he was that evening.

It was, indeed, a prodigious *tour de force*. London had never been so grandly, so poetically, nor so fully, presented to the world. The effects of light and shade were masterly. The weird pictures of docks and river, and refuge, and slum in the darkness of the night, were those of the imaginative mind that had illustrated the *Legend of the Wandering Jew,* and the *Inferno* of Dante; but they were real also. Within the covers of this immense album lay London in light and shadow, as seen by a poet.

The existence of the album was bruited about, and the news soon found its way into the papers. The *chroniqueurs* knew more about it than the artist and the author. It was reported that we had concluded a treaty with an eminent firm of London publishers for a great book. Even the title was invented for us—" Typical London." The rumour exasperated Doré, who was afraid that it would be prejudicial to our interests when we were ready to treat for publication. He wrote to me (Oct. 5, 1869):—

"Pray do your utmost to put a stop to this; or, when we do submit a proposition to a publisher, he will be surprised to find the work in the market, and will endeavour to take advantage of the false position in which we shall appear as persons who are under an engagement with the public to produce at any cost. This is very serious; and do what you can to put an end to the premature paragraphs. All kinds of publicity as to the vivid impression London has made upon me are good no doubt, except publicity about a treaty made with a publisher.

"The subject continues to delight me, and I am entirely at your disposal to begin, directly your affairs will allow you to come to Paris."

On the morning of his arrival in Paris, at the end of September 1869, after a short holiday in the country, he sent his faithful servant Jean to me, asking me to breakfast with him.

"I shall be delighted to see you again," he writes, "and to have a long talk over our projects."

The talk ended in the settlement of the plan of our work on London.

The business negociations for the publication of the book at the end of 1869 were difficult, and, to Doré especially, very irritating. He was more than once on the point of breaking them off. His irritable nature was jarred by rough remarks. He wrote me long letters of pain and remonstrance. He was worn out by a weary day we spent in a *salon* of the Moulin-Rouge, fighting over petty details. He was himself tenacious in making a good bargain, but he could not tolerate, the broad basis being established, a wrangle over the exact centimètres each drawing should be, or who should pay for *clichés*. He was as careful about my interests as about his own; and when he thought I was not handsomely considered, his spirit was up at once, and the gallant, whole-hearted friend, became fully apparent.

The negociations were brought to a conclusion in the spring of 1870, whereupon Doré wrote to me: "I congratulate you, and congratulate myself, on the news you lately sent me; for I saw difficulties in all these delays, which enervated me. Courage, then, and draw us up a masterly plan. I suppose that from this time you are heart and soul in the great work, deep in the studies and enquiries it necessitates. *À vous de cœur*. G. D. I am going to work with both hands, so that I may get to London in February." But the spring passed, and he never found time to cross the Channel.

Our enterprise was destined to receive a rude shock before we had proceeded far with it. On the 17th of July 1870, I received a brief note from the Rue Bayard: "I am leaving to night (for London). I don't know where I shall lodge, so let us meet to-morrow, Saturday, at eleven o'clock, at my gallery in New Bond Street. I shall wait for you." He never came. War was declared; and Doré wrote: "Excuse me, my dear Jerrold, for not having replied sooner. The agitation which has pervaded the country for the last few days is, as you must imagine, an obstacle to my journey to London at this moment. I am even on the eve of my departure for Strasburg, to embrace my soldier brother, who expects, from one moment to the other, to cross the Rhine with his squadron. It will be the end of the month before I can join you."

It was after many months of bitter experience that we saw him once more in London. He remained in Paris throughout the siege, and many are the stories told of his generous help to those who felt the privations of it, through their poverty. He himself bought and carried provisions (then at fabulous prices) to his suffering friends. He went to the fortifications and the outposts, as his series of powerful cartoons of the siege attest; and in May 1871 he had found his way to Versailles. He wrote,* immediately after the entry of the Versailles troops, that he was still detained there by the vigorous measures adopted by the military authorities :—

"I write to you, under the weight of the profoundest grief. Our poor capital is in flames; its palaces destroyed—its finest streets, and all that made

---

* To Messrs. Fairless & Beeforth of the Doré Gallery.

it beautiful. As I write, I have before me immense volumes of smoke, rising to the heavens. In the whole history of the world, I don't think there is a parallel instance of so sanguinary a drama, and of such ruin. In spite, gentlemen, of my ardent desire, and serious reasons, to go to London, it is absolutely impossible. My presence is necessary in the midst of my family (part of which, however, is separated from us), in Paris, and we are without news from them for a week past."

We shall glance again at Doré during the siege.

When he reached London, at length, he was in a state of profound dejection, from which we could, with difficulty, rouse him at intervals. It was not before the war was over—that is, in January 1872, that the first number of *London: a Pilgrimage*, appeared.

Our correspondence, in the course of our common work on London, was extensive, although we met often and spent hours over the breakfast-table in consultation. "My innumerable engagements," he writes, "make my life an almost perpetual slavery." He was careful and anxious as to the most trifling details. The exact measure of an initial letter, a trifling alteration in a design, the illustration of any incident we had seen in common, the dates of the despatch and arrival of *clichés*, drew rapid notes from him, often roughly illustrated. For instance, the Derby number of the work gave us much trouble. "You will receive," he wrote, "within forty-eight hours, proofs or photographs of all I have done. I have thought that the number should be more fully illustrated than the rest; and I have tried to scatter through the text the popular types and scenes of the road to Epsom and on the race-course. You will find, my dear Jerrold, that these sketches will involve hardly any alterations in your text, for they are, naturally, of things we have seen together. Thus, you must have mentioned the carriages filled with jovial people, shooting peas and throwing dolls at their neighbours. You have not forgotten the scene near the race-course, the

LIFE OF GUSTAVE DORÉ.

"LONDON: A PILGRIMAGE."

groups of humble families lunching on the grass—the bivouac of the poor. I have drawn a group of little children making up a sweep, like the grown people. You have, of course, mentioned all the games of the race-course, as that with sticks thrown at cocoa-nuts, the man trying the strength of his arm, and the boxer's tent (you remember we went into one).

I have drawn a family of country-people, sitting upon their luggage, who can find no lodging in London on the 30th of May." (See p. 192.)

He was anxious to hear the opinion of the publishers on his drawings, as they arrived. Were they satisfied? He had himself closely watched the engraving of every block. He was irritated by the

LIFE OF GUSTAVE DORÉ.

smallest objection, and dejected by a hint that any block was not all that could be desired. The trials of the war had aggravated his natural sensitiveness. It

had been remarked to him that there was no railing round his statue of Peabody. He protested to me angrily that to put one would destroy the moonlight effect he had managed, by which the figures were thrown up. When I went to him in Paris, after the siege, I found him sad and distressed at the defeat France had suffered. The loss of Alsace was a cruel blow to him; and he said to me that he should never set foot in Strasburg again. It had been his dream to end his days there. Four of his dogs were rolling at his feet. "But where are the pugs?" I asked. "They ate five for me," he answered, looking down tenderly at those which had been spared.

It was the end of July 1872 before he brought his *London* drawings to an end, and could cross the Channel to settle with me the way in which we should wind up our "pilgrimage."

I had proposed, while we were first travelling about London, and Doré was executing the large drawings for his album, that we should open with a general description of the river—from Sheerness to Maidenhead; and we were to arrive by the London boat from Boulogne. I insisted it was the only worthy way.

As the English coast is made, a white fog is thrown about the ship, daintily as a bride is veiled. The tinkling of bells is heard around. We anchor. Our whistle answers the screams of other ships. We are of a fleet in a fog: undoubtedly near England. It is a welcome and an exquisite sight when the first faint beaming of the morning light smiles through imprisoning vapour. The lifting of the silver veil, as I have watched it, vanishing into the blue above, leaving the scene crystal clear, is a transformation that would give the pilgrims, it seemed to me, the best first glimpse of Albion and the broad mouth of the silent highway to London. The water alive with ships: the ancient ports nested in the chalk: the Reculvers, brought to the edge of the rock : the flaunting braveries of Ramsgate and Margate, with the ship-loads of holiday-folks passing to and from the port : the lines of ocean ships and coasting vessels bearing, as far as the eye can reach, out from the immortal river, with the red Nore Light at the mouth : the war monsters lying in the distance by Sheerness : the scores of open fishing-boats working for Billingsgate Market—the confusion of flags, and the astonishing variety of build and rigging—are a surprise, absolutely bewildering, to all who, having the faculty of observation, pass to London this way for the first time. A tempting route to travel, had we not been in haste to open upon the heart of London.

But by Greenwich we often lingered and lounged —over our work. We watched, one lazy day, the ebb and flow of London's commerce by water, from the windows of the "Ship." While the pencil

worked, we ran through groups of subjects to be done. During our planning, I cited Isaac Disraeli on local descriptions: "The great art, perhaps, of local description, is rather a general than a particular view; the details must be life to the imagination; it is suggestive rather than descriptive." He gives a good illustration of the writer who mistakes detail for pictorial force, and gives five hundred verses to the description of a palace, "commencing at the façade, and at length finishing with the garden."

Lounging and chatting against the railings of the "Ship," with the after-dinner cigar, the artist caught the suggestion that would realise the scene. A striking pictorial fact is enough. Selection is the artistic faculty. We agreed that London had nothing more picturesque nor striking to show than the phases of her river, and her boundless docks. And hereabouts we tarried, week after week, never wearying of the rich variety of form, and colour, and incident. My note-books were filled with studies that were to be made before we entered the streets of London. Our accumulated material would have filled half-a-dozen volumes. London an ugly place indeed! Doré soon agreed with me that it abounded in delightful nooks and corners; in picturesque scenes and groups and

LIFE OF GUSTAVE DORÉ.

figures; in light and shade of the most attractive character. I planned several chapters on work-a-day

London, of which the workmen's trains, and the crowds passing over London Bridge, were to be the

key-notes. We were to analyse the crowds of toilers, and present to the reader a gallery of types—as, the banker, the stockbroker, the clerk, the shop-boy. Instead of separate types, we gave comprehensive pictures.

Our original plan took the form which, with Doré's approval, I shaped into the following remarks:—

"We are Pilgrims—not Historians; travelling by the same highway as that by which the Potters of London, and the Dinanters of Dinant on the Meuse, carried on their commerce six hundred years ago, we approach London. Upon its bosom cargoes were borne to the ancestors of Chaucer. It is an ancient tide of business and pleasure indeed.* We are true to remote amicable relations between the two foremost nations of the earth—we, French Artist and English Author—when we resolve to study the

---

* There seems reason to believe that an extensive trade existed in the thirteenth and fourteenth centuries, between London and the town of Dinant on the Meuse, in the purchase, that is, of its manufactures of brass vessels, for which the town is still famous. The "Potters" of London, according to Mr. Riley (*Memorials of London and London Life*), were makers and sellers of vessels of *metal*, and he notices accordingly transactions between them and the Dinanters. Among others, Baldwin le Chaucer is entered as being indebted in £6 10s. to Nicholas de Woderseye, "Merchant of Dynaunt."

greatest city on the face of the globe together. Under the magic influences of its vastness; its prodigious, unwieldy life; and its extraordinary varieties of manners, character, and external picturesqueness; a little plan, that peeped out of a few pleasant days' wanderings through the light and the shade of London, has grown into a broad, serious, and very

responsible purpose. Some happy memories of trips through strange places have been nursed into preparations for a pilgrimage that shall traverse London from the Pool to the Slopes of Richmond.

"The population of every city may be sharply parted into two sections, by no means halves, viz., those who work, and those who are able to choose, or are

"LONDON: A PILGRIMAGE."

compelled, to live, without work. These two sections have been subdivided in many fanciful ways. There are the people, for instance, who will not work, and are without honest means; then again there are the people who are incapable of work, as the halt, the sick, the blind. The workers have been split up into hundreds of divisions, as Mr. Riley* shows, centuries ago, and in recent times by Mr. Henry Mayhew. But from that November day in 1419 (the third mayoralty of Richard Whityngton), when John Carpenter concluded the Liber Albus, down to the present time, no satisfactory, and certainly no complete, analytical survey of London has been made; no labour fairly comparable with the learned and methodical report on the trades of Paris, over which Horace Say presided, has been attempted in regard to the English metropolis. Mr. Charles Knight's extensive series of articles on London are brought into only a filmy connection by an analytical table of contents. Mr. Henry Mayhew's *London Labour and the London Poor*

---

* In his introduction to his *Memorials of London and London Life*, when touching on early trades and forgotten names of trades, and the surnames derived from them, he instances Roger the Flaoner, as probably a maker of flans, or flauns, "a light cake once much in vogue and not much unlike a pancake." Flan is at this time the popular name all over Paris for plain crust tarts holding fruit.

is but a brilliant fragment on the wage classes and criminal classes of the metropolis. In brief, an authoritative and a complete analysis of London

La salle des grands Tonneaux
chez Barklay perkins

commerce and London work remains to be written; and then we should have no full view of the metropolis.

"LONDON : A PILGRIMAGE."

"Mr. Peter Cunningham and Mr. John Timbs are admirable and searching authorities, who give vast masses of antiquarian and other information, for the use of the historian, and for the cultivation of the lettered Englishman. From these methodical chroniclers of our own time, back to the days when Chaucer sang of the Tabard, is a span of centuries, rich in lore, in song, in spirit, and satire, and pictures about the great city which threatens to spread from the source to the mouth of the Thames. It was a place of great traffic and great merchants in the time of the Emperor Nero, according to Tacitus. That which is to be gathered from the poets, the historians, the voluminous memoir writers, English and foreign, the ballad and pamphlet collectors, has been industriously ransacked again and again. The subject is, and has been to many generations, so engaging that enthusiasts have fastened upon parishes and streets. To be the historian of a London alley is fame enough; to be chronicler of the London of his own time was to secure the writer a living name through ages— as witness, William Fitz-Stephen, Stow, Lydgate, John Taylor the Water-poet, Gay, and many others. They who know their London of to-day love to read authentic descriptions of the Maypole that was in the Strand, and the headlong games at foot-ball that were played there. The royal water pageants when the river was the City's main highway; Raleigh gazing upon the tide from the Tower; the gibbets* that fringed the river as warnings to the evil-doer; the salmon-fishing by London Bridge; the wild fields where now are narrow thoroughfares—hundreds of associations of the olden time which stimulate the imagination and help the Present to realise the Past —are lovingly preserved.

"Just as the mind is delighted with a line from Steele's description of a summer boat-trip from Richmond, quoted by Knight from the *Spectator*,† as realising a delightful scene and contrast with the utmost vividness; so we fondly hope to please the

---

* Such spectacles may frighten crows,
But never scared a thief.—*C. Denis.*

† "Nothing remarkable happened in our voyage; but I landed with ten sail of apricot boats at Strand Bridge, after having put in at Nine Elms, and taken in melons."

"LONDON : A PILGRIMAGE."

imaginations of future generations, as well as to present an acceptable picture of London life and London exteriors to our contemporaries.

"How little the London of even fifty years hence will resemble the marvellous city of to-day—webbed as it already is with railways, and honey-combed with pipes—may be anticipated by any person who will make an estimate of the changes which the last forty years have seen. Mr. Knight's *London* of 1841 is a book of the past. His streets and his Cockneys— even those of Dickens—are of another generation —the like of which we know no more. His picture of 'a plug in a frost' is a part of London history; it has ceased to be *our* plug in a frost—and the figures are less familiar to our sight than Chinamen. It is the prodigious fund of human energy that moves for ever along the banks of the Thames which makes the surfaces of London life as shifting and evanescent as clouds before a gale. The force which never rests is for ever producing new forms, so that he must be alert who aspires to catch the manners, living as they rise, in London.

"We are pilgrims: not, I repeat, historians, nor antiquaries, nor topographers. Our plan is to present London in the quick to the reader—as completely as we may be able to grasp the prodigious giant, and dissect his Titan limbs, the floods of his veins, the iron beams of his muscles! We approach him by the main artery which feeds his unflinching vigour. We shall examine him at work and at play; asleep and in his wakefullest moments. We shall pay court to him in his brightest and his happiest guises: when he stands solemn and erect in the dignity of his quaint and ancient state: when his steadfastness to the old is personified in the dress of a beef-eater, or his passion for the new is shown in the hundred changes of every passing hour. 'Human destinies look ominous without some perceptible intermixture of the sable or the grey,'* so we shall approach him also in his sickness, his poverty, his evil-doing. If, as Jean Paul tells us, play is the first poetry of the human being, the poetry of the grown man lies in his work; his chivalry amid the sick and old, his mercy to the weak of purpose, and even the base in nature, affect a large proportion of London life that cannot be passed over by the self-respecting pilgrim. It is a weak stomach that is sipping always what is sweet.

"Our object is to seize representative bits of each of the parts which are included in the whole.

"Each function of London life comprehends the

---

* Hawthorne: *Blithedale Romance.*

most striking varieties of men, manners, and rewards. Taking a philosophical view of armed authority mounted for the common protection, the field-marshal is at the top of the ladder, and the beadle at its base. There is a distinct affinity between the west-end club and the bar parlour: the priest, the schoolmaster, the writer, the man of science, and the artist. Threads hold together the great house in St. Swithin's Lane and the pot-house loan society. There is a link between the dealer in horses and the wig of Mr. Speaker: between the foibles and follies of the great, and the vices and crimes of the humble. Kung, who is greening his old tea-leaves upon copper pans under celestial rule, is beholden to the little tea-party in Camden Town, and the local doctor again profits by Kung's rascality. A folly dropped into the fashionable waters of the West, raises a ripple presently in the saddest places of poverty and crime.

"It is among the working population of a community like that which has been busy by the banks of the Thames from the days of Nero—and has raised Rome upon British ruins, and British upon Roman again—that the true, innermost secret of the mighty fact London must be sought. How the conglomerate millions act and re-act upon each other; draw their wants from every corner of the globe;

split up industries into a hundred sub-industries, and then set to work to divide these, till ingenious man is lost in wonder over the infinite methods which competition has invented of earning a leg of mutton;—suggests a long and patient study, that cannot be without strong interest to intelligent humanity, nor devoid of use in the hand of the philosopher and historian.

"The first glance at this subject is confounding enough to slacken the courage of the most methodical and the toughest inquirer. I remember being struck, after travelling through one of the great pine forests of Sweden, with the factories of Norrköping—where the forest is split into lucifer matches. Here were the princely capitalists to the beggars: gentlemen in chateaux, purveyors of stock-in-trade to the great army of Rags! There was lately a lofty palace in Victoria Street, Westminster, the fiery streams from which are in direct communication with our gaols and workhouses. 'Blue Ruin' was the particular formation of which its corner-stone consisted. There are men whose pernicious commercial activities represent a township of pauperism: there are others on whose heart and honour the hopes of a thousand creatures are hinged. As we take nearer views, passing from the general surface that is brilliant to the underlying force, we find the same humanity—only the circumstances differ. Here, as in the high region, are the men who work honestly, and the sluggards and cowards who prey upon work—who will pick dainties from the needle of the seamstress. We touch the gates of the gaol; we hear the oaths echoing from

the casual ward. Also, we are bound to mark and record that we see the thousand end honest lives in misery for the ten who sink to pauperism, vagrancy, or crime. It is not possible to overpraise the greatness of heart with which the English working-classes have passed through famine. They alone have known how to starve for an idea. In approaching the sadder parts of the great metropolis, in which stubborn custom and purblind speculation have doomed them to abide, the poverty of one man re-acting on his neighbour and lack of money forcing the unfortunate to the companionship of drunkenness and crime, we seek the completeness of our picture, in the hope and belief that this completeness will be its chief value. Hard, solid work—work that makes millionnaires and leaves the worn-out fingers of the heroic honest man cold upon a pallet—work is the Key to London. In the serried legions of the distressed, battling for an independent crust and loathing the unearned crumb, there is a spectacle of moral grandeur which covers all the crime and vice and drunkenness. There are a hundred daily heroes for one craven wretch.

"If this pilgrimage through London should not afford the rich and well-to-do a higher estimate of the hand-to-mouth population than they have yet formed, chiefly through the police courts and poor-law records, the pilgrims will be justly convicted of weakness and narrowness.

"Those who can and do work are emphatically—London, and the great city is their inheritance from countless generations of workers, stretching back to those rich English merchants whose fame reached the ancient Romans. They make the laws and make the laws obeyed; they grace the senate and the bench; they preach from the pulpit, teach in the school-room, spread daily history from the printing office; speed ships to every clime; make London the chief granary of the world; send railway navvies to the Japanese; deal in anything the earth produces, and invent against the keenest the means of cheapening in order to hold a market. It is a French saying that wine, now-a-days, is made with everything—even with the grape—a compliment to commercial ingenuity which may be applied in London as well as in Paris. Privat d'Anglemont once wrote a lively book on the unknown trades of the capital of which he was the reigning Bohemian—and dived under the surface far enough to reach the breeder of gentles for anglers, and the painter of turkeys legs to give the birds a fresh appearance. Our neighbours are ingenious, but they have not overmatched London ingenuity in the art of contriving strange occupations.

"London wears a dismal exterior to the eye of the foreigner, because all London means work. The State Secretary, in his severely appointed room, receiving a deputation, has a hard-worked appearance, and looks dressed for downright business. In the clubs men split into groups, and are all, or nearly all, intent on some mighty affair of the day. The streets, west as well as east, are filled with people who have errands. They are not sad men and women, but they are seriously devoted to the thing in hand. Young peers—heirs to fat slices of counties—are in the throng, repairing to committee sittings, public meetings, board appointments. Old men, retired from business, are nevertheless going to business. "Better rub than rust."

That is a duke, with the bundle of papers under his arm. Here is a Member of Parliament, with his documents for the long day and night of work before him in a bag. Many of the pale men in wig and gown, pacing Westminster Hall, are slaves to fashionable society, as well as barristers in large practice, and they sit up studying their briefs after the rout is over. Their luncheon is in a sandwich box, so that nature may not rob them of an hour in the best part of the precious working time. The ordinary daily labours of a city alderman, who is in business as well as on the bench, would fill the week of an Italian, and leave him exhausted on the seventh day. There is not a happier man than this same alderman, and his content is never so hearty as when he is speeding from one duty to another. His features

are set; his manner is solid; he looks into no shop, heeds no passer-by; directness is his quality—it is that also of the crowds threading their ways swiftly on all sides. Energy and earnestness pervade London shops, and are of fiery intensity in the popular

markets. Take the Whitechapel Road on a Saturday night; or Camden Town; or Knightsbridge; or the Borough; or Tottenham Court Road: the vehemence of the street traders is alarming to a stranger, who anticipates a score of cases of apoplexy. St. Martin's-le-Grand, when the boxes are about to be closed! The Docks, when the wind has wafted a fleet home from the downs! Or Petticoat Lane on Sunday morning! Or Billingsgate, when the market opens! Here, emphatically I repeat, is London."

Doré was pleased with the comprehensive scale of my plan, for he saw in it ample scope both for the play of his imagination and his observation. We even talked about treating Paris on the same scale and method; but long before even the abridged *London* we published was finished, his mind had turned to other subjects far away, and chiefly to his great pictures and the cultivation of his power as a landscape painter. He had engagements to fulfil for his Doré Gallery that were enough to monopolise the energy of the hardest worker.

But the parts of London that riveted Doré's attention—for they touched his charitable heart, and they are also the more picturesque—were the abiding-places of the poor. Where the struggle for life is ever severe, as in London, the wounded and disabled in the battle must be in considerable numbers. The London army of Lazarus bewildered and horrified the artist, as we lingered in the by-ways. I pointed out to him how our subscription lists and fancy fairs display the open-handedness of all who have money,

"LONDON: A PILGRIMAGE."

when a pressing occasion calls forth the latent charity of the most commercial of races. And thus the relief of the multitude is connected with the pleasures and the Christian charity of the rich. Some of the spare riches which flow from work and

trade are drawn back to the young, left alone and helpless before they can join the ranks of labour, and to the denuded invalids in whom there is no more possibility of work.

"We will do a great work," he said again and again, as I laid the foregoing development of our

LIFE OF GUSTAVE DORÉ.

labour before him. But the scheme was cut down ultimately by two-thirds; and we skimmed the surface where we had hoped to probe the depths.

CHAPTER XI.

GUSTAVE DORÉ IN LONDON.

As I shall show, it was the siege of Paris that finally took all the youth out of Gustave Doré. Before, the great man could not repress the *gamin*. After, the abounding spirits, the love of athletic tricks, the wild forms of humour, even the practical jokes, the romps with his dogs, seemed to have fallen away from him. He re-appeared in London depressed, serious, and bent on transacting the business he had on hand at his Gallery, about his great picture, "Christ leaving the Prætorium," which had lain rolled up and buried beyond the reach of German shells during the siege, but was now to be submitted to the judgment of the London public.

LIFE OF GUSTAVE DORÉ.

I was fortunate enough to be very useful to him throughout the negociations which ended in the establishment, by Messrs. Fairless and Beeforth, of the Doré Gallery in Bond Street. "I should like to have twenty quires of paper under my hand," he writes (January 5, 1869), in his impulsive way of exaggerating any service rendered to him, "to cover them with the warm thanks I owe you for the great and excellent service and the proof of friendship I have just received from you. I am hastening to thank M. Fairless for acceding to my views; and, under these circumstances, I do not hesitate to promise him all the success he can desire, and to discount the future. When you are passing New Bond Street, press home the conviction you have created in M. Fairless; and believe in the impatience I feel to have the pleasure of thanking you in Paris."

When, on the 10th of July, he arrived at Morley's Hotel, after the siege, it was to resume our wanderings about London, as well as to see to the installation of the first great gallery picture; and it was during the many days we spent together that I remarked the profound change which had come over him. His sensitiveness was now morbid. A feeling of resentment against his French critics appeared to have become fixed in his mind. When I met him at breakfast in the morning, at his hotel, he would indulge in a burst of anger and regret that he had undertaken to illustrate *London*. He feared that the illustrator would be again welcomed at the expense of the painter. This dread remained with him whenever he took up his pencil.

Thanking me for something I had written deprecating the perpetual repetition of the statement that he was hasty and careless as an artist, tossing off paintings as well as drawings without giving a second thought to them, he said (21st January 1873): "Thank you particularly for the theme you develop in regard to the prejudice raised against me on account of my alleged hasty productiveness. This cannot be too often attacked."

"They will not accept *Doré peintre!*" he would exclaim. I had urged him to send two of his landscapes to the Royal Academy, and we often discussed the subject. But he always came to the conclusion that he would be rejected, and that his thousands of illustrations, as he bitterly expressed it, would be thrown at his head. He would eat his cutlet in sulky silence, and I would leave him to speak first. He would, at last, break away from his gloomy reverie, call for the coffee, almost tear the end from his cigar with his teeth, and, when he had taken a few strong pulls at it, dash into a fresh subject, and a brighter one.

Then we would issue forth on the day's travels, generally calling at the Gallery in Bond Street to begin with. Doré was never tired of glancing

into his Gallery: it was his sole consolation, as a painter. I found his old eagerness as an observer, and his animal spirits as a humorist, revive by short fits and starts when we made our way behind the scenes of London. He was enchanted with Petticoat Lane, the sailors' haunts in Ratcliff Highway, Drury Lane by night, the slums of Westminster, the thieves' quarters round about Whitechapel, and the low lodging-houses. The long black kitchens of these houses had a particular charm for him. The groups of street-folk, eating, lounging, drying their clothes at the common fire, sorting their baskets; the heavy toil- and care-worn sleepers in the shadowy dormitories; and the children tumbling about in rags—constituted scenes that never faded from his memory. He noticed, as Dickens would, old toy-makers, making card-board cabs in a corner. He was fond of roaming about the docks. He was particularly impressed with the van-loading in Thames Street. Almost his last water-colour drawing was a scene from this street. He made some studies of the flower-girls by the Royal Exchange; but when he painted or drew them afterwards, he put French baskets on their arms, and was impatient when I pointed this out. He painted an English drunkard with a French measure of wine before him. The Field Lane Night Refuge, with a clergyman reading in the midst of the waifs and strays of our cruel London life, inspired him with one of his finest drawings. Tiger Bay, in the heart of Rascaldom, supplied him with a score of "types." We were presented to "the strongest woman in Shadwell"—a brazen creature, with a brutal face, and the muscles of a navvy.

"That is not a type," I said to Doré, as we turned away—"but a monster."

"She is the ideal of ferocious animalism—a hideous

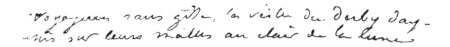

excresence of civilisation. The latent brute beast in humanity, has burst out into this hideous spectacle. Yes, she is a type—of the wild human animal."

We visited the opium-smokers in the room described by Dickens in *Edwin Drood*. The old woman was

GUSTAVE DORÉ IN LONDON.

there, in bed, mixing and smoking her opium, while her tame mice ran about the ragged and dirty bedclothes. The man's place was vacant: he was undergoing "a month of it" for begging, she said in a hoarse voice. Doré watched in silence, while I and the inspector who was with us, talked. He grasped my arm as we went out into the night, and said, "C'est affreux." He could not shake off the effect, even when we were witnessing the humours of the "sailors' hops." But now and again, as I have said, a flash of the old brightness would pass over him. One Sunday, when he had been lunching with me, he proposed to drive to Hampstead to see the Cockneys disporting themselves. As we went along he talked about music with a lady—an accomplished amateur—who was with us, and sang snatches from various operas, as their merits were touched upon. While we were crossing the heath, he suddenly burst into a Swiss air in his slight tenor voice with extraordinary agility; then suddenly he relapsed into the sad thoughtfulness which had become his chronic state.

We went to the theatre and heard the song of the "Little wee dog"; and on the following morning Doré burst into my room, singing:

"Oh vere oh vere is ze leetle ve dog,
Oh vere oh vere is 'e?"

dancing round and round in imitation of the actor; and still dancing as he left, down the passage back to his own room. I found him, an hour afterwards, at his drawing table in deep melancholy. On the morrow of the Oxford and Cambridge boat-race (we had dined in the evening with the crews), he sang, at the breakfast table,

"For zey are jolly good fellows!" *

winding up with a "Heep! heep! hoorah!" Then he fell into his dreamy mood, and said, turning to me a very grave face, "Do you know, *mon ami*, it was *assommant*, this 'heep! heep! hoorah!'"

He chafed under his ignorance of the English language, and was always going to study it in earnest. He would get me to give him English words and phrases while he painted. He never found time to study; but his tenacious memory enabled him to store up many words and phrases, so that he

---

* The author of the obituary notice in the *Times* justly remarked: "It is to be noted, however, that Doré, though he studied England closely, never quite entered into the spirit of English things, and his illustrations to his friend Blanchard Jerrold's *London* were hardly a success. He never mastered our language either, though he spoke it with a true French intrepidity. It was funny to hear him misuse shall and will; and exclaim, 'Will you that I shall tell you now what I will do?' He took a long time in learning that the French 'Mon Dieu' must not be translated literally in current conversation."

managed to get about London. But he said, in 1879, at the rate he was progressing he should begin to speak fluently in about five-and-twenty years—"that is, when I am about to die."

We were dining together in the coffee-room of the Westminster Palace Hotel, while some twenty gentlemen, at a centre-table, were celebrating the success of some scheme of theirs before a Parliamentary Committee. I explained this to Doré, who was amused; for the party were eating in solemn silence—one man occasionally breaking it with a few words in an undertone to a neighbour. At last, one of the diners ventured to address a question in a loud voice to the man at the head of the table.

"Ah! le bavard!" said Doré.

As an instance of his penetration, I would note that, one morning, when we were strolling down St. James's Street, he suddenly pointed to a tall man opposite who was daintily picking his way, and leaning upon the arm of a companion. Doré, fixing his eyes upon him, said:

"That must be one of your great men."

It was Lord Beaconsfield.

When we went together to Newgate, he remained in a corner of the prison-yard, observing the prisoners taking their exercise—a moving circle of wretchedness. He declined to make a sketch. As I have observed already, he was shy with his note-book, and would ask me to stand before him when he ventured to cast a note or two into it. His habit was to pause awhile and take in a scene; and, in the evening at his hotel, to fill a sketch-book with notes of the day's observations. As a rule they were remarkably true and vivid. In Newgate, he asked the turnkey, who accompanied us, to leave him for a few minutes at an opening that commanded a view of the yard. When we returned to him, he had not used his pencil, but his eye had taken in every detail of the scene.

"I will tell you," he said, "what most of these men are." He pointed to a common thief, a forger, a highway robber, an embezzler; and the gaoler was astonished. His guesses were, mostly, quite correct.

The next day when we met, he laid before me his circle of prisoners. It was a chain of portraits from the poor frightened little postman, who had succumbed to temptation in his poverty, to the tall officer who had cheated a widow out of her last mite.

His observations, in the parks and in society, on English female beauty, were curious. He seldom drew a beautiful female countenance. At the Opera, he would survey the boxes with his glass, and pick out a

pale, attenuated tamely fair woman, and say—"Elle est belle." The piquant beauty, the laughing eye and rosy lip; the pink-and-white young girls to be seen cantering in the park on summer mornings, drew no admiration from him, as his drawings showed. He was struck by the majestic, the commanding—what we call the queenly types of loveliness to be found in drawing-rooms; and he was touched by the sad beauty to be seen in poor street flower-sellers, lavender-vendors, servants, even in rags; but archness, brightness, youth with its natural witcheries, could not arrest his attention as an artist. He failed, in short, to catch the typical female beauty of England. His Belle Anglaise is beautiful—but she is scarcely English. The only finished study of a sparkling, mocking beauty, he ever painted, to my knowledge, was a portrait of Adelina Patti before her marriage. His Sleeping Beauty in the *Contes de Perrault* is no enchantress: she is the failure of the work—she is even grotesquely out of drawing. His mediæval damosels are dolls. His caricatures of Englishmen and Englishwomen were the conventional French types of our race. His Englishmen, before he became familiar with the streets of London, had red hair, the projecting teeth, the long chins, and open mouths of the caricaturists of the *Journal pour Rire*; and his women were but exaggerations of

LIFE OF GUSTAVE DORÉ.

what he selected as English beauty. The *Anglais à Mabille,* a popular lithograph for many years in Paris, was by Doré. With a white hat thrown back, dressed

in a light suit, sitting at a table, and with drooping mouth and prominent eyes, staring at the spectator, and showing the teeth which have been compared to tombstones, this Englishman at Mabille has been the delight of the Paris flâneur for many years. Doré was well satisfied with it, albeit he never acknowledged publicly that he was its creator; for he executed it on a large scale in oil, and it hung for years in the ante-chamber in the Rue St. Dominique. It was after his visits to London that he removed it.

Doré delighted in his annual trips to London during the season; and was charmed by the welcome he received in society. The Prince and Princess of Wales invited him to Chiswick, and received him at a *diner intime*; and his name was to be found in the list of those entertained at what are called "the best houses." At Chiswick he was introduced to the Queen, and Her Majesty held a long conversation with him, in the course of which she said she hoped to see him at Balmoral. Doré ventured to make some remarks on the influence of the Prince Consort on art, that were very graciously received. The Princess Louise delighted him by accepting one of his sketches. Lady Combermere gave a dinner in his honour. Archbishop Tait held a grand banquet in the Guard Room of Lambeth Palace, at which he was the principal guest. When he was the guest of the Lord Mayor, the ladies stood upon their chairs to look at him and wave their handkerchiefs. He was a great attraction at fashionable fancy fairs, to which he contributed drawings liberally. He went to stay with the Orleans family when they resided at Twickenham. His love of music drew him to Lady Downshire's entourage. His friend, Canon F. K. Harford (himself an accomplished artist), escorted him to Lambeth Palace and to Dean Stanley. He and Colonel Teesdale became fast friends, and travelled to Scotland together, as we shall see. Sometimes he would stay for five or six weeks, drawing and painting, first in Jermyn Street, then at Morley's hotel, then at the Westminster Palace, and lastly at the Bath; and giving his afternoons and evenings to drives, calls, dinners, and receptions. His faithful servant, Jean, accompanied him in his early visits; and although this honest old trooper could not speak a word of English, he would execute the most difficult commissions, with the utmost correctness, even to the purchase of the particular paper, pencils, brushes, and canvases his impatient master required. Doré was perpetually expressing astonishment at Jean's ingenuity in these respects. To brave Jean all he did for his master was a labour of love.

Life in the hurly-burly of the London season, however, soon palled upon the worker, who in Paris lived a retired life with a group of intimate friends about him. He tried to tear himself away many times before he actually left. His table was covered with invitations—some from persons he had never seen, the Leo Hunters of the present generation.

One of these, which he accepted, led to an experience of a Sunday afternoon in a middle-class upstart family, which he described with that graphic force he had in conversation.

An elderly gentleman and his son had paid two visits to the Gallery in Bond Street, had examined a picture very attentively, and had made inquiries as to the price of it. After the second visit, the son called and left a letter for Doré. It was an invitation to dinner in a fashionable square, for the following Sunday. Doré tossed it aside, saying, contemptuously, he knew nothing of the people. He was asked to remember that the gentleman who had invited him, probably wished to see him on the subject of the picture he had examined so closely. Doré, after much persuasion, and several refusals, was prevailed upon to accept the dinner of the unknown connoisseur.

The dinner was early. Doré arrived at the appointed hour, and was introduced to a family of persons who could not muster twenty words of French among them. They were a solemn, ceremonious group—with airs, not of cultivated, but of rich people.

When dinner was announced, Doré was aghast to find that he was the only guest. His description of the gloomy afternoon he passed, was a picture of the dulness of the rich commercial class. He was hungering for a cigar; and, at length, the host suggested to him that if he smoked his son would accompany him in a turn in the garden of the square, where he could indulge for half an hour. In all that cavernous house, there was not a corner where smoke was permitted. Doré described himself as sauntering in the square with the youth appointed to follow him —his prisoner. "I felt ready to seize him by the throat, to strangle him, and run away," he said, holding up his hands like claws, and putting on a diabolical expression.

And, the host bought no picture, and was never seen again. He had enjoyed his Sunday lion all to himself, and this was his sole desire.

We were a small party at dinner one evening at Very's, when the conversation fell on the study of the figure. Doré described, in his own bright and earnest way, how he had studied it for many years.

"You must know every muscle, every fibre, every movement," he said. "This knowledge is to be got at only by going to the hospital dissecting-room, as well as to the living model." He wound up with an energetic expression, stretching out his arm, and clutching at an imaginary object as he spoke, "*Il faut*," said he, "*fourrer la main dedans.*"

London as I have remarked, was illustrated by Doré, while he was in one of his *grincheux* moods.

PUGILISTS' TENT, EPSOM.

It was a great success to the publishers; it was hailed as an extraordinary presentation of London, by the pencil of a poetic observer; and to Doré it brought a good financial reward. Yet he was never content while engaged upon it, and his ill-humour increased as he approached the end. He had been disappointed by finding the colossal "London" album left on his hands.* It had been carried to America for sale, and had been returned. Nobody would bid his price, which was not less than £1,000. He was told that he had failed to realize the characteristics of the Saxon race. He had not got nearer the true types of English men and English women, than Gavarni. This was severe condemnation. Its effect fell, in part, upon the guide and companion of his London wanderings.

"You know," he said, " je vous en veux."

He was dissatisfied with his work, and I was to blame, because I had done my utmost to keep him from the very errors with which his English reviewers reproached him—as making street lamps project from the walls, his Norman arches to London bridge, and many other evidences, not of haste, but of disregard of details. His boat-race drawings were full of blunders. At the end of our London labours, Doré sulked awhile. I knew it would pass, and waited. But I was roused to write a formal protest when I

---

* Yet he was generous, even under his bitter disappointment; for he dismounted the more important drawings, and distributed them among his friends.

found that he had issued a French édition of our *London* discarding my text, and putting M. Louis Enault in my place.*

It was an unhandsome action, and it parted us for a year.

To Doré's honour, be it said, he was the first to take a step towards a reconciliation. On his annual visit to London, after our quarrel, he came to me suddenly before leaving on his return home, walked straight into my library, held out his hand, and said:

"I couldn't leave without seeing you." He knew he was in the wrong. He had behaved ungenerously and unfairly towards me, in return for months of labour which I had devoted to him, apart from my proper share in our common undertaking. His vanity had been his enemy here, as it had been on other occasions. He must appear before his countrymen

* *Londres.* 1 vol. 4to. Par Gustave Doré. Texte par Louis Enault. 1875-6. MM. Hachette et Cie. Boulevard Saint Germain, 77, Paris.

LIFE OF GUSTAVE DORÉ.

as the sole discoverer of the hidden ways of London. It must be the London of Doré, and of Doré alone. Courbet once said of Doré, "*Il n'y a que lui et moi.*" There were times when Doré said to himself, "*Il n'y a que moi.*"*

We had a long and, in passages of it, an angry discussion. But he could not, and did not, justify himself. He broke off into other questions, suggested friendly meetings, and then stopped again and again, looking with very searching eyes at me, and saying, "But—since we are no longer friends——"

In the end we parted on the old affectionate terms; and the bitter subject was never mentioned more by

---

* There was a strong affinity between Gustave Doré and Gustave Courbet. They both came from south-eastern France. As boys they were familiar with the same scenes. Courbet was some thirteen years Doré's senior, and was born at Ornans, in the Franche-Comté, in the sweet country of the Doubs—a region for far and wide all natural beauty. Courbet, like Doré, began by caricature, at his school and in his native town. He was a passionate student of nature—a man of original genius; but an egotist who held that, as an artist, he could do no wrong. He has left fine work behind him, as his "Burial Scene at Ornans," now in the Louvre, "At Bay," and other broad, bold, and true hunting-pieces; and some fine portraiture, as the "Belle Hollandaise"; but, unlike Doré, he had no imagination, no poetic insight. His strength was rude, and coarse, and turbulent. He was a violent man in all things; and he will be remembered most vividly for his share in the destruction of the Vendome column, an act that drove him, in irreparable disgrace, to die in an obscure Swiss village by the banks of Lake Leman.

either of us. Doré could not rest while at enmity with anybody who had once been his friend. Testimony to this noble feeling in him was borne by several of his old companions after his death.

Paul Dalloz, who had been intimate with Doré for thirty years, wrote to me of him :—*

"Everybody knows the works of the artist, full of the past, the present, and the future; I knew something more and better than his glory—I knew his big heart. The irascible, agitated, irritable man, had a tenderness which he thrust under the rough exterior, but which betrayed itself nevertheless. An example. A discussion on art had separated us for a moment. A few days passed : then the door of my study opened : it was Doré.

"'Let us embrace one another,' he said. 'It is too stupid to quarrel with friends. We will talk no more about painting, but only of drawings. Then, you were perhaps in the right. I have thought it over.'

"We hugged one another. He had been the first to come back. He was a better man than I. And he has gone the first. It is perhaps justice, for the next world is, doubtless, better than this. But I have a friend the less, and a friend like this one. It is a heavy blow, I assure you."

* Letter to B. J.

LIFE OF GUSTAVE DORÉ.

Albert Wolff has described a quarrel with Doré. He had touched the same ever open wound. He had written an article on one of Doré's pictures in the Salon, in which he was warm towards the illustrator of Rabelais and Dante, but cold towards the painter. The critic and the artist had been friends for fifteen years; and this article parted them for five. Then, one summer evening the two met face to face in the Champs Elysées. It was Doré who advanced with outstretched hand, saying: "Is it all over?"

"As you please," was the critic's cold reply.

Doré hesitated; but his better nature prevailed over his pride, and, passing his arm within that of Wolff, he said: "I must speak to you."

He was a better man than M. Wolff. Hereupon the two paced about under the trees, amid the crowd; while Doré, who wore his heart on his sleeve, poured out his plaint. Wolff said no tragedy had ever stirred him so deeply, as the story of Doré's sufferings under the cruel indifference of his countrymen towards him as a painter. He appeared to be the most miserable man in all Paris, smarting under the injustice of the world. The tears stood in his eyes while he recounted his sufferings. He who had worked so prodigiously, who was filled with the noblest ambition, who loved art passionately for its own sake, was misunderstood, neglected, put aside. Had he his time to come over again, he would not make a single drawing. He would not illustrate the smallest volume.

Yet it was in the years when he worked the greater part of his time, in his drawing-studio in the Rue St. Dominique, that he was happiest. No blyther

ORLANDO.

spirit ever toyed with the laughing hours, than Doré when he broke away from his blocks and plates, and went out to amuse himself at a first night at the theatre, or at Rossini's.

When, on the 29th of February 1864, Rossini kept

LIFE OF GUSTAVE DORÉ.

his seventy-second birthday, Doré was of the little dinner-party. "As usual," according to M. Louis Engel, " a musical soirée followed; but between the two, Gustave Doré, the *enfant gâté* of the house, gave a terpsichorean, vocal, and instrumental performance in honour of the host and the few intimate friends assembled before the soirée, dancing a *pas seul*, singing, with a tenor voice which reached easily the C in the chest, a song, '*Que c'est comme un bouquet de fleurs*'; and then he played a solo on the violin, making an immense caricature of a certain violinist, which caricature, however, showed to what an extent he had mastered the mechanism of the instrument."

In Doré's dining-room, by the hearth, was a framed portrait of the maestro, with the following inscription :—

Souvenir de tendre Amitié
Offert à Gustave Doré.

Qui joint à son genie de Peintre-dessinateur les talents de violoniste distingué, et de tenorine charmant s'il vous plaît.

G. Rossini.

Passy, 29 Août,
   1863.

It was one of Doré's most valued treasures.

DORÉ'S MUSIC MASTER.

CHAPTER XII.

DORÉ'S SHAKSPEARE.

IT has been remarked by M. E. Forgues, in that chapter of his *Book Illustrators of the Nineteenth Century* which is devoted to Gustave Doré, that it has become already impossible to obtain a complete list of the works on which Doré's pencil laboured. Many have already disappeared; and some of his early work, albeit ill-engraved and printed on bad paper—as the first edition of *Rabelais*, bound in blue paper, the *Labours of Hercules*, the adventures of three artists, and *Sainte Russie*—fetch high prices among book-collectors. But some of his early pencillings have disappeared altogether. It is no loss to art. When he was contributing a page of caricatures weekly to the *Journal pour Rire*, or, during the Crimean war, tossing off battle-pieces for the *Musée Anglais-Français*, he threw out ideas roughly by the score, which are interesting now

ORLANDO FURIOSO.

only to the student of his progress. In the *Ménagerie Parisienne*, an extravagant pictorial review of eccentric Parisian life, there are indications of the power which was developed afterwards in *Rabelais*, then in the *Contes Drôlatiques* and the *Wandering Jew*, and finally in *Croquemitaine, Don Quixote, Ariosto*, and the *Crusades*. The progress is swift, but it is steady from the early hack-work for papers, the albums, like the *Trois Artistes Incompris*, and the cheap books of Bry and others, to the superb works to produce which Doré educated his own school of engravers,* and had recourse to houses of universal renown, as Hachette et Cie., Hetzel, Mame of Tours, Charpentier, Michel Lévy Frères, Garnier Frères, and Dentu.

It has been said that Gustave Doré was avaricious, that he toiled and moiled for money, rather than for a love of his art and in order to do justice to his powers. The charge is devoid of foundation. He was a "man of order," as he was fond of repeating. He had a rough method of keeping his accounts. He deposited his business memoranda in a range of cigar-boxes. He would thrust agreements, money,

---

* Pizan, Pannemaker, Pierdon, Brevière, Maurand, Boetzel, Hébert, E. Deschamps, Dumont, Delduc, Fagnon, &c. All these, for instance, took part in the engraving of the *Contes de Perrault*.

securities, carelessly into a draw within reach. He could not let them interfere with any discussion in hand, nor with brush or pencil; but they were not mislaid, they were not lost. They found their way to his cigar-boxes in due order. His studio table was littered with letters, sketches, books, presentation copies of music, cigars, match-boxes, scraps of statuary in plaster or bronze; and he would plunge his hands into the depths of the tumbled mass in search of something, very often with the help of Jean. He would generally find what he wanted. His memory was seldom at fault. In his transactions with publishers and others, he carried all the conditions of his bargain with faultless precision. He set a high value on his art-work, and he exacted it resolutely directly he was able; but he believed absolutely that the thing he sold was fully worth the price he put upon it. He proved this by the courage with which he spent his own money in some of his larger ventures. He threw out the bank-notes he earned in what is called "pot-boiling," upon the dreamland in which he lived.

He even seriously embarrassed himself when he undertook to bring out the *Inferno* at his own cost. Not only did he invest his own labour, but he undertook to pay the engravers. When he had in this way produced some twelve or fifteen of the page blocks, he found himself at the end of his tether. He had disbursed all he could spare.

"He came to me at this time," says M. E. Templier,* "as sad and gloomy as he was generally lively at this time of his life. I asked him what was the matter? He described his predicament to me; and we arranged to pay him for all the drawing and engraving he had produced, and to bring out the work at the expense of the firm. Later we shared the profits of the first and subsequent editions." It was in this way that his first great work in folio was carried to a successful issue.

Campbell's *Last Man* was a subject that captivated Doré's imagination, but which he could never realise to his satisfaction. He promised himself the pleasure of doing it if his *Ancient Mariner* succeeded, as a companion volume; but Hood's poem brought him a heavy loss. "Alas!" he wrote in 1876, "it is not the *Last Man* I am thinking about just now, but the *Mariner*, the sale of which gives me anxiety. I cannot undertake another work without seeing a return of some of the expenses that I have made for

---

* One of the partners in the great firm of Hachette et Cie., who was Doré's friend, and to whom I am indebted for valuable information concerning him.—B. J.

this work, and they are really enormous. The press and the public look upon it with sympathy, but my purchasers are few. I have spent about £3,500 on the engraving and printing of this book. If I could see only the half or third of it, I should at once undertake something more, for I am impatient to do so. I hope that when this new production of mine becomes known in society (and I consider it one of my best and most original) an impulsion will be given at once to the sale. Let us live and hope—this is my device. I am moreover iron-plated with courage and perseverance."

Then he turned to other subjects, as to the illness of Lady Augusta Stanley, for whom he felt a deep respect,—sending at the same time assurances of his affectionate sympathy to the Dean.

Doré's earnings, like his rates of production of illustrations, have been exaggerated. He received, as a rule, 500 frs. or £20 for his large folio drawings, and for this sum he sold his entire copyright of them. This was his general custom—at least with MM. Hachette et Cie., who published his principal works*; and it was the plan that he himself preferred.

---

* This firm published: 1. The *Inferno, Purgatory, and Paradise*; 2. *Don Quixote*; 3. *Atala*; 4. *The Ancient Mariner*; 5. *Orlando Furioso*; 6. La Fontaine's *Fables*; 7. Taine's *Journey to the Pyren-*

DORÉ'S SHAKESPEARE.

LIFE OF GUSTAVE DORÉ.

At this rate Doré would receive 38,000 francs (£2,720) for his *Dante*; £2,400 for La Fontaine's *Fables*; £1,000 for *Atala*; and £3,600 for *Orlando Furioso*. In addition he had, in some instances, his foreign copyrights, and for some of these he obtained considerable sums of money.

The curious reader may make an approximate estimate of the main sources of Doré's income as an illustrator, on the bases I have indicated, by reference to the bibliography of the works he illustrated.

This income was fed by many minor streams. The work scattered over illustrated periodicals, as we have had occasion to note again and again, was prodigious. At the same time Doré cast forth separate drawings,* in abundance; and some of these cartoons are valued by his admirers as more precious than any of his paintings. He had a thirst for money—not to be spent in pleasures, or frivolities, but because he had dreams not to be realised without fortune. The money and drawings he gave away, showed the charity and

---

nées; 8. *The Idyls of the King*; 9. *London*; 10. *Le Roi des Montagnes*; 11. *Histoire du Capitaine Castaquette*; 12. *La Legende de Croquemitaine*; 13. Saintine's *Chemin des Ecoliers*, and the *Mythology of the Rhine*; 14. *Ségur Nouveaux Contes des Fées*; 15. Mayne Reid's *Habitation du Desert*, &c.

* Among the fine drawings Doré has left is one in the Print Department of the National Library, entitled "Frère Angel." It was intended to illustrate George Sand's *Spiridion*.

ORLANDO FURIOSO.

the generosity of his nature. He was utterly careless about his personal expenditure. All humble folk who did him a service he paid lavishly. He could not pass a beggar and refuse him his groat. He was without suspicion. His money lay about at his London lodgings, as he had emptied it from his pockets. The servant one day picked up a *rouleau* of Napoleons he had left rolling upon the table. Poor as his English was, he managed to make his way about London in hansom cabs; and he paid the fare he was asked. It was sometimes extravagant; but he became impatient if a friend interfered. Time was too precious to him, and life was too short, to be troubled by the impositions of cabmen. He would argue this, and prove that it was bad economy for a man of intellectual habit to allow his mind to be distracted from a train of thought, or a point of observation, by the trifles of every-day life.

"The man was a rogue," he would say; "but what have we to do with that? It is not our mission to reform him. Let us forget him as quickly as possible, hoping that he will not get too drunk with his overcharge."

While we were breakfasting one morning, a note was handed to Doré. A French chroniqueur, of whom Doré could not speak without scorn, wanted £5 to

ORLANDO FURIOSO.

carry him back to Paris. While Doré folded the money in an envelope, he said: "This is for a gentleman who is never tired of attacking me, and who will fall upon me to-morrow if he has the opportunity."

I have passed in review the career of Doré as an illustrator; and prodigious as the work is at which we have glanced, it appears to the friends of the artist but the *disjecta membra* of the prodigious range of creations he had in his mind when he first studied the page of Rabelais. In the notes on his life, which he has left in the hands of Dr. Michel (Doré's nephew by marriage), he has enumerated the authors who were to figure in the Library to be illustrated throughout by him. It comprehended about forty universally-known writers. They appeared to be packed pell-mell in his busy brain. Homer and Thomas à Kempis, Anacreon and Ossian, Montaigne and Lamartine, Hoffmann and Plutarch. It was in 1865 that his notes on his career were closed. He had already published seven volumes of his ideal library. "I pause," he said in conclusion, "for I am trenching on the future, and this is no longer biography."

He went forward with his noble purpose after this. He completed his *Dante*, he put forth his *La Fontaine*, his *Ariosto*, his *Tennyson*, and *Hood*; but the crown

ORLANDO FURIOSO.

of his labours as an illustrator he was not permitted to complete. He has left only a few jewels of it.

"My Shakspeare! My Shakspeare!" he cried on his death-bed. "I must get up quickly to finish it!"

"Come and have a talk, over a feed of oats," he wrote to me in 1879 (Nov. 16). We discussed the old subject, Shakspeare; and I advised him to publish it in separate plays. In December 1879 I heard from him that he had been for some weeks almost exclusively engaged on his *Shakspeare*. He was working on the *Tempest*, and believed that he had struck out some original ideas. "*Romeo* is begun," he added, "*Timon* is ripening, *Julius Cæsar* is coming out, and *Macbeth* is nearly finished; in short, all is going well."

I was to open negociations for him with a London house; and he estimated the value of a complete Shakspeare by him at £40,000!

Alas! *Romeo* was never to be finished; *Timon* remains a mere shadow upon many soiled sheets of paper; *Julius Cæsar* lies scattered upon pages of scratches and confused lines, intelligible only to the imagination that is extinguished; and *Macbeth*, one drawing of *King Lear*, and some water-colour drawings of the *Midsummer Night's Dream*—in all some twenty Shakspearian creations—alone peer out, in a

DORÉ'S SHAKSPEARE.

few settled forms, from the shadows of Doré's tomb. When I looked over the stacks of his drawings, lying upon the floor, in the Rue St. Dominique after his death, I saw that he had covered hundreds of sheets of drawing-paper with rough Shakspearian notes, showing that he had meditated over every play; having read and discussed Shakspeare's text with his friend Canon Harford, the writer of these pages, and other Englishmen.

SECOND PART.

CHAPTER XIII.

DORÉ THE PAINTER.

BETWEEN "the painter's painter," Franz Hals,—the perfect master of the technical side of his art, the most skilful practitioner of his handicraft, who has been ranked with Velasquez, of whom Fromentin said "no man ever painted better, and no man ever will,"—and Gustave Doré the painter, the objective, realistic artist sees no kind of affinity. And he is right. The Dutchman was the consummate workman, and this only. Doré was the creative artist, to whom the brush was an instrument for giving concrete form to an idea. The work of Hals at Haarlem betrays no intellectual force. We behold, and devoutly admire, the greatest technician of his school,

DORÉ THE PAINTER.

whose craftsmanship was an education to Ostade and Brower, and even to Rembrandt. We may see distinctly in his immense portrait groups what was

wanting in Doré to make him a consummate painter as well as a wholly satisfactory creative artist; and we may as plainly discover in the great scenic canvases of Doré the extraordinary poetic and intellectual qualities, wanting which the transcendant Dutch craftsman remained only a perfect craftsman, even to his eightieth year. With an imagination like Doré's at the handle what might not such a workman have produced? Hals began to paint the highest examples of his matchless technique at the age when Death laid his hand upon the dreamer of dreams, Doré. Even his worshipper, M. G. Van Reusselaer, admits that the worship of such technicians as Hals and Velasquez has sometimes induced a disregard, even a comparative contempt, for the other and more subtile artistic factors which must go with splendid workmanship to make up a splendid art.*

Gustave Doré, in his lifetime, chafed and would not be comforted as one of these more subtile factors, who were wronged and degraded by the comparative disregard and contempt of the worshippers of the painter's painter. That he should not have suffered this scornful and ignorant neglect of his contemporaries to ruffle his life, and finally to destroy his happiness, is unquestionable. He should have gone manfully and serenely on his way, leaving the care of his fame to the justice of Time. He should have

* *The Century*, vol. xxvi. No. 3.

DORÉ THE PAINTER.

rested content with the realisations of his imagination, with his many noble dreams and aims, with the strength that was in him—and none better than he knew it was in him—to come out of the contest with glory. It was his misfortune to be swayed by "the last infirmity of noble minds." He hungered for fame. He worked for immortality. His sense of his own power, and of the range of his creative force, was so high, that the acknowledgments of the world always fell short of his own estimate of his deserts. And he went to work again, in a passion. A larger canvas, a bolder flight, a more audacious challenge— sculpture or etching or water-colour drawing, if they would not have his painting—must decide between him and his enemies.

This impetuous temperament of the Alsatian, who fell crying "J'ai trop travaillé" at fifty, had nothing in common with that of the easy Dutchman, who went on gaily and patiently reproducing his brown, and grey, and golden tones till he was eighty, upon subjects always ready for him, and that required for their treatment the freedom of hand, the frankness, correctness of form, the breadth and harmony, the spirited grouping, in short, all the qualities and attainments which the good craftsman has at his ready command, and which were under the supreme control of Hals. Doré would hardly have been able, in his early manhood, to answer the old academic test of study: "Where do you put in your brown tree?" In the work of Hals, that went on steadily improving with practice, as pianoforte playing, there was no strain upon the painter's brain power. An easy-going, even bibulous Dutchman, he covered his canvases, took his pleasures, and went peacefully to his rest in his eighty-second year, having been honoured throughout his life as a glory of the Dutch school. He had the advantage which Doré craved in vain. Hals's countrymen honoured his genius in his life-time; Doré had to seek his laurels beyond the frontiers of the country he so passionately loved. We must go back to Jehan Cousin,* chief of the French Renaissance, if we seek an artist who shall remind us, by his versatility, the many forms of art he used by turns, and his powerful and overpowering originality, of Doré. Cousin was architect, sculptor, painter (chiefly of glass, but in oil also), engraver, writer on artistic anatomy and perspective; in short, an artist who sought every way of expressing himself—from illustrations to "emblems" and miniatures in a *Livre d'Heures*, to a monument as ambitious as

* Born towards the close of the fifteenth century.

DORÉ THE PAINTER.

that of Admiral Chabot in the Renaissance Museum of the Louvre, and historic painted windows like that describing the last judgment in the church of St. Romain, at Sens. His copy of it in oil is now in the Louvre. This remarkable artist was also an illustrator of books, which were published in France during the reigns of Henri II. and his successors, save one, the *Emblemata Fortunæ*, which has only recently come to light. The master of Sens was more unfortunate than Doré, in that his best work as an illustrator of books lay *perdu* for centuries. Both have made a deep impression on the art of their common country. Doré in his later days used to say that if he could live his life over again, he would not touch illustrations to books. And yet it is not unlikely that, centuries hence, he may be recalled vividly to the mind of posterity by his *Contes Drôlatiques* or his *Dante*, as Jehan Cousin has just been recalled to his countrymen by his animated pen-and-ink illustrations to the *Emblemata Fortunæ*. Cousin's finest paintings on glass have been shivered; but his exquisite ivory statuette of St. Sebastien remains to bear testimony to the genius of the master of Sens. It is only three years ago—some three centuries after his death—that his statue was set up at Sens.

Gustave Doré, albeit he was one of those phenomenal

masters in art who spring up at intervals, and give it a fresh channel and a stronger tide, like Cousin, Holbein, Hals, or Hogarth, and who, as the French say, *font école*; was deficient in staying power. He has been called, by turns, the Hugo and the Dumas of French art. He had the impetuosity of Hugo, his sense of grandeur, conceptions akin to his of sublime, ideal effects of nature, the vision and the faculty divine, that roamed and observed in Paradise and in Hades; but he had not Hugo's intense and most tender human sympathies, his love for the humble and forlorn, his mighty arm to smite the oppressor. Doré's sympathies and brotherly love of humanity were not motive forces in his studio. He had, however, a calm majesty in his grander conceptions, that is wanting in all Hugo's creations. The difference may be seen once for all by contrasting Hugo's *Visions de Dante*,* a great and stirring poem, with Doré's *Enfer*. In Hugo, it is Hugo the generous politician and the philanthropist speaking throughout, the characters being mere *portes-voix*. The frail dramatic web disappears. Sublime visions are conjured up, but we recognise the voice of the author of the *Legends des Siècles* throughout. It is

---

* *La Légende des Siècles*, vol. v. 1883. Paris: Calmann Lévy.

DORÉ THE PAINTER.

a drama read in a monotone by one voice of our acquaintance.

Doré had the true dramatic instinct along with a poetic imagination, that enabled him to give individuality to every character. There was a vraisemblance permeating the entire vision. Here the awful scene had the stillness of death upon it; and there the cries of the damned smote to the marrow of men's bones, and to the inmost recesses of their hearts. Then the ultimate dawn suggested the cool zephyr, and the notes of happy waking birds. Hugo is ever the prominent figure on the stage. Hurry, turmoil, passion we have by turns, but we cannot keep our eyes off the manager. Doré, by his dramatic instinct, was strong where the greatest of French poets has ever been weak. This instinct was as conspicuous in the artist as it was in Alexandre Dumas.

The whole truth seems to be that Doré's poetic power was closely akin to that of Hugo, and that the extraordinary resources he had for telling his story dramatically with pencil and brush, linked his genius with that of Dumas.

If he had only had some of Ingres' staying power! The deep poetic heart possessed every moment of Ingres' long and most noble life. With a loving care the Viscount Henri Delaborde—a refined and an accomplished critic—has collected into one handsome volume an account of the great artist's life, a selection of his MS. notes and letters, and a list of all his works, down to his pencil drawings. The portrait, by the delicate hand of Morse, is that of a thoughtful, quiet man. The fine brow covers earnest, fixed eyes. The lines of the mouth are delicate—as they always are when the head is that of a delicate, fine, fastidious thinker. Whether Delaroche's "Execution of Lady Jane Grey" was painted to prove that the mouth is the most expressive of the features or no, is of less importance than the indubitable fact that in the picture the mouth, unaided, expresses all the pathos of the scene. In the portrait of Ingres the corners of the mouth are drawn slightly down, as they quivered in the flesh when the master was under the spell of the gracious and splendid power with which he was gifted.

I venture upon no criticism on Ingres' place in art. His flag will be planted only after a pitched battle that has yet many years to last. The life of the artist who, even in his eighty-sixth year, was surprised by Death in the midst of his work is deeply interesting. He passed from his studio to his grave. When the crucifix was put between the waxen hands, the mark of the pencil was still visible

DORÉ THE PAINTER.

upon the fingers. If Doré, I repeat, had only had the staying power of the grand old painter, he might have out-distanced all his contemporaries, and died an octogenarian.

SKETCH MADE AT SCHOOL.

CHAPTER II.

EARLY PAINTINGS.

"Let us not raise a building upon a single column,"* said Sainte-Beuve. The subject of this biography reared the edifice of his fame upon many columns. He was a mere gamin when, shortly after his arrival in Paris, he was taken by his family to Boulogne-sur-Mer; and, having witnessed a storm and shipwreck there, painted in oil a picture of the lifeboat, and presented it to the Humane Society of that

* "Ne batissons pas tout un édifice sur une seule colonne."—Sainte-Beuve's Essay on Victor de Laprade.

EARLY PAINTINGS.

port. It still hangs in the principal room of the institution, and is dated 1849; it is, therefore, the earliest known oil painting by Gustave Doré. The incident described in the picture was a stirring one. The lifeboat had put out to a lugger in distress off the port; but the fury of the gale had thrown it against the jetty, and upset it. It floated keel upwards, and seven of the eight brave fellows who manned it were drawn ashore by ropes. The eighth was given up as lost, and the boat was carried some way along the coast by the current, followed by a crowd—young Doré being in the midst of it. The boat grounded at last, and the sailors who had followed hastened to right it, thinking they might discover the body of the lost man in it. To their astonishment, they found him clinging to the bottom, alive. He had had the presence of mind to take up this position when the boat turned over upon him, and he had floated in his dark prison for upwards of an hour. He was carried back in triumph to the house of the Humane Society. Doré was so deeply impressed with the scene that he put the finding of the man upon canvas, in a rough, broad fashion. As a work of art the picture is worth very little; but as Doré's first picture, painted while he was a collegian, it is interesting; and the Boulonnais may well be proud to possess it.

LIFE OF GUSTAVE DORÉ.

The grand effects of a tempest off a sea-port were congenial to the ardent temperament of the young artist. His imagination "rode the whirlwind."

It is curious to contrast the turbulent and tumultuous art-life of Doré with that of one of our most refined and deep-seeing classical landscape-painters, Samuel Palmer. Both are known early. Palmer was an exhibitor at the British Gallery as a lad, and on his fourteenth birthday heard that his first exhibited picture was sold. He was, like Doré, a musician and a reader; but, unlike him, he was content to dwell all his life with nature in the quiet of a Kentish village, and to find all his delight in his violin, his books, and his landscapes. The light of his genius shone, like that of the glow-worm, in lonely, silent places; while that of the French dreamer and worker was borne aloft through the storms of life, a beacon seen from afar under a tumultuous heaven. While Palmer took his inspiration under a hedge, and cast it upon a lane, a farm-yard, a flock of sheep following the shepherd to the fold, Doré's imagination filled the nature his restless eye surveyed with

"An ampler ether, a diviner air."

He was stirred by mighty hosts of men, by the wars of the elements, by the mysterious, the unfathomable, the awful. His spirit was moved by fierce contentions. In his Bourg copy-books, the illustrations are Minerva slaying the giant Pallas, Vulcan overcoming Clytius, and the like. His infantile scratches are attempts to represent the shock of battle. But his imagination had, as I have already remarked, a tender, a sentimental side. Charity was the virtue he specially loved. Like a true Frenchman, his heart was alive to the miseries of poor children. He revelled in fable, for his fancy could play freely with it. We have seen that when he was a child, hardly seven years old, he made a series of pencil illustrations, which he called "Dr. Fox," and that the future illustrator of *La Fontaine* was only ten years old when he executed a series of very careful and dainty drawings of "The Bee and the Fly," "The Bear and his Journey," "The Owl," "The Two Mice," &c. In all his infantile work we are reminded that the child was father of the man—save in this, that the boy caricaturist left no traces in the matured artist. After *Rabelais* and the *Contes Drôlatiques*, the pictorial satire on Russia, and *Don Quixote*, we find hardly any traces of the humorist. The artist advanced out of the realms of caricature, to which fortune condemned him when he produced in the company of Daumier and Gavarin, to the solemn scenes of the *Wandering Jew*

Dante, and the *Bible*, and the enchanted ground of *Milton*, *La Fontaine*, *Ariosto*, *Hood*, and *Tennyson*. And while he fed his imagination on the works he illustrated, he strengthened himself to take the commanding place he coveted as a painter.

He began to work with his brush almost at the same time that he fell in with M. Philippon. During the years of his youth, in which he threw off sketches for the *Journal pour Rire*, the publications of M. Bry, and other popular sheets by the hundred, he kept the supreme object of his ambition constantly before him. He welcomed his popularity on wood, because it promised him the means of becoming immortal on canvas. He broke his days into two, and sometimes into three parts. The mornings were devoted to his work for the publishers, the afternoons to painting, and, often, the evening to more work for the publishers. His early work for the weekly illustrated miscellanies was irksome drudgery to him; and it was only when he was able to illustrate a favourite author, or work out a subject of his own, that he became reconciled to the labour of illustration. His heart and soul were in his studio where his woodblocks, his plates, his lithographic stones, his pens and pencils were not to be seen. It was to excel as a painter that he studied anatomy, buried himself in

EARLY PAINTINGS.

the forest, scaled the Alps, and filled his albums with pictorial notes. His *Don Quixote* was nothing to him beside the paintings of Spanish subjects it enabled him to design and execute. His *Dante* was most precious to him because it led him up to perhaps his most perfect work, his "Paolo and Francesca da Rimini." His *Milton* charmed him because it drew him to the "Victor Angels." His illustrated Bible was precious for the sacred scenes it fixed in his reverential mind —his "Triumph of Christianity," his "Dream of Pilate's Wife," his "Christ leaving the Prætorium," and his "Entry of Christ into Jerusalem." But his painting brought upon him the great sorrow of his life.

"One day," M. René Delorme tells us in his biographical sketch, "one sad day, on which Doré had been wounded in his proper pride as a painter, he said: 'However, I ought to have expected this. Long ago it was foretold that painting would bring despair into my life. I was not taller than that — when the prophecy was uttered. It has been terribly realised. You will hear the story of my first box of colours. Here it is: I was a little fellow, but I had long ago despised the harmless colours without poison in them which my prudent parents gave me. I aspired to colours in tubes—to colours *pour de vrai*.

EARLY PAINTINGS.

Well, one day when I was going to Josserond, a charming corner in the department of the Ain, to spend a week with one of my father's friends, an oak box, with brass handles, with pencils and tubes, was brought to me. I was mad with delight. I wanted to begin at once, but I was prevented. The carriage was ready. We started, but it was dark when we arrived. I was forbidden to open my box; I was ordered to bed, and the light was put out. Impossible to close my eyes! At the first peep of day I jumped out of bed, took my box, and went down to the court-yard. But alas! I had no canvas, no cardboard, no panel. These had been put beyond my reach. I was dying to begin. I squeezed some colours upon my palette, and the freshness of them intoxicated me with delight. Nothing is more stimulating than a new palette. I remember there was a green from which I could not withdraw my eyes—a lovely green, a Veronese green in all its glory!

"'But what was I to paint, and on what?

"'As I put this question to myself, my eyes fell upon a poor chicken, well-formed, but with dirty-white plumage, that was pecking about near me.

"'Its colour was frightful. It was an error of Providence to make fowls so ugly, when they might have the tints of the parrot. I resolved to repair it at once. The bird made some difficulties, not understanding that I was working for its good; but I was tenacious, and I went on to the end. It was soon perfect. It is true I exhausted my entire tube of Veronese green upon it; but what a splendid bird! It was a pleasure to see it strutting about in all the brilliant colours of the spring.

"'This work of art accomplished I went to bed again. I was awoke by a great disturbance of many voices in the yard. The peasants had assembled, and were terror-stricken; for there is a local legend in which a green fowl bears an awful part. It is a sign of famine and pestilence. I ran down and confessed that I was the culprit. When the clamour had subsided, and I ventured to make my appearance, an old peasant-woman said to me in a prophetic voice:

"'"You have made people cry; your turn to cry will come, with your painting."'"

It came, and more than once. It began in 1855, the year in which he made his first serious appearance at the Salon. He had already exhibited some vigorous drawings of forest-mountains, and two or three paintings; but in the year of the Universal Exhibition he first sent forth from the studio, which was filled with his early paintings, generally on an immense scale, his challenge as a painter. Unfortunately, the best of

EARLY PAINTINGS.

these was rejected. The "Battle of the Alma," "Evening" and "The Meadow," were hung, but the landscape was skyed, to the great regret of his college-chum and critic, Edmond About, and the "Death of Rizzio" was rejected.

Let us turn back for a moment to the year 1853, when he exhibited a picture of rare excellence.

It was when his brush approached children that the depth of human tenderness in Doré came fully out. Among his early pictures (it has been called his greatest) is his "Famille du Saltimbanque," exhibited at the Salon. The story is told with great dramatic force and pathos; the colour is good but coarse, and deficient in delicate tints, as most of his work was; but the studies of character are very fine and subtle. Indeed, it is impossible to forget the picture; and none can see it without feeling a swelling at the heart. When, in the course of its strange fortunes, it appeared in the window of a Paris picture-dealer, the crowds who paused to contemplate the pathetic drama of the acrobat's life blocked the pavement all day long. It spoke to their hearts. The family is one of vagabonds. They are tempting the public to the show by the flageolet of a drunken man. The Hercules stands sullenly near a woe-begone woman, and the little boy Hercules is in a corner, the tears trickling down the most awful child's face ever realised by a painter. Forlorn, waif, with protuberant muscles and empty belly, and the marks of a childhood of vice and cruelty. The visages of this unhappy, brutalized family are made more hideous still by the theatrical rags with which they are bedizened. The old man with the flageolet leering in his cups from under a cocked hat, is the repulsive figure. The woman is stony, hard, hopeless, horrible even with her stage-jewellery, waiting for death to end this misery of the street. There is an exquisite touch of feeling in the dog, with his nose fondly laid upon the poor child's lap. Even the dog is deplorable, with a hat and feather on his head. To see this picture, the work of a very young man, is to be converted to an abiding faith that the creator of it had genius, and of the highest order.

Doré afterwards painted a companion picture—the "Wounded Acrobat"—before which it was hardly possible to restrain one's tears. The boy of the troop has fallen, and is hurt. His mother holds him to her breast, and the father looks on in grief, the dog watches in evident distress—and all this feeling is seen through the paint and spangles of street performers. The faces of the father and mother, seen through their coarse paint, are realised with the

EARLY PAINTINGS.

cunning of a master. If Doré had left only these two canvases his place would be safe among the great artists of his epoch. In these subjects his lack of refinement is a gain to him.

The appearance of the famous young illustrator as a painter raised a host of detractors; but Theophile Gautier bore in mind the *gamin de genie* with whom he had travelled, and with the many lights of whose genius he was familiar, and stood by him, saying, "M. Gustave Doré possesses one of the most marvellous organisations as an artist that we know. His illustrations to *Rabelais*, the *Contes Drôlatiques*, the *Legendes Populaires*, are masterpieces, where the most powerful realism is combined with the rarest fancy. His studio is crammed with immense canvases sketched with a dash which exceeds that of Goya, there thrown aside, there re-touched; and in which, in a chaos of colour, bits of the highest order shine—a head, a torso, a limb thrown down with the vigour of Rubens, Tintorette, or Velasquez. Even now, through the mists, a ray of genius starts; yea, of genius—a word of which we are not prodigal. It is understood that we speak of the future of the artist. The draughtsman has already taken his rank."

In this, written by the first art-critic of his time, there was enough to serve Doré as a shield against

EARLY PAINTINGS.

the malice of his foes—a small fry, but a very abundant one. M. About followed, telling him in a letter that he was original, that he imitated nobody, and that soon he would be imitated. Both critics dwelt on the original point of view of a battle, in Doré's "Alma." Theophile Gautier remarked that Doré had departed from the old groove, and painted a combat of soldiers. In the conventional battle-piece, the general and his staff occupy the foreground; but in the young artist's battle the Zouaves, from the foreground, pour like a torrent upon the Russians. The confusion is terrific. There are no details; and yet the spectator is impressed with the sense of the life-and-death struggle going forward from the foreground to the distance, peopled with those indefinable but impressible hosts of men which Doré could create with a few strokes of his pencil. Gautier said that the picture appeared to have been painted with such feverish activity that the artist had lacked time to wipe his brushes, and to have produced certain muddy tints in consequence. This observation probably took all the honey out of the praise. It distressed Doré beyond measure to say that he was a rapid painter. M. About told him that he was the Zouave of painters, meaning to please him. He was not tickled, he was stung—as he was stung every time he appeared at the Salon with the observations of academic mediocrities who had mastered the mechanism of their art, but had none of the life, the creative power, "*talent facile!*"

It was most unfortunate that in 1855 his most highly-finished and vigorous picture was rejected; and that it was destined to lie *perdu* for some twenty-

EARLY PAINTINGS.

five years.* The "Death of Rizzio" is, perhaps, the most satisfactory work, as regards technique and colour, Doré has left behind him. It was painted in his twenty-second year! The drawing is daring and vigorous, the colour is rich and harmonious, the grouping is striking and original, and the murderers' heads are wonderful studies. The figures are solid and thoroughly studied as those of Velasquez. Both Theophile Gautier and Edmond About had predicted for this production of the young painter an uncommon success. It would have answered the malicious murmurers of "*talent facile*"; but the fates were unkind, and kept it for a quarter of a century from the public view.

The objections which had been made to the "Battle of the Alma," in 1855, were renewed, and with increased vigour and malevolence, when, two years later, Doré sent to the Salon his immense canvas—about fifteen feet square—of the "Battle of Balaklava." It was a *tour de force*. The fighting hosts were rendered as only Doré could render the tumult of thousands of men. It stirred the blood; it amazed the observer who endeavoured to analyse it and get order out of the multitude; and it commanded the

* It was found in London, cast aside with lumber, by Messrs. Fairless and Beeforth; and was placed in the Doré Gallery, opposite the Francesca.

admiration of the crowds who were still under the excitement of the war. At the same time it gave rein to the tongues of the mockers, who resented the appearance of Doré's prodigiously vehement individuality in their midst. He was of no school. He was Doré, the creative genius of still unfathomed power. One of the sneerers passed before the great canvas, with his cap on his ear, and tossed at it the mot—it was all but a *buisson d'écrevisses.** But the trusty Gautier stood by the painter, and picked out of the hosts of fighting men, groups that he declared to be unmistakable marks of genius of a high order that was trying its wings.

The picture was bought for Versailles, where it figured for years among the Crimean battle-pieces; but it was taken down and put aside, even before the painter's death, nor can it be said that Doré's fame will suffer by its removal. It was an extraordinary effort for an artist of twenty-five, full of promises that have since been, for the most part, realised; but its crudities in colour, and its general violence as a composition, rendered it unworthy to remain in a national collection as a representative emanation of the artist's power.

* Referring to the red-coated English soldiers in the foreground.

CHAPTER XV.

1860 to 1870.

In what may be called the second epoch of Gustave Doré's career as a painter, viz. the years which lay between the exhibition of the " Battle of Inkermann " (1857) and the breaking-out of the Franco-German war, the character of his subjects, as well as his mode of treatment, underwent changes that manifested steady progress, the result of persistent study. After the publication of the *Inferno*, a page from which he amplified into a vast picture which was exhibited in the Salon of 1861, he felt a longing to refresh his mind with lighter and brighter themes. As we have seen, he took up the *Tales of Perrault*, in order to get quit of his visions of Hell; and when, with his brush, he returned to the inspiration of Dante, it was to deliver himself of the sweetest and purest of his creations—his "Paolo and Francesca da Rimini."* When he painted this picture he was in the full enjoyment of his powers as an artist. His mind was unclouded, his life was happy, he was young, and, which is the essential thing, he felt young. The "Francesca," the "Neophyte," and the "Titans" progressed together in the company of a majestic landscape—"Evening in the Alps."

The immense canvas on which Doré set forth Dante and Virgil, in the awful gloom and desolation of the frozen circle of Hell, where Virgil meets Ugolino, was on too vast a scale.† It was a prodigious sketch, full of power, in the cruel episodes, as where the two hideous heads are in a frozen hole,

---

* Canon Harford possesses the two original Francesca drawings made by Doré, before he painted the picture, or even published his Dante. The second drawing represents the sin which sent Francesca to hell. In presenting the two to his friend (Jan. 1870), Doré said the pair might be called *le baiser sur la terre* and *le baiser dans l'éternité*. They were Doré's first drawings cast upon paper in 1862, and are among his most beautiful compositions.

† It now adorns a music hall in New York. It was one of the pictures that figured in the original exhibition of Doré's paintings at the Egyptian Hall, Piccadilly, in company with the "Baden Gaming-Table." This exhibition was ultimately dispersed, owing to the difficulties of the director.

one gnawing the other. The damned are indeed tortured! The swollen veins, the bleeding wounds, the hopelessness and the agony, are told in downright touches that curdle the blood. The painter has faithfully rendered the poet; the imaginations of the two are in harmony; more so than in Delacroix's "Virgil and Dante in the Bark of Charon," which is in the Luxemburg. It is an awful vision of frost and shadow and suffering; but there are violences in it that shock; realities too plain for a poetic vision. Dante and Virgil are shades in a boundless vault, wherein the imagination has fearful play; but the damned in the foreground are as human as the patients in an hospital theatre, or a town mortuary. It drew forth bitter criticism; but such judges as Maxime du Camp did homage to the original genius of the painter. This picture was the striking and powerful work of the Salon of its year.

It may be said that from 1860 to 1870 Doré's education as a painter was in progress; and that during this period he replied to the hostility which met every step he made, with a proud and defiant consciousness that he was conquering the difficulties of oil painting and approaching mastership in technique.

If his pictures are taken chronologically, the student

of them cannot fail to remark a constant steady advance in executive excellence, from the " Battle of the Alma" to the "Vale of Tears." The courage manifested in this prolonged struggle to overcome the disadvantages of a deficient art education in his youth, is of a heroic type. It had its reward, albeit the artist did not live to enjoy it.

I think it is Mr. Hamerton who has regretted that Doré, when he felt his ground as a painter, altered his scale, and took to immense canvases. But *il voyait grand*. His *Wandering Jew* was a series of the largest wood-blocks that had ever been engraved. In his earlier time his canvases were of unusual size. The "Massacre of the Innocents," which lay against his studio-wall for years, and which he drew forth and finished only in 1869, was of scenic proportions. When he etched his "Neophyte," it was upon a copper-plate of extraordinary breadth. He took to water-colours only in 1873, but at once began to enlarge the ordinary scale of the aquarellistes; and he painted his mother's portrait the size of life. As a sculptor he was impatient to raise trophies of stupendous proportions; and, when he died, he was planning a studio that was to exceed in size that of the Rue Bayard. It was remarked to him that people had not houses big enough to hold

THE SECOND EPOCH.

his canvases, and that connoisseurs would welcome small highly-finished pictures from his brush. He cramped his hand over a few cabinet subjects, and produced some landscapes, every part of which was patiently elaborated; but he took no pleasure in these little works made for the market. He would say that he could paint with the minuteness and breadth of Meissonnier; but his hand was not at ease with small brushes. It had swept so long over broad expanses, and become so accustomed to effects wrought on a large scale, that it trembled and was uncertain when boxed within a few inches of space. The hand that smites the anvil cannot adjust a watch-spring.

There can be no doubt that Doré's method of producing the effects of light and shade, of which he was a master, by a tint of shade out of which his design was picked in Chinese white, told against him when he first took to oil as a vehicle for the production of effects on a large scale. He got the effects of the scene-painter. He produced broad washes. His painting was deficient in solidity, and in variety in the shadows. Ink gave him all his shadows upon wood; but when he came to colour he forgot, in his earliest works in oil, the infinite varieties in the tints of shadow in nature; so that he was monotonous

LIFE OF GUSTAVE DORÉ.

and coarse, and flat, when one looked closely into his broad masses of shadow. To the end his painting was deficient in the delicate gradations of colour. His shadows were often inky. Master as he was of chiaroscuro, he neglected the wealth of transparent colours at the oil-painter's command.

This defect, I repeat, was the consequence of his familiarity with the few materials of the illustrator. He was by nature a colourist; and this is, perhaps, most apparent in his earlier works—certainly in his " Death of Rizzio," and in his " Francesca "; but his 40,000 drawings, or whatever the startling number may be, accustomed his eye to white and black, and destroyed its sensitiveness to the finer gradations of colour, which are to be found in the greyest of landscapes and the most sombre of forests. It has been remarked that the only artist who has shown a mastery over " gloom and glare " equal to Doré is Rembrandt; but in Rembrandt's deepest gloom you will find variety of colour—and in this, as a painter, he has the advantage of his modern rival. In his boundless invention Doré is *facile princeps*.

The detractors of Doré have said many false things about him, as that his illustrations were executed with the help of pupils, or assistants. The absurdity of the statement was obvious on the face of it to the

LIFE OF GUSTAVE DORÉ.

student of Doré's manner, and of the peculiarities of his touch. As a matter of fact, every line and touch in his designs was drawn by his own hand. It was reported, also, that he worked in a sumptuous studio; whereas there was not an ornament, and hardly a bit of carpet in it. He committed many oversights and errors in the swift realization of the creations of his sleepless imagination. In the hewing of timber in Lebanon for the temple of Solomon, the giant trees are represented as smoothly sawn down—all the woodmen having axes. It would be impossible to saw down trees of this girth. The error is repeated in the last plate of Tennyson's *Vivien*, and once or twice in *Atala*; again in the *Fables*. His geology is often at fault, making his rocks formless confusion. He has been attacked for his false heraldry. Sometimes his blunders are gross, as where, in illustrating the reign of Arthur, he has cut on the walls of Almesbury the modern arms of Great Britain.* The ark of bull-rushes in which he

* "They are not the Welsh dragon, nor the white horse of Hengist, nor the cross and martlets of the Confessor, not the two lions of the Norman Conqueror, nor the three lions of the sons of Eleanor of Aquitaine, nor even the quartering of France and England assumed by Edward the Third; but the bearings first quartered by George the First, including the escutcheon of the kingdom of Hanover!"— *British Quarterly Review*, No. xcvii. Jan. 1, 1869.

placed the Infant Moses, both in his Bible and in his painting, could not float—it must topple over. The same remark applies to the floating bier bearing the body of Elaine.

But albeit these deficiencies and oversights mar the perfection of his work, they take little from the grandeur or the grace of his creations. They leave us in the presence of the most prolific and poetic painter of our epoch.

Between 1860 and 1870, in the course of which the illustrator sent forth his *Inferno, Purgatorio,* and *Paradiso* of Dante, his *Tales of Perrault, Croque-mitaine, Don Quixote, Atala, Munchausen,* the *Bible, Paradise Lost, La Fontaine,* the *Idylls of the King,* and an extraordinary mass of minor book-work, he painted his "Tapis Vert," the "Neophyte," "Paolo and Francesca da Remini," many Alpine and Swiss and Spanish landscapes, "Andromeda," the "Famille du Saltimbanque," the "Gitana," the "Alsatian Family," and Vosges landscapes, the "Portrait of Rossini," the "Titans," the "Flight into Egypt," and the "Triumph of Christianity." It was said of the "Gitana" that it sufficed to make his name memorable. Within this limit he also began his "Prætorium," and worked upon his "Massacre of the Innocents." To this studio work his whole heart was given. The illustrations had begun to be irksome to him, since he perceived that they impeded his progress as a painter. Giving a friend his portrait, he wrote over it, "Qui de livres il faut illustrer, pour s'illustrer soi-même!"

His portrait of Rossini dead showed the excellence he had attained in technique before 1870. I was with him when he brought the pencil-sketch from the Maestro's death-bed, and watched his sad contemplative face as he examined it and prepared to elaborate it upon the canvas Jean had prepared to his hand. He worked patiently and affectionately to get the exact death-mask of the dear friend who had delighted in his violin performances and in his boyish gambols. The hue of recent death is rendered with marvellous fidelity. The drawing is careful. The great composer is defunct indeed ; but the fine points of his countenance are preserved and idealized. It is death, peaceful, beautiful, and impressive—but not painful. The picture made a strong impression, both in Paris and in London ; but he was loth to exhibit it, and it took some time to overrule his repugnance.

He wrote to a correspondent in London :—

"I thank you especially for what you say of my painting representing the person of my dear and regretted Maestro Rossini. The sentiment of piety

THE SECOND EPOCH.

which dictated this picture causes me to regard it with a particular affection; and I am made very happy by hearing that the London public are attracted by, and interested in, this my profoundly affectionate souvenir of the great man whose friend I had the honour to be, and whom I saw almost in his last moments."*

He made a bold and successful etching of the picture on copper.

It is in his "Paolo and Francesca" that we find Doré's power and command of his material, as a painter in oil, at their best. I have already described this as his purest and most accomplished work—satisfactory in every respect. The drawing is not only unexceptionable, it is lovely in the harmony and broad and bold sweep of the lines. There is in it evidence of study of the great Italian masters; but there is no copying, no servility. The modelling of the shoulder of Paolo has been likened to that of St. John in the Michael Angelo in the National Gallery; but it is a mere suggestion, as the blue of the mantle may recall the colour of Perugino, and the tresses of Francesca those of an angel by Francia. This is only to say that the painter has studied well;

* Letter to Miss Amelia B. Edwards, May 9, 1869.

his picture is his own, stamped in every part with his original genius, chastened and educated.

If we pass from the "Francesca" to the "Neophyte," the "Titania," the "Victor Angels," the "Flight into Egypt," to the "Triumph of Christianity," and then to such robust and impressive landscapes as "Evening in the Alps," the "Prairie," the "Pine Wood," near the artist's beloved Barr (whence he played truant when he was a child in a blouse), and to the forest depths of Hohwald, we get a full view of the level Doré the painter had reached at this time. Of all these fine pictures, the "Neophyte" is the best known, and deserves to be the best known. The double row of old Carthusians seated in their stalls, with the young novice awakened from the dream which has led him hither to a full and sudden sense of the doting, leering, coarse, and sordid set of men, each stamped broadly with a marked individuality, among whom he has cast his lot, tell a sad story of youthful enthusiasm and faith destroyed. The effect made upon the beholder is very painful. Doré, standing one day by a friend who was examining the vigorously-drawn picture, wherein the light and shade are scattered with masterly effect, leading up to the central figure—the Neophyte—said, pointing to him:

"He will be over the wall to-night."

THE SECOND EPOCH.

The "Victor Angels," from Milton's *Paradise Lost*, is a poetic conception of the good and evil hosts, after victory, rendered with broad touches. The rebellious hosts lie beaten, aglow under the rays of the setting sun; while Michael and his white victors are massed in such groups as Doré knew how to create with a few passes of his brush or pencil. It may be fairly said that it is a lovely scene, or vision, in which we recall the work of the illustrator of the Bible and of Milton. The "Flight into Egypt" may be taken as a companion picture to the "Victor Angels." The group repose under the shadows of the Sphinxes. The scene is bathed in the glories of the after-glow. Rest and thought and suggestion are in every part of the canvas.

Another note is struck in "Titania," where the scene teems with fairy life. Even the leaves of the trees are fairy platforms. The incidents of impish activity, at its height under the moonlight, in the leafy court of Queen Titania, are infinite, so prolific is the fancy of the painter, who appears to have given himself up, after his severer studies, to a laughing holiday in fairyland. We have a foretaste of the Shakspeare it is his hope to bequeathe to posterity, and on which he thought and talked for many years before his death. The defect in the scene is the occasional

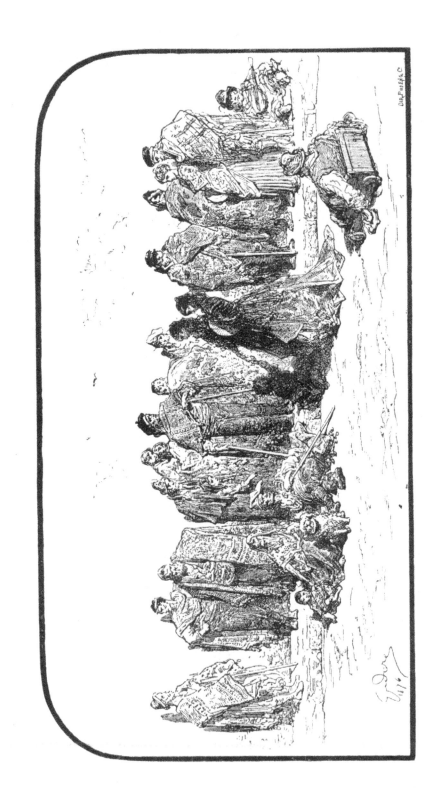

THE SECOND EPOCH.

crudity of the colour, or rather the absence of the variety always apparent in nature. The blue moonlight is in sharp contrast with the greens of the landscape. The beauty of the position lies in the richness of the filling in of the composition. The tiny folk are as multitudinous as a swarm of fireflies.

Passing from the crude blues and greens of Doré's fairyland to his Barr and Hohwald forest pieces, and to his "Evening in the Alps," we light upon three landscapes of the most vigorous, truthful, and impressive kind. The "Evening in the Alps" has been likened to the Alpine pictures of Calame; but it has in it a power over the imagination, an emotional force, beyond Calame's reach. Mr. Tom Taylor, after trying his word-painting on it, fairly gave way and remarked: "Before this picture, as before the nature it represents, the writer feels so strongly the inadequacy of language that he renounces the attempt to put into words what M. Doré has so powerfully conveyed with his pencil."

The picture is true to nature in all particulars, for it was the nature with which Doré had been on familiar terms from his infancy; to which his heart responded; and every turn, effect, and witchery of which was an old friend. Nobody has ever treated the vagaries of snow-drifts and settlements upon mountain flanks and ridges with Doré's strength.

In the first London exhibition of his paintings, which was held in the Egyptian Hall in 1868, the principal work was the "Baden Gaming-table"; in the second, held at the German Gallery in Old Bond Street, the "Triumph of Christianity" was the chief attraction. It was a picture nearly ten feet in height, by seven feet in width. The idea embodied in this ambitious and complicated work, that cost the artist infinite labour, is, as Tom Taylor pointed out in his description of it written to guide and inform visitors to the Doré gallery,* the same which Milton described in his "Ode to the Nativity!" He remarked: "It is the more interesting to compare the painter's work with the poet's, as M. Doré, when he painted his picture, was unacquainted with Milton's ode." So closely does the painter's vision of the overthrow of Heathenism by Christianity resemble the poet's that, as Mr. Taylor points out, some passages of the poem might serve without alteration as descriptions of parts of the picture.

* The Doré Exhibition at the German Gallery, and that which has kept its doors open for fifteen years at the gallery bearing the painter's name, owe their success to the enterprise and energy of Messrs. Fairless and Beeforth, between whom and Gustave Doré a cordial friendship grew up that lasted till his death.

THE SECOND EPOCH.

I will quote Mr. Taylor's brief guide to the incidents of the picture: "In the upper portion of M. Doré's great design Christ bearing his cross stands as the central figure of a glory whose light, emanating from him, bathes in its prismatic radiance myriads of heavenly hosts, ranged orb after orb, and rank on rank; some with golden harps of praise, others with shields of pearl and swords of light, soldiers of Christ armed for the conquering work of the Word. In the centre stands Gabriel, the angel of grace; before him Michael, the angel of power, shoots down to drive away the false gods, whose dominion is subverted by the coming of the Son of Man. Far below in the darkness of the shadow of failing Heathenism floats the earth, which till now has been the place of power for false gods, and of worship of their idols, the work of men's hands. Below the radiant form of Michael the powers of Heathenism, Greek, Roman, Babylonian, Assyrian, Egyptian, Scandinavian, and Celtic, are confounded in what is at once precipitate flight and headlong ruin. The central figure of the rout is Jupiter, the father of gods and men in the Greek mythology, still wearing his royal robe, attended by his eagle, and grasping his thunderbolt, but with his crown falling before him into the abyss. Juno, his Queen, cowers helpless as she is swept down at his side.

Chronos, or Saturn, the father of Jupiter, bearing his symbolic scythe, is involved in the ruin of his progeny—the Prince of Time fleeing before the Lord of Everlasting Life. With these disappears into outer darkness Dagon, the god with gold-horned human head and arms, and the belly and tail of a fish, worshipped by the Philistines and Phœnicians off the coasts of Tyre and Sidon. This was the idol that fell upon its face to the ground before the Ark of the Lord at Ashdod, when the head and both palms of the hands were broken off. It was before the altar and in the house of Dagon that the people of Gaza were gathered together for a great sacrifice and rejoicing, when blind Sampson bowed himself with all his might between the centre pillars of the house, and buried the lords and the people beneath its ruins. The connection of Greece with Phœnicia, through the invention of letters and many arts, explains the juxtaposition of Dagon with Jupiter. Fading into darkness to the right of this central group are the other chief deities of Greece and Rome. Phœbus Apollo, the sun-god, in his car drawn by white horses, now dazzled by the Day-Spring from on High; his sister Luna, Diana, or Hecate, Queen of Night; Venus, Mercury, Minerva, helmed and armed; Pluto, god of the nether world, with his wife Proserpine, and Ceres,

THE SECOND EPOCH.

her mother. Bacchus crowned with vine-leaves, and hiding his eyes from the celestial glory, forms the proper link between the gods of Greece and those of Asia, the hybrid monsters of Nineveh and Persepolis —made up of man and eagle, lion or bull, Baal and Nisroch, Remphan and Moloch, who fill the foreground on the right-hand of the picture."

And so on. Mr. Taylor was a scholarly guide, and passed from one part of the picture to the other with admirable method, showing how the gods of the ancient Celt and Teuton on the left centre of the picture balanced the group opposite. Œsus, the Celtic Mars, the Norse All-Father with his two ravens whispering tidings of the world in his ears, Thor with his hammer, Balldur, Bragi, and Freyia the Norse Venus, are among the overshadowed deities. Then come the many-tinted gods of the Nile, the scarlet Ibis making the happiest passage of colour on the crowded canvas.

Taken as a pictorial marshalling of the ancient and barbarous faiths that faded like the stars at the rising of the sun before the light of Christianity, as " a painted Pœan," the picture is one of Doré's most remarkable works. It is worked out, in every part, with unusual care as to details. The scenes of groupings are masterly, and the general design is powerful; but the colour, in the mass, is opaque and hard, and dusty. The observer has only to compare it with the Paolo Veronese's "Glory of Venice" in the Palace of the Doges at Venice—a design akin to Doré's—to see where the French artist, with all his fine drawing, his imagination, and his skilful grouping, has failed. Doré's subject, however, appealed to all Christendom; and when the picture was submitted to the public, just before the breaking out of the Franco-German War, it at once made his name known in every part of the British Empire. It commanded an immediate success.

PRÆTORIUM (FIRST SKETCH).

CHAPTER XVI.

"CHRIST LEAVING THE PRÆTORIUM."

GUSTAVE DORÉ was travelling to Sydenham, in the company of his friend Canon F. K. Harford, to dine with Mr. George Grove,* when the conversation fell upon some religious subjects. Doré said he was hardly an orthodox Christian, a member of a church, a man with his faith pinned to any ritual. He was led to make this remark by an observation of his friend, that there were high and grand paths of his art on which he had not yet ventured—there were Biblical themes which should fire his genius—he had yet to give to the world the sublimest emanations of his power.

Doré gazed dreamily, as his wont was when an idea struck him with force; and then, turning earnestly towards the Canon, he said that his religion

* The Biblical scholar, now Sir George Grove and director of the Musical College.

lay folded within one chapter of the Sacred Writings. He then began:

"'Though I speak with the tongues of men and of angels, and have not charity, I am become as sounding brass, or a tinkling cymbal. And though I have the gift of prophecy, and understand all mysteries, and all knowledge, and though I have all faith, so that I could remove mountains, and have not charity, I am nothing.'" It was after pauses, recalling the words and meditating on their meaning, that he continued: "' And though I bestow all my goods to feed the poor, and though I give my body to be burned, and have not charity, it profiteth me nothing.'"

And so he went on, not omitting a word, to the thirteenth verse. It was, he said, his creed. A man must be a good man to his fellows in thought and in deed. He had faith, hope, and charity; but to him "the greatest of these is charity."

"You know that I am not without religion," he wrote in 1873; "and I sometimes think that if trials and sorrow are a law imposed upon us by Providence, an end to them is vouchsafed to those who without weakness have drained the bitter cup to the dregs."

Again, on his mother's death, and on the morning of her funeral, he wrote from his solitary chamber to his friend Canon Harford: "You are a priest, my

"CHRIST LEAVING THE PRÆTORIUM."

dear Frederick; I adjure you, then, to offer up prayers to-day for the repose of her sweet and holy soul, and for the salvation of my reason, which I find touched in a singular manner by the cruel despair and dejection which lie before me in the future." In another letter he signs himself "G. Doré, *chrétien militant.*"

After dinner, at Mr. Grove's table, and over a cigar upon the lawn, the subject broached in the train was resumed; and Mr. Harford drew Doré's attention to a passage in the life of the Saviour which had not, so far as he knew, been treated by a painter's hand. It was the moment after judgment when Christ came forth from the Prætorium, and before he had taken up the cross. Mr. Grove endorsed with his authority as a Biblical scholar the statement of Mr. Harford, that this passage had never been pictorially treated. It was fortunate for Doré that among his most intimate friends in England he included the Reverend F. K. Harford, the divine, the scholar, and the accomplished artist. They had met in Paris during the Exhibition of 1867; and their acquaintance soon ripened into a cordial friendship. They began talking about Shakspeare in the studio in the Rue Bayard; and when Doré visited London, it was to the sympathetic attentions of Mr. Harford that he owed much of his success in English society. The artist checked his gamineries, selected his friends with discretion, and, which was most important, was led into that serene atmosphere where he found higher and purer inspiration than he had felt before. His thoughts took a serious turn. A new world opened upon him. He came into contact with Mr. Gladstone, Dean Stanley, Dr. Tait, the late Archbishop of Canterbury, and other elevated minds.

It was, in short, owing to the serious and cultivated society that was opened up to him in London that Doré's mind took a new direction, some fifteen years before his death, and that he buckled on his armour to do mightier work than he had yet achieved.

The first of his sacred subjects was that which originated in Mr. Grove's garden at Sydenham—"Christ leaving the Prætorium." The canvas, twenty feet by thirty, was stretched in 1867, and Doré began the labour that was to end only in 1872, when the finished picture was despatched to London.

The intimate friends who watched the growth of the great picture, which the painter regarded as the highest achievement of his life, and which brought him more satisfaction than any other emanation of his genius, were witnesses of the most patient industry, the most lavish expenditure of energy and of thought

STUDY OF THE SAVIOUR.

"CHRIST LEAVING THE PRÆTORIUM."

on the part of the artist. He made studies for every figure. He listened to every suggestion. He executed the scene again and again in black and white. The anxious days and nights he gave to the figure of the Saviour were many. I reproduce only a few of them in these pages. Each group was the subject of a separate study. The picture so engrossed him that he found it irksome to divert his attention to work of illustration he had in hand (and it was overwhelming, as he wrote again and again in his letters). It was while we were making our "pilgrimage" about London together that he was most anxious about *le grand tableau*—his way of describing it; and this preoccupation led his mind away from the subject we were treating in common.

Strolling up George Street, Hanover Square, I drew his attention to the fashionable church for weddings. It was a leaden, grey morning, and he paused to observe the scene. But his mind was far off. The church, with the statue in the distance, gave him the idea for part of the background of his picture. There is the temple on the right and the statue in the centre, with Doré's imagination marked upon them. In Paris, when he was painting in details of the scene, he would nod from the top of his ladder, or from his elevated platform, continue his labour awhile, and then run down the ladder, deftly wheel it aside, and run to the farthest point of sight, and remain smoking and contemplating the prodigious thing which was growing under his hand. His eyes would presently turn upon you, to read in yours the effect produced. Unlike the vain mediocrities who must not be seen at their work, and who veil as an awful mystery the unfinished picture, which time will surely cover up soon enough, Doré loved the companionship of his few intimate friends while he painted, welcomed candid advice, would listen earnestly and weigh thoroughly any objection or suggestion. He was free to confess a mistake, as we have seen. One day he showed me a Swiss landscape he was finishing; I objected to a certain harshness which appeared to me to be in some contrasts of tints. He listened, with his eyes fixed on the parts to which I pointed; and then he fetched his palette, mixed some transparent browns, and rubbed the colour in with the palm of his hand. Having stepped back to take in the effect, he said: "You were right; let us to breakfast."

When he had a great picture in progress—as the "Prætorium," or the "Vale of Tears"—the departure from the studio for breakfast was effected after frequent pauses. He would turn to look at the work from every corner. His eyes were fixed upon it while

PRÆTORIUM (SECOND SKETCH)

"CHRIST LEAVING THE PRÆTORIUM."

he put on his coat, while Jean was fetching his hat, while he lighted his cigar. At the door he would stop and take a last look. It filled his mind as we walked to the restaurant. He talked about it over the coffee. When he got back to the studio his eyes remained fixed upon it while Jean drew off his coat.

But during the years when his mind was fixed upon his first great sacred subject his absorption in it was extraordinary. The labour told severely upon his nervous system; for it was while the great Scriptural subject was in progress that he completed his illustrations to Dante *Il Purgatorio e il Paradiso* (1868), and his *Idylls of the King* (1869).

The few sketches that will be found in this chapter are but the barest indication of the tentative sketches, the studies of heads and groups, the amendments of the general composition and effects he wrought in the evenings of the days given to the picture. His patience was pathetic. The earnestness he gave to the perfection of every figure, and to its relation to the whole, was admirable. His heart and soul were in the effort he was making.

Originally the scene was bathed in light. There were brilliant masses of colour. The hosts of people, acting under a common impulse, were grouped and piled up, as only Doré could manage masses of

LIFE OF GUSTAVE DORÉ.

humanity. The painter was at last almost satisfied with his work; and his mother would follow him to the studio and sit enchanted before her son's handiwork.

Mr. Harford arrived in the Rue St. Dominique on a visit, to inspect the great picture, and with strict injunctions from Doré to criticise it frankly as a Biblical scholar and a connoisseur.

The friend made the tour of the studio, noticing all the minor work in it, but saying not a word about the great canvas, Doré's anxious eyes following him. They went away presently to breakfast, as usual, at the Maison Rouge; and it was only after an embarrassing pause that Doré said:

"You don't like it."

Canon Harford confessed his disappointment; and in the evening, at home, they discussed the subject. The frank critic remarked that the sky should be overcast; that the awful morning should not be one of sunlight; that the entire picture should be toned down and darkened until the eye was led up to and fixed upon the figure of the Saviour.

Doré sat thoughtful and dejected. His mother protested that her son's masterpiece should not be touched. On the following morning Doré quietly asked his friend to meet him at the studio. He was

FIRST SKETCH OF THE CHRISTIAN MARTYRS.

"CHRIST LEAVING THE PRÆTORIUM."

distressed at the objections the justice of which he could not but admit. The time for sending in pictures to the Salon was at hand, and he had been building high hopes upon the work he had laboured at for two or three years. But before his critic and adviser came his mind was made up, and he was ready to receive him. He mounted his ladder before the glowing canvas, bearing a prodigious palette and brush. Turning to his friend as he entered, he said:

"Tenez!"

And with broad sweeps of deep neutral tint he proceeded to cover the upper part of the picture, working with feverish activity in order to obscure all the bright lights and get at a rough idea of the picture as it is now realized. The change was amazing; the figure of the Saviour stood well out in commanding majesty in the gloom of the sorrowful morning. When his mother saw it she burst into tears.

From the altered picture Doré turned to a small canvas and rapidly sketched in a subject that he had pondered and discussed for a long time—the "Christian Martyrs." He had only a few days; but he bent his utmost energies to realize his vision, so that he should not be absent from the Salon.

He had imagined a Roman amphitheatre by night,

in the reign of Diocletian, after a great festival, of which Christian martyrs had been the victims.

The moon lights the scene. The sated wild beasts prowl lazily about the silent and deserted arena, amid the bodies of the martyrs. A serene dome of star-lit sky covers the dreadful space, and out of it descends a sweet host of angels, bearers of the martyr's palm of the slaughtered and their attendants to heaven. The awful beauty of the vision is purely poetic—it has been described as idealistic to a fault— and it has nothing theatrical about it. To say that the stars look like electric lights, and that the whole resembles a drop-scene,* is to endeavour to be *spirituel*, even at the expense of truth. There is a flood of blue light over the picture, but it is true to nature—it is moonlight upon a grey scene. The drawing of the amphitheatre, and the cold hazy atmosphere in it, are dainty and correct. The fault of the picture lies in the ghastly realism of the preying animals, the smears of blood, and the crunching of bones. Many of the artist's noble conceptions are defaced by these violent contrasts, which are vulgarities in idealistic pictures.

* M. Jules Claretie applies this epithet indiscriminately to Gustave Doré's paintings. In this instance he admits (in *l'Art et les Artistes Français*) that the picture is, "*N'est pas réellement désagréable.*"

"CHRIST LEAVING THE PRÆTORIUM."

Within a week after Doré had the blank canvas before him he had told one or two of his friends that he had a little surprise for them. It was on the social Sunday evening which closed every week at his house. When the guests had assembled, singers (Alboni being generally of the number), artists, men of science, savants, the faithful Jean wheeled an easel into the middle of the room and displayed, for the first time, the " Christian Martyrs." It had been painted within a week!

Doré, always afraid of his Paris critics, drew his friend Mr. Harford aside and said: " Don't say anything about the time it has taken me. They 'll say I paint one picture at least every day before dinner."

Albeit this poetic canvas was painted in a week to fill the gap in the Salon made by the withdrawal of the " Prætorium," it was not exhibited before 1874, when its impressive beauty extorted praise from a few, at least, of Doré's brother artists.

To this period of his life, when he worked hardest while he suffered most, Doré owed the origin of the constitutional disturbance which undermined his health and led him to an early grave.

The picture which cost the artist the heaviest labour, both mentally and physically, was brought forth in pain and sorrow. For when it was little more than half-finished the Franco-German War broke out, and Jean was called upon to unroll it, to fold it carefully up, and bury it underground beyond the reach of the enemy's shot and shell. And the artist, whose patriotism was intense and all-absorbing while the country was in danger, went forth bravely to do his duty as a National Guard when the Germans closed round Paris.

PRÆTORIUM STUDY.

CHAPTER XVII.

THE SIEGE OF PARIS.

"You have understood, dear friend," he wrote on the 27th of July 1870, "the sad reason why I have put off my projected journey to London—a gigantic and terrible war, which puts France in a fever and on fire! You will understand how, under such circumstances, I should be disinclined to be absent from the country where all are uniting against the common danger which may come. Then, again, great news are expected from day to day; and in London they would be a day later. My brother Emile, the captain, has just written to us that his division is about to take the field!

"But, in the midst of these dark skies, an item of news has reached me from your country, like a ray of sunlight. You probably know it already, and your friendly heart must have already been touched. The Queen of England has just done me the great honour of buying one of my works* for her gallery, and I cannot express the proud pleasure that this has given me, and the gratitude I feel for this high mark of kindness."

His last letter from Paris before the siege was dated September 13th:—

"I believe, dear friend, I am taking advantage of the last mail to England; for the enemy is at the gates of Paris, and we are expecting, every moment, to hear the sound of the cannon. Our misfortune is immense, and our agony is terrible. How shall we escape from the abyss of blood in which poor deserted France is plunged? No hope, no solution appears on the horizon; and yet it would be hard to think that our poor France—so innocent of this war—might be the object of universal disaffection!

"I shall carry with me when I go to the ramparts,

* The "Psalterion."

my dear friend, the object,* so well chosen, which your affection has addressed to me. As I have said, I think it will be to-morrow. I pray you, my dear Harford, offer up a prayer that the drama which is beginning may come speedily to an end, and that the mourning already upon us may not cover the whole of France.

"Adieu; it is with a heart much troubled, but with my entire affection, that I embrace you."

He buried his great picture, that the German shells might not reach it; and turned to his duty to his country in danger. With his faithful and valiant servant Jean, who was an old soldier, he went to his service as a National Guard; and the two posted themselves at all kinds of posts of danger while the master made sketches of the bastions, the skirmishes, and all the episodes of the defence of beleaguered Paris. Jean, Doré reported, performed prodigies of valour in his service; but he made light of his own pluck in tranquilly sketching under fire. This is the account he gave of himself to a fair correspondent in England†, who had thought of him, like scores of his English friends, with the deepest anxiety :—

"Despite much suffering, fatigue, and privation

* A silver drinking-flask of quaint design sent to Doré by his friend Canon F. K. Harford.
† Letter to Miss Amelia B. Edwards, 17th February 1871.

of every kind—especially towards the close of this cruel and tragical trial, which has proved fatal to so many—I have come out safe and sound, as have also the few members of my family who preferred to remain within the walls of Paris. As for military service, I have not been called out—not, that is to say, as a soldier for outside fighting. The limit of age exempted me so far; but I served in the National Guard both in Paris and the suburbs, receiving no more glorious wounds than some bad colds and severe attacks of rheumatism. Staying thus in Paris, I have witnessed many dramas and episodes of ruin, in which, despite the gloom of the theme, you would, I think, be interested. I could furnish you with many vivid scenes and descriptions to which your pen could add the colouring of romance. . . . I have good news of my brother, the captain of artillery, who has been a prisoner-of-war at Coblentz ever since the capitulation of Strasburg, which he helped to defend."

Later on he wrote:—

"I thank you a thousand times for this mark of interest, coming at the end of our most sinister and fatal crisis; and I hasten to tell you that, despite unnumbered menaces and miseries, and despite imminent danger of fire (many houses very near to us having been burnt down), we are safe. As for our belongings in the Rue St. Dominique, we have escaped with a few scratches to some pieces of furniture which were dragged out into the street to make part of a barricade close against our house. My eldest brother, who lives in the Ternes quarter, has been less fortunate. The whole first floor of his house was wrecked by shells thrown from the Asmières battery, and he had the furniture of two rooms shattered to pieces. Dear Mademoiselle, the weight of so much pain, the infliction of so much damage, will long oppress us. There is not at this moment a single Frenchman who has not suffered in some way, either by the loss of friends, relations, or property, to say nothing of political hatreds not yet extinguished. As for our poor Paris, I hardly dare to look about me. Paris has irretrievably lost all that beauty which was her ornament and her crown; and, in truth, we may have been very near to seeing this immense city reduced to a mere heap of stones, for it is said that a general and wholesale conflagration was planned by these nameless monsters."

Strasburg, where he had hoped to finish his life when his work was done, was for ever lost to him; and the part of Paris which was his studio and his mother's house half laid in ruins, left Doré a saddened man. He could smell the smouldering ashes

LIFE OF GUSTAVE DORÉ.

of the Palais d'Orsay from his bed-room window; he could see the ruins of the Tuileries directly he turned into the Champs Elysées from the Rue Bayard. To pass from his work to his club (the Mirlitons) in the Place Vendome, he had to skirt the charred shell of the Ministry of Finance, and to step over the broken masses of the Vendome column. He had learned to abhor the devastation and the horrors of war. In 1866 he had been moved by the struggle between Prussia and Austria to produce two powerful drawings—"Peace" and "War." Peace lies upon a happy village. The sheep are trooping to the fold, a lover is talking to his mistress at her window, the last load of the harvest is coming in. War has come upon the scene, like a pestilence. The houses are riddled with shot, the dead and dying lie about, the cattle are rushing away in terror. A bayonet glances through the window where the lovers were courting. In 1866 the artist saw only the terrors and savagery of war, and had renounced battle-pieces.

But when war broke over his country, his exultation knew no bounds; and he seized his pencil, and it became a weapon in his hands by which he stimulated the ardour of his countrymen. The large drawings which he sent forth during the war are so many patriotic inspirations. The Black Eagle advancing upon prostrate France, as she lies with her sword broken; the "Chant du Départ" when France, erect, advances with her cohorts, pointing her sword towards the enemy, and bearing a flaming torch in her left hand; the noble design of the "Marseillaise"—a radiant figure above the advancing armed hosts *en route* for the Rhine; "L'Armée Terrible"; the "Country in Danger," in which a winged France is striking with the hilt of her sword at a man's door bidding him to come forth; " Le Rhine Allemand," where the earth opens on the passage of the army towards the river, and the soldiers of other days rise to cheer their young descendants on their way; the "Enigma," or the Sphinx; and finally, his beloved "Alsace," represented by an Alsatian woman in mourning holding the tri-colour to her heart. These noble drawings from the inspired pencil of the incomparable draughtsman and master of light and shade, acted like warriors' hymns upon the French people. They crowded the windows of the print-shops, to gaze upon and gossip about them. No wonder that the creator of these spirit-stirring appeals to the patriotism of his countrymen in the hour of danger, who could sketch quietly at the outposts under fire, and who was remarked all over his quarter for the steady help he tendered to his friends and neighbours when food and fuel were hardly to be had in the hard winter of 1870-1, enjoyed such a popularity as not all the Art Academies in the world could have given him.

He painted only one picture during the siege—that of a Sister of Charity bearing away a wounded boy: one of his tenderest and most successful subjects. Afterwards he made a picture of his "Alsace," and sent it to the Salon with the title "She Waits." This appeared to the authorities to bear a threat addressed to Germany; and at their suggestion the original title re-appeared. The picture is now in the possession of the Baroness Burdett Coutts.

LIFE OF GUSTAVE DORÉ.

CHAPTER XVIII.

THE COMPLETION OF "CHRIST LEAVING THE PRÆTORIUM."

WHEN the war was over, and the Commune had been crushed, Doré took heart, and, turning from his drawings of the siege as from the recollection of a nightmare, bade Jean unroll his great picture, that he might give himself up to it and complete it. He had another cause for sadness. During one of his visits to London he had met a lady who became the idol of his dreams, and about whom he talked and wrote unceasingly—albeit he never told his love to the object of it. In a letter, dated November 1873, and many subsequent letters, he bemoaned his fate, and said that even work would not efface for a short time the beloved image. He vowed that he had not made a single step towards forgetfulness. But he worked on, so that in April 1872 he was able to throw open his studio and invite the critics and connoisseurs and

STUDY OF THE SAVIOUR. PRÆTORIUM.

"CHRIST LEAVING THE PRÆTORIUM."

fashionable world of Paris to come and see the wonderful picture he was about to send to his gallery in London.

"I think," he wrote, "if you were in Paris just now you would be able to amuse yourself at my studio watching all Paris there. It is a perpetual crowd. At last I have finished my picture, have put it in a fine light, and have invited all Paris to come and judge it, up to the end of this month, stating that it must go to London next month. I assure you that if my success in London is as great as it is here just now, I shall be very pleased. You have no idea how the last month's work upon it has increased the effect of my (I should say our) picture; for you have taken so affectionate an interest in it that you ought to feel equal emotion with myself as to its reception in London."

The " Triumph of Christianity " had prepared the way.

In his *Rembrandt et l'Individualisme dans l'Art*, Alte Coquel fils remarks that he is persuaded that in religious art particularly, and indeed in all art, individuality or spontaneity is the essential quality. The artist must express that which is within himself, and in his own manner, apart from the schools. He must toss aside conventional forms and ideas, which have been the bemummying wrappers that have bound students in academies, and destroyed that which was vital and precious in many. The very strong cannot choose but burst the fetters, and create their own methods, like Rembrandt. The original spark is extinguished in the feebler natures. In religious art that only is true which is individual; that alone impresses the beholder which has moved the soul of the artist. He who gives himself entirely up to his inspiration, discarding the schools and closing his eyes upon received and generally adopted art-conventionalities, is in a position to speak straight by his pencil to the hearts of men. It is the individuality of the painter which strikes the chord of sympathy; and when he has established an understanding direct between himself and the beholders of his creations, he may snap his fingers at the conventional critics of lines (a line is not a good line to them until it has been worn to a groove) and the crowd of folk who never think for themselves, but have their standards of taste prepared for them as regularly as their beds.

In a letter announcing the forward state of his "Vale of Tears," Doré refers to it as the most truly religious and Christian work he has done, and as a "more personal creation than all the others." It was begun in tears; and he said that perhaps the

DORÉ IN HIS STUDIO. (From a Photograph.)

sorrow in which he was working cast its tenderness into the subject he was treating with all his heart and strength.

In the "Christ leaving the Prætorium," the spectator who approaches it in a Catholic spirit is not critical about the relative proportions of the figures, the unfinished drawing, the deficiencies in technique in short. He feels himself in the presence of a commanding genius, who has conceived a mighty scene, full of emotion, of grandeur, and of power. It is the conception, the creation—not the perfect painting of legs and arms and heads, the harmonious grouping, the happy and delicate combinations of colour—by which the observer is held spell-bound.

Anna Perrier, writing immediately after Doré's death, and in reply to something I had written about him under the influence of grief at his sudden loss, has touched, and with admirable precision, the lines of argument I have adopted to defend him against carping, unsympathetic criticism. I have insisted that paintings are not of necessity pictures. Anna Perrier has some valuable remarks on this point, which may be remembered with advantage in the presence of Doré's great Scriptural canvases or scenes.

"I am neither an artist nor an art critic," says

this lady; "yet I am ready to enter the lists on this issue on the side of Doré against all the art critics who have slighted him, and many of the artists who have been preferred to him, and to say boldly that the first aim and object of pictorial art should be to reach the intelligence and to touch the sensibilities; and that inasmuch as Doré aimed at and accomplished this, insomuch is he superior to every artist who either does not aim at or who cannot accomplish it. Without undervaluing accuracy of drawing or correctness of colouring, I will maintain that the utmost perfection attained in these will not compensate for the lack of the higher attainment, and that even errors or shortcomings in these—supposing for the sake of argument that there are such errors or shortcomings in Doré's works—may be pardoned when we have in them such sublime conceptions of great actions and events, such stirring and also such faithful records of human passions and feelings. An artist may paint with the most precise accuracy a female human form, and call it Phryne, or anything else he pleases; but it is, after all, nothing more than a specimen of the perfection to which he has brought his hand in the use of brush and pencil, and the accuracy to which he has trained his eye in distinguishing form; and if this be all that is required in the painter's art, then I do not know why his art should be placed above the art of making boots or coats or weaving lace, in all of which arts delicacy of manipulation and accuracy of form are as conspicuous as in his. No, no; a specimen of painting, mere painting, may be an admirable study in which to train the hand and eye of future artists; but it is no more a picture to give pleasure to the minds of the spectators than a single passage from Shakspeare is a play, or four lines from Pope is a poem. From the former we may certainly see with what force a command or remonstrance can be expressed in a few words, and from the latter with what perfection our rather stubborn English language could be compelled into the most softly-flowing iambics; but we should hardly admit the claim of either writer to be a dramatist or a poet if neither had produced a play or a poem. Just so, if artists give us only 'studies,' we may not be justified in denying that they could give us pictures if they chose; but we are quite justified in denying that the works which they do give us are equal to Doré's, which fulfil in the painting art what 'Othello' and the 'Rape of the Lock' fulfil in poetry.

> Oh that I were a painter to be grouping
> All that a poet drags into detail,

said Byron; and nothing that has ever been written conveys a truer idea of what the painter's aim should

LIFE OF GUSTAVE DORÉ.

be or of what is the test of his genius. If he does not present to the mind through the eye what the poet does through the ear, he is not—whatever his dexterity in mere manipulation may be—an artist, but an artificer; and greater is his blame if, capable of being the former, he contents himself with being the latter, and is satisfied with showing mere dexterity in work without any regard to the value of the work itself. I think art critics are not quite free from the blame of having encouraged by their adulation of mere dexterity this sacrifice of the higher purposes of art to the lower. Whether the fact that a sufficient knowledge of technicalities and a glibness in expressing that knowledge are things easily 'got up,' while a capacity to sympathise with a grand idea or a noble conception is an inherent quality not to be acquired, and difficult even to be simulated, may be the cause of this adulation, I leave to the critics to determine. One objection which may be made to what I have said I take leave to anticipate. It may be urged that the great masters of former times gave us what may be called mere 'studies,' and that such studies show unquestionably the genius of the painters as well as their other works do. I say no doubt this is true; but, in the first place, those great masters did not give us only 'studies,' and in the next place those 'studies' had a character, an individuality, conspicuously absent in the 'studies' of our modern painters. A head by Rembrandt or Holbein—whether it be a veritable portrait or the painter's own conception of a human face—is not a mere accurate drawing of a set of human features, or correct colouring of a human complexion, but has the attributes of the mind, portrayed or conceived, which belong to that face, stamped upon it. Meantime we do not care to have whole galleries of mere 'studies' by either old or modern masters. They would not compensate us for the loss of one picture; for the lack of Murillo's 'Holy Family,' of Francia's 'Entombment'; for the want of Wilkie's 'Blind Fiddler,' or Hogarth's 'Marriage à la mode'; of Herbert's 'Judgment of Daniel,' or Doré's 'Christ leaving the Prætorium.'"

If perfect technique be the aim and the end of art, its professors have been greatly over-estimated. To fall foul of Gustave Doré, and to deny him the first rank as an artist, albeit he has left us a gallery of his creative work in which tens of thousands, nay, millions of people—and not the merely unintelligent or uninformed—have sat and felt the better for the sitting, because faults or incompletenesses in execution are to be found by the expert in the corners of canvases teeming with noble thoughts, is not to harm

"CHRIST LEAVING THE PRÆTORIUM."

him, but to lower the mission and the aim of art. It is, as the lady I have quoted remarks, to lower the artist to the artificer.

Gustave Doré was a creative poet who, as Byron expressed it, grouped all that a poet drags into detail. The idea, and the effect of it upon the beholder's heart and mind, were the precious parts of art to him. We have seen how he contended for this view when as the *gamin de génie* he travelled with Théophile Gautier. Sitting before this majestic vision of the Saviour leaving the Prætorium, the beholder is transported to the place, the morning, the awful event.

Doré's power of realizing space and indicating multitude is here transcendant, as it is in the " Entry into Jerusalem." It is the sense of the artist's prodigious vitality and individuality, informing every part of the canvas, which fixes the attention and acts upon the emotions. The vigour in the drawing is that of the master working out an idea that has entire possession of him. The idea is profoundly pathetic. The Saviour comes forth clothed in the majesty of the godhead, and passes, apart in serene composure, through the tumultuous street-host, to Golgotha. Behind, in the gloom, Pontius Pilate and Herod foregather—the former already conscience-stricken. Near the Saviour are three of the chief

"CHRIST LEAVING THE PRÆTORIUM."

priests, one of whom is triumphant Caiaphas. Then there is the shadow of the down-cast Judas. The Roman guard violently hold back the surging crowds in the foreground, amid whom is the sorrow-laden Virgin Mother and the swooning Mary Magdalene. The Jewish rabble, as cowardly as cruel, look their hate, but fall back before the silent majesty of the Condemned.

The effect of the genius of the artist is direct and commanding. Crowds upon crowds have taken their seats before the picture, and remained long before it, speaking together in whispers. To them Doré has been, in truth, "the preacher painter"; and his weak points have been lost in the marvellous force and majesty—the thought and emotion—of the scene as a whole. The types of physiognomy, the picturesque costumes, the skilfully balanced groups, the multitudes never confused in their vastness, are evidences of the labour and the study given to every part of the subject. But that which is immortal in the work, and will put it on a level with the masterpieces of the Italian masters of the sixteenth century, is the conception of the coming forth of the Saviour from judgment, and the broad and simple treatment of it.

CHAPTER XIX.

1870 TO 1880.

IN the Rue Bayard there were not the stacks of pictures which had astonished Gautier, About, Taine, Claretie, and other observers in the Rue Monsieur le Prince. Jean kept something like order in the establishment, and only the works in progress, together with a few decorating the walls, appeared to the ordinary visitor. Vosges and Swiss landscapes,

Spanish subjects—as beggars at a church door, dark ladies in the dazzling southern sunshine, dancers, gipsies, &c., painted in solid colour, with deep blue sky, old favourite studies of years ago; dark scenes from London life, a dainty bit from Ariosto, a mother suckling her child—one of the most perfect and refined bits of colour the artist ever laid upon canvas—a portrait of Philippon, Rossini dead, with his flaxen wig crowning the waxen features, an English flower-girl whom I have christened Peggy,* one of his great Scriptural pictures, and other religious subjects, in the foreground. These were the canvases amid which his friends wandered, smoked, and talked of late years. There was the most delicate and highly-finished portrait of a prima donna, apart upon an easel, for some time. But it suddenly disappeared—the lady had married. A tender chord had been broken.

The artist was not fortunate in his serious attachments; for he would have married, had the fates been kind, an Englishwoman, he always said, because an English home-wife was his ideal of a woman, and home was the atmosphere in which he had lived all

---

* Poor Peggy sells flowers from street to street
Till—think of this, ye who find life sweet—
She hates the scent of roses.—HOOD.

his life. He was admired by women, and was courted by them; he had *tendresses*; but his heart was never satisfied. The *grande passion* about which he talked and wrote, and which really troubled his repose and made him unhappy for a time, was a dream that never, as I have already remarked, took the shape even of a declaration.

The beautiful face that disappeared from the easel faded also out of his life; and he died in a bachelor's home, where he strove to conjure up, to his dying day, the echoes of his mother's voice.

The change in manner noticeable in the last ten years of Doré's life began with the war and the siege of Paris. When I met him after the siege I saw, in the morning we spent together, that a cloud had settled upon him. He was serious, at times morose. The sunlight had passed out of that happy life, which could rebound after a blow, and laugh while the tears were still in the corners of his eyes. The extent of the difference was apparent only to those who had known him as I had, from his earliest manhood, when he had uncontrollable bursts of animal spirits, and would play gamin tricks, vault over railings, go through conjuror's pranks, indulge in feats of strength, and talk well and solemnly on serious subjects—all within the space of a single hour. He walked demurely to the Maison Rouge, he ordered breakfast like any heavy bourgeois, and hardly noticed the respectful salutes which always greeted him. Sometimes he would stand over the fountain-basin where the live fish were kept, watch their movements, and plunge his arm in to catch one; and then turn away with dripping hands into the street, and get back, a little doggedly, to the studio and to work. At other times we strolled in the Champs Elysées, discussing his plans. But the old laughter hardly bubbled for a moment, even in many walks. The boy had gone out of the man.

Disappointments and trials he confided to me, but which are not for the world's ear, weighed upon him, when he wanted all his courage to rise erect and strong out of the tumult and heavy care of the wartime. He was soured as well as grieved; and he used to say that if it were not for his Bond Street Gallery, where his work was generously appreciated, and for the projects he had to realize, he should give way.

He had become a middle-aged man. He had reached his "forty year," and he felt it as a burden suddenly put upon his shoulders. The *quarantaine* had struck in tones that smote as a *glas funèbre* upon his ear.

LIFE OF GUSTAVE DORÉ.

In work, and in work only could he find consolation, and the courage to look cheerfully forward. He had yet many visions to realize. His brain was full of ideas. His mind had been directed to the Bible, to Christian inspirations, to the triumph of Christianity, Christ leaving the Prætorium, the Christian Martyrs, the dream of Pilate's wife, the Ascension, and so on to Scriptural subjects yet to be realized. At the same time, his chastened genius turned lovingly back to the tranquil grandeur of Nature; and henceforth he drew his inspiration from the Bible and from the wilderness. It was from under the cloud of disappointments and troubles, of a heart unsatisfied and a life disturbed at its centre, that his imagination took its grandest flights with the Apostles, and caught its most impressive effects of *la grande nature.*

In one of his letters " I firmly believe," he said, "that *we workers* have the best health, and for the simple reason that our lives are more uniform. Idlers always fancy that we must be tired, and are astonished to find that we do not wear out faster than themselves. Now, I am one of those who believe that even excessive intellectual work, if it is pursued steadily and continuously, consumes one less rapidly than idleness, intemperance, or *ennui*." And so he

LATER PICTURES.

LIFE OF GUSTAVE DORÉ.

turned for consolation to the studio, and to his dreams. It consoled him to express them in many ways. In his later years sculpture became the delight of his life; and he shut himself up in the little studio within the big one, and gave form in clay to his ideas. Or, when he felt disinclined to sally forth from his home, he would work at his etching, and, as he said, almost poison himself with the fumes of the acid. But moments came, at this time of his life, when he could not work in oil, or clay, with point or pencil. He would suddenly break away, and seek quiet and health in walks and climbs among the Swiss and French mountains. But even in these later days there was a painful drawback. For he could not return to Barr and its surrounding Alsatian loveliness—the black pine-forests and the embattled heights and the grandeur of the views from St. Odile, where he had first learned to love nature—all this romantic region had passed into the hands of the Germans; and he had said that he would see it and Strasburg no more. The landlord and landlady of his humble hotel still say to the passing traveller: "Le pauvre garçon, comme il était content chez nous." But he could not be content with Prussian helmets gleaming in the streets of his little town.

He went away from Paris early in the year 1873,

STUDY FOR THE DREAM OF PILATE'S WIFE.

LATER PICTURES.

travelled for some ten weeks, returned to old haunts in the south of France, and then got as far north as Scotland. He wrote, on his return to the Rue Bayard* : "Henceforth, when I paint landscapes, I believe that five out of every six will be reminiscences of the Highlands; of Aberdeenshire, Braemar, Balmoral, Ballater, &c. I hope to go back there again and again. I went with a party of friends, under the pretext of salmon fishing; but, unskilled as I am in that kind of sport (which is not easy!), I caught, as you may suppose, very few fish, and soon devoted myself exclusively to the catching of landscapes.† I took a good many notes and jottings in water-colour —the first time I have tried that medium. I have employed it solely in obtaining qualities of *intention* or *impression*; and it is in this respect of these effects only that I ask your indulgence for the water-colour sketch which I venture to forward with this, and of which I beg your acceptance."

I shall touch upon Doré's work in water-colours presently. He returned to Paris in 1873 to complete the "Night of the Crucifixion," and the "Dream of Pilate's Wife," which had cost him much anxious meditation.

* Letter to Miss Amelia B. Edwards.
† See Colonel Teesdale's letter for full account of this expedition.

LIFE OF GUSTAVE DORÉ.

The "Night of the Crucifixion," painted in 1872-3, and exhibited in the Salon in the latter year, is a powerful imaginative composition of the most impressive and emotional kind; but it is not on a level with "Christ leaving the Prætorium."

"And it was about the sixth hour, and there was a darkness over all the earth until the ninth hour.

"And the sun was darkened, and the veil of the Temple was rent in the midst.

"And when Jesus had cried with a loud voice, he said: Father, into thy hands I commend my spirit; and having said thus, he gave up the ghost.

"Now when the centurion saw what was done, he glorified God, saying: Certainly this was a righteous man.

"And all the people that came together to that sight, beholding the things which were done, smote their breasts, and returned."

This is the final and terrible scene of the drama of the Passion to which Doré devoted the reverential poetic power that was in him, and which had been strengthened and chastened in the four or five years he had given up to Biblical subjects. The scene is Jerusalem, filled, under the awful gloom, with excited and lamenting hosts, overwhelmed with the crime just consummated, and held in check with difficulty by the Roman guard. Out of the distant darkness, in which Calvary is seen by the glare breaking in the sky through the sable clouds, the lightning flames like a sweeping sword, reflected wildly here and there upon the dark masses of retreating men and women, and the arms of the soldiery. The masterly chiaroscuro of "the preacher painter," as Doré has been called, is used herein with an effect that thrills the beholder. M. Claretie calls it a phantasmagoria. The eternal prattlers about technique, albeit it is carefully painted throughout, pick it to pieces; but to the imaginative mind it appeals with irresistible force. It stirs the blood; it quickens the beating of the heart. The figure of Judas, casting a black shadow before him, is a touch of genius. But there is thought in every stroke of the brush, an idea in every corner of the scene. Some of the figures are slovenly in drawing, albeit there is more elaboration of detail than is customary with Doré; the gloom here and there lacks transparency; but there is sublimity in the conception. It is such a vision as no other painter of the artist's time could have designed or realized.

As I have said, the mind of the painter was given up to sacred themes, and to the cultivation of his real gifts as a poetic landscape painter. These almost monopolized his energies for the last fifteen years of his life, his illustrations being now subordinated to his painting. In 1873 he exhibited at the Salon, with the "Night of the Crucifixion," "Mont Blanc from the Breveut," and "A Torrent near the Grimsel." In 1875 he turned from his Biblical subjects and his landscapes awhile to complete his *Dante et Virgile visitant le septième Enceinte*; but the truant quickly returned. The "Soldiers of the Cross" and the "House of Caiaphas" (1875), The "Battle of Ascalon" (1876), "Ecce Homo" (1877), "Souvenir of Loch Leven," and "A View in Aberdeenshire" (1878), The "Ascension" (1879), the "Falls of Garry, Perthshire," and "Loch Carron" (1880)—these, with many water-colour drawings, and his finest pieces of sculpture, filled the years succeeding the war down to 1880.

"You will find me," he wrote to Mr. Harford (Nov. 1875) "with magnificent landscapes, and at work upon the big picture the 'Entry into Jerusalem,' with which you will be prepared to find fault, but which pleases me entirely. This thing, vivid with light, is a relief to me after my scenes which are nearly always dark—a reproach that has been launched at me with good reason. I saw the Prince of Wales here, and shook hands with him on his way to the railway-station—also our good Teesdale, who

FIRST SKETCH OF CHRIST'S ENTRY INTO JERUSALEM.

was quite unhappy at not being of the company, and who passed a few days with me."

While he was finishing the " Entry into Jerusalem " (1876), Mr. Harford left Paris, and Doré wrote to him to say how he missed him, and wanted to turn to him to ask his advice, adding : " You may boast, my dear friend, that your visit has enabled me to settle several points—amongst others the head of Jesus, executed under your superintendence, and which will be, I think, a magnificent success. I have followed your suggestion also for Claudia Procula; I have drawn around her a kind of court of Roman women, which makes a very good effect." And then he says he has just heard of the death of Lady Stanley. " What a sorrow it must cause the Dean, to find himself alone, after having had for companion this *âme d'élite* and this elevated mind! Convey to him my sincere and affectionate sympathy."

But the head of the Saviour in the Prætorium picture remains, on the whole, the finest head of Our Lord Doré put upon canvas. There is a sacred majesty in the figure : there is radiance and there is intellectual dignity in the countenance beyond any other approach to the unrealizable ideal I can call to mind. It was the result of many studies, and of the most earnest discussions. The reverential labour lying behind the white-robed figure that is the glory and inspiration of the scene, is known only to the few friends of the painter, who were near him through the anxious years of the picture passed in the Rue Bayard.

CHAPTER XX.

DORÉ THE FRIEND AND COMPANION.

LET us now turn awhile from Doré, painter and sculptor, to Doré the friend and companion, before and after the war. In the course of his career Doré had three *ateliers*. His first was in the Rue Monsieur

LIFE OF GUSTAVE DORÉ.

Le Prince, the second was built out of his mother's house; and the third was an old gymnasium in the Rue Bayard by the Champs Elysées, which he turned into a studio. This *atelier*—incomparably the finest in Paris—was a monument that did honour to its owner. Not because it was admirably conceived in every part, and furnished, like the artist's home, with an eye to comfort as well as to the harmonies; but because it was the realization of a dream of Doré's boyhood. When the hard classical masters of the Rue Bonaparte turned a cold shoulder upon him, and even his way to the walls of the Salon was not clear, he resolved, as he painted valiantly in the modest studio which he built out from his home—afterwards the great *salon de réception*, where he gave his pleasant Sunday evenings and his musical *soirées*—that he would erect his own exhibition-room, and stand alone in the midst of his creations, challenging the criticism of the world. In the early days of our friendship we talked this over in the Rue St. Dominique, sitting near that picture of a corn-field which is now upon the walls of the gallery in Bond Street. Doré's plan of life was formed then; and the spacious work-room or hall was realized as, in the flush and heat of youth, he designed it. He even worked already beyond the limits of his dream. Twenty-five

DORÉ THE FRIEND AND COMPANION.

years ago there was no thought of the Doré Gallery in Bond Street.

The work done already was immense; but it had not yet taken all the boy out of the man. As I have said, you had to catch Doré in the vein to discover the humorist, the conversationalist, and at times the *farceur* in him. When he had, accidentally, a friend or two who had dropped in at the studio in the morning, and whom, in his hearty, hospitable way, he had invited to breakfast round the corner at the Moulin Rouge—and where could man make a better breakfast on a summer morning?—and when these were familiar spirits, Doré would toss his paint-covered coat aside, throw himself upon his back on a rug, and, before going out, let his pugs and his terriers run over him, and have a rough play with him, while Jean held the unpainted coat ready for his master, chiding at the same time any of the dogs that threatened to take advantage of their master's condescension. The agility with which he would spring to his feet, and execute two or three gymnastic *tours de force*, singing and talking and tossing repartees the while, would surprise many an admirer of a genius that, in the manifestations of it known to the world, appeared to be wholly absorbed in grand poetic flights. In his youthful time Doré was, as we have seen, a notable gymnast; and afterwards, when he was at work upon one of his immense canvases, it was delightful to see the spring and quickness with which he mounted his ladders, moved about his platforms, and ran down to look at his effect from a distance.

Let us follow him to the Moulin Rouge. Never was the human frame filled with intenser life. I have known only one individual in whom the faculties of observation and apprehension were as acute and unresting as those of Doré; and that was Charles Dickens. It is easy to see why Doré delighted in the author of *Pickwick*, and was for ever talking about him. Doré recognised in the great novelist powers akin to his own.

Doré, however, had only fitfully that which never forsook Dickens, viz. the power of enjoyment, the delight in life, the love of laughter. But when Doré *was* in the vein, his spirits knew no bounds. His fund of anecdote, his humorous observation, his store of reading, and, which was more important, his store of thinking, all heightened by a marvellously strong and faithful memory, commanded the table. His language was richly varied with Rabelaisian flavour at times; but never charged with such despicable slang as that with which the *gommeux* defile the language

DORÉ THE FRIEND AND COMPANION.

Pascal spake. From extravagant liveliness Doré would lapse in a moment to a serious mood. This was a marked peculiarity of him, and indicated the swift rate at which his thoughts travelled, and how deep and thorough was his earnestness. We were laughing our heartiest over an *omelette aux rognons*—Doré's favourite breakfast-dish—and a bottle of St. Julien one morning at the Moulin, when one of the party, a forlorn failure in art, to whom Doré had been a true friend, talked about some whimsical experience of his when he was studying anatomy in the hospitals.

Doré's face grew grave as he listened. The jest passed by him; but the anecdote drew recollections to the surface of his mind; and he began to talk about the necessity of studying the figure from its innermost recesses. The old artist would not agree with him; whereupon Doré reiterated his assertion, and clenched it by bringing his fist smartly upon the table, and repeating his old way of putting the question, "Si; il faut fourrer la main dedans."

While we laughed at the force of the expression, which I had heard before in London, Doré fell into a reverie, and his eyes seemed to be wandering over far-off and sad scenes. From this he broke suddenly, springing to his feet; and while ringing for the cigars carolled the roulades in *Dunque io Son*, in that rich, sympathetic voice which only his intimate friends have heard.

These gossips with old companions were Doré's delight. He went into "the world." He was to be seen on first nights at the theatre; he was a steady frequenter of the opera; and, in the season, he was at the great official receptions, the embassy festivities, and the most brilliant of the private *soirées*; but he was not fond of society, for the sufficient reason that it interfered with his art. Although, through a long, hot evening, he would take nothing more than a couple of glasses of water, the heat and the crowd and the talk told upon him; and he wanted a cool, refreshed brain and a steady pulse at six o'clock in the morning. His pleasure was his quiet evening at home, talk in the company of a few cultivated friends —he affected the society of doctors particularly—and music among musicians, as Alboni, Duprey, &c., and without an audience of mere toilettes.

I have already remarked that Gustave Doré was, chiefly, a solitary man. Since he was a boy, and the delight of that Bohemian club of men of genius, where art and song, and wit and humour, filled the laughing hours in the *caveau* behind Notre Dame de Lorette, it is doubtful whether he has ever been seen in a *café*. He delights in saying that he lives the

DORÉ THE FRIEND AND COMPANION.

life of an Arab. Plain living and high thinking are his choice, albeit all forms of luxury are at his command. During the twenty-five years I knew him he lived in his mother's house, in the Rue St. Dominique St. Germain; in the midst of the ministries, embassies, and sombre hotels of the old aristocracy. It was here that it was delightful to see him.

You passed under a great gateway, peculiar to the quarter, across the yard, up a broad staircase to a spacious apartment, graced with French taste in the hangings and the furniture; but having, superadded, that air of quiet and comfort which distinguishes a well-appointed English home. You saw that all these perfect appointments, these masses of curious and beautiful things, these artful fillings up of corners with valuable nicknacks, and this crowding of treasures upon the walls, were the long result of time. The story of many quiet, happy, active years lay, plain reading, before you. The folios, books, and albums; the musical instruments, the proofs and finished plates, the costly presents—tributes from far and near, from strangers and from loving hands; the pug superbly cushioned in a corner by the armchair of the lady of the house, whose loving spirit followed every footstep of the illustrious son (as much a boy to her then as when he tripped home daily from the Lycée Charlemagne); and finally Gustave Doré himself, who came forward from an inner sanctum to greet you, a pencil in one hand and a cigar in the other,—made a delightful impression on the mind of the visitor. Doré had not, in his address, the ceremonial courtesies of the conventional Frenchman. His face brightened swiftly as Dickens's used, and he got quickly through the *banalités* of meeting, to touch the subject on which his vehement, unresting mind was bent. If he were in a sad or moody temper you would see and feel it at once, as he led you to his work-place; for he must get on with his work while he talks. If he had a grievance or a wrong, you would know it. He was incapable of concealment. He would throw down pencil or brush or graver, toss his hair back, and give you, in a burst of anger, all that was upon his mind. But the storm was short, and was generally dispelled by some sudden reference to a picture in progress, an idea not yet attacked, or some sketch caught up from the mountain of papers, blocks, and drawing-materials which were spread upon a long table in his room beyond the *salle à manger*.

Doré made no mystery of his art, like many *poseurs* who were not worthy to light him to bed. He was open to discuss his plans with any friend for whose

GITANAS, GRANADA.

DORÉ THE FRIEND AND COMPANION.

opinion he had the least respect. He was thankful for a suggestion; if it touched him his fine, penetrating eyes were raised from his drawing and fixed intently upon you. His earnestness never knew abatement. He had that in an extraordinary degree which Lord Lytton has called the best majesty in man. So that you could seldom tempt him out of the realms of art. It was his work and his play. Doré's great London trouble was that he could not get the early *café-au-lait* which he had at home, as he set to work at six o'clock in the morning. Careless busy-bodies have been wont to talk about the extraordinary rate at which he produced picture and illustration; the fact being that the sustained power with which he could labour was beyond that of any artist of the age. I called in the Rue St. Dominique one morning, and found that Doré was not at work in his usual room. His servant directed us to the top of the house. There, shut in an attic, he was bending over the copper plate of the Neophyte. He was finishing his first great etching. Against the wall were two rejected plates, each nearly finished.

"Yes, this is the third," said the etcher. "You see I have the patience of the ox."

In London he would have the keys of the gallery

in Bond Street at night, that he might be able to go there and have some hours in the morning at one of his pictures, before anybody, save the market-gardeners, was stirring. He had been many hours in his little studio at home in the Rue St. Dominique, before he sallied forth, past the old Corps Législatif, across the Place de la Concorde, to his great *atelier* in the Rue Bayard.

The generosity and warmth with which he acknowledged the least tribute paid to his genius were manifested in letters like the following, addressed to me in October 1879:—

"My dear Jerrold,

"Above, behold the beautiful portrait of your friend, taken while he was reading the glorious page of which he has the honour to find himself the object. The roses of modesty invade his countenance, which will be suffused for many hours with this incarnate emblem of the happy emotions and overflowing jubilations of self-esteem *en fête*. It is enough to make one succumb to the sin of vanity from which you declare me to be exempt. Three portraits in this tone would make me lose the 'unspoilt' and the 'unconventional' with which your pen has invested me, and exchange these gifts for Byronian fatuity and *personalisme*. Be this as it may, I promise that I shall never present myself to you in these new colours, but always as you have known me, which is something less *embêtant*, is it not so? than an *orgueilleux*. You pay me, my dear friend, the great compliment of saying that success has always left me unchanged, in the midst of so many contrary examples; and I shall endeavour to remain as before, even after the ovation you have raised to me, and which is a success. Still, a little time ago, I felt a peacock-tail growing upon me as a lady translated and read to me the Review. In a word, my dear Jerrold, I should like to be able to borrow your style for a quarter of an hour, in order to convey to you the pleasure the generous lines your friendship has devoted to me have given me. Thanks also for having thrown out a few words about the Shakspeare. I am at the same diapason in regard to this; and I am organizing my affairs so that I may be able to give to this great subject the greater part of my time. No doubt even next winter I shall have some results I shall be able to show.

"I returned only yesterday from passing six entire weeks in that enchanting region called Glion, the Righi Vaudois.* Didn't you tell me you were there

* We were to have met there in the following autumn.

last year? I found myself in pleasant company among some distinguished countrymen of yours; clergymen, doctors, &c. I should have been well looked after, you see, if death had threatened me. The mornings and all the wet days were given up to my lucubrations on Shakspeare. The amount of paper I blackened cannot be described; but it is certain that in a short time my Glion room assumed the aspect of that in the Bath Hotel which you describe. It was, perhaps, even worse. The work of departure was heavy, when I came to arrange the masses of paper, and I thought I should never get through with it.

"Thanks again, and a hundred times. I hope to say all I have written, and more, over the ragout of omelette and kidneys, for which I have, it seems, a remarkable weakness."

Directly I reached Paris he sent Jean to meet me with a cheery message: "Here is a sunny day," his message ran, "for the smiling *bosquets* of the Moulin Rouge. Come at twelve, and we will breakfast."

It was our custom to meet in this way when I was in Paris. Jean would come with a rapid word from his master, and himself persuade me not to refuse "Monsieur," who was waiting for me. Many of these pleasant little notes lie before me; and most of them are cheery in tone. Even one, dated May 1880, betrays a lively mood, albeit the great cloud was gathering over his home that was to make him a sad man evermore.

"All right!" it ran; "Sunday at half-past eleven, I shall expect you. Reopening of the Moulin Rouge, and resumption of our conversation. — Yours, G. Doré."

The conversation was, as usual in that year, about Shakspeare, and the best form to be given to it. Doré strongly inclined to my opinion, that the work should appear in separate plays; so that each issue would be a separate and complete book. I urged this form of publication, moreover, because I thought it would moderate the rate of the artist's work, and lessen his anxiety.

The following letter is offered as an illustration of his method of correspondence, and as a specimen of his hurried caligraphy:—

Paris 7 Janvier 1881

à mon tour, cher ami
de vous adresser tous
mes voeux affectueux de
bonne année pour vous
et les vôtres et de vous
remercier pour votre
bon souvenir. J'espère
que ce sera le milieu de
l'année dans laquelle
nous entrons, que vous
verrez disparaître enfin
des dernières traces du
mal qui vous a si
longuement éprouvé et

que vous ayez jusqu'à en
effacer le souvenir.
Quant à moi je dis adieu
sans peine à une année
où chaque épreuve douloureuse
entre toutes m'a été infligée
sans compter bien d'autres
encore; car les malheurs
sont certains sinistres
animaux qui ne viennent
qu'en troupe; je m'efforce
cependant de m'armer d'espérance
vous savez que le courage
ne me manque pas
j'ai toujours aimé
le combat et jusqu'à

la foi que l'annexion

Andrè lement à vous

Doré

J'ai reçu la romance que
Madame Arnold a eu la
gracieuseté de m'adresser
Je l'ai fait jouer au piano
par un ami et c'est très
sincèrement que je lui
envoie tous mes compliments

DORÉ THE FRIEND AND COMPANION.

Among his more intimate London friends Doré ranked Colonel Teesdale. Their friendship is admirably described by Colonel Teesdale in the following letter* :—

"My first acquaintance with Gustave Doré must have commenced about the year 1869, or probably somewhat before. At all events he was then in London, beginning to make studies for the work which you wrote and he illustrated. I was able to show him some small civilities, and the acquaintance so commenced soon became a very great and intimate friendship. At that time I was in the habit of going to Scotland every year when possible, to fish amongst all the beautiful scenery of the Deeside; and it seemed to me that no one would appreciate it more than Doré. He was not, however, an easy man to get away from his own *milieu*, and it took a long time to determine him. At last we made a bargain that if I went to pay him a visit in Paris he would return with me to London and then come to Scotland.

"I was received at his mother's house in the Rue Saint Dominique with the greatest hospitality, and

* Letter from Colonel Teesdale to B. J., dated 13th July, 1883.

had the privilege of seeing what his domestic life was. His dear good mother had a perfect *culte* for her famous son, and treated his every want as if he were still a child. Their love for one another was very touching, and as Gustave's imagination was always at the gallop he never seemed to think or care for the wants of every-day life. He used to put on the clothes that were most comfortable, eat at any time that he felt hungry, and drink wine and water if he should be thirsty. At the same time nothing could be good enough for his friends. When the Sundays came there was always a *réunion* of intimate friends, and after dinner there was an adjournment to his home studio, where he used to make his drawings and sketches, but did not paint. I recollect that once when we arrived at the room there was a large canvas there representing a man hanging. The place for the face had been cut out, and his old servant Jean had inserted his own in the orifice. The effect was extremely grotesque, and after that canvas had been played with enough four or five more were brought in succession, each more ridiculous than the other, and the guests were invited to furnish the faces that were left vacant. Generally there was some excellent music, and Doré would sometimes be persuaded to play the violin himself, which he did admirably, but

ENTERING THE ARENA. SPAIN.

always in a strange, weird way peculiar to himself.*
I don't think that he knew a note; but he had complete mastery of the instrument, and often when he was tired of painting in the Rue Bayard he would take up his fiddle and play until he felt rested.

"In spite of all the immense amount of work that he produced he never seemed to apply himself steadily to any one subject, but rather to keep several in hand at the same time. Painting, illustration, and sculpture were all in hand at once. I was once with him in his studio about two o'clock, when, seeing a new canvas he said: 'Let us make a picture'; and before darkness came he had composed nearly the whole of 'The Crusaders,' such as you may see it now. Of course I speak only of the charcoal sketch. That is a fair illustration of how quickly he could embody his ideas. At other times I have seen him working most laboriously on wood-blocks, and going into the minutest details—particularly in the *Orlando Furioso*.

"When I prevailed upon him to come to Scotland with me, we travelled from Paris to London together;

---

* He inclined to the sentimental and tender. He was fond of Strauss' waltzes, saying there was a certain melancholy that attracted him. His ear was sensitive and correct; and he soon threw in a second to anything he heard with skill and precision; and his knowledge of music was extensive, as he would prove when he gave an idle hour to "pianoter."

and in the first days of April 1873 left by steamer for Aberdeen. I had not, until then, had an idea that my friend had such a horror of the sea, *la grande vague*, as he used to call it. Our passage was good enough, but for some four-and-twenty hours poor Doré remained in his berth and would not be comforted. Between Aberdeen and Ballater there is already some tolerably good scenery to be seen from the Deeside Railway, and from Ballater to Braemar is one of the most beautiful drives in Scotland; but to all this Doré was unable to attend through complete prostration. He, however, soon recovered when we were at our journey's end, and was enthusiastic about the wildness and beauty of the country. The salmon fishing turned out to be a perfect failure; and after two or three attempts he quite gave it up and occupied himself with his sketch-book. I was fishing then on Colonel Farquharson's water, and two of his stalkers, Sandy McClaren and Angus, were constantly with us. Before we left Doré made admirable likenesses of them in pencil and gave them to the good old fellows, by whom they were very much prized. His book, from one end to the other, was filled in an incredibly short space of time; for as soon as we came home and had dined he would spend two or three hours in finishing the memoranda he had made during the day, with water-colours, ink, or anything that came under his hand. I once saw him take his coffee and pour it over a page to produce a tone that he fancied. He worked with anything. The end of a pen, his finger, a thumb nail, anything seemed to do; and yet from these rapid sketches he subsequently produced some of his best and most finished work with wonderful fidelity.

"After leaving Braemar we went to Ballater, visiting Balmoral and Abergeldie on the way. Doré had then the illustration of Shakspeare in his head, and many were the discussions that took place every evening; and if we wearied of them Doré would borrow a fiddle and play about the village and on the bridge, to the great delight of the country-people.

"It was somewhat difficult to follow Doré in conversation, though at times he was very brilliant and amusing. His imagination was so fertile that when once he took up a subject that interested him he elaborated it in such a way, and built up so many original theories upon it, that one could hardly follow him; and he became so abstracted that no remark or question was heeded. He often made himself very unhappy by fancying that people were determined to injure him in ways that would never have entered any other man's head. He invented many sorrows and troubles for himself in that way, and, on the whole, was not what we should call a happy man. One of his greatest griefs was the want of appreciation shown to him by his countrymen. Nothing would have given him more real satisfaction than to have had real success in Paris; but for various reasons this was always denied to him. He lived too much in a world apart from any clique—too much alone; he was too original, and produced work of every kind without keeping to one *spécialité*. Jealousy of every kind was the result, not only in France but in England; and the dread of having a picture of his refused was the reason why no work of his ever appeared at the Royal Academy.

"' Je scais ce que je vaux,' was a common phrase of his own; but over-sensitiveness was his weakness. Apart from the artistic side of his character, no more genial, unaffected, kinder man ever lived. He could be like a boy, full of life and spirits, when the cares of his career were forgotten; and he was the truest and most thoughtful of all friends. Nothing seemed to escape his memory. We corresponded regularly for years. His letters were just like the man, full of feeling and thought for others, and at the same time full of fancy and considerable humour. The death of his mother, and shortly afterwards the death of his

THE RETURN FROM THE FÊTE.

old servant Jean, were blows from which he never seemed to recover. We never met after that, as I had my own troubles at home; and when I was last in Paris he was travelling and trying to bring himself to face the lonely life he would have to lead in the big house of the Rue St. Dominique, without the care and love he had been so accustomed to all his life.

"I lost my mother on the 30th December last (1882), and Doré, who loved her well, sent a magnificent wreath from Paris to be placed on her coffin, with such a letter as only the truest and most affectionate of friends could write. Before those flowers had quite faded I heard, to my horror one morning, that my dear friend had gone too. No one who knew him well failed to love him. One could see that in the small circle of his intimates at his home and from the devotion of those who were nearest to him and knew him best.

"I fear that I have given you too personal a description of my acquaintance; but the fact is that it is beyond my power to describe fully all that there was in such an exceptional nature. I have never known anyone with whom I could compare him, as his mind was as original as all the work that he produced."

LIFE OF GUSTAVE DORÉ.

CHAPTER XXI.

THE DEATH OF MADAME DORÉ.

IN the winter of 1881 Gustave Doré lost his mother; he never recovered from the shock.

"I have been so cruelly absorbed, dear friend, for the last three weeks," Doré wrote to me (March 25, 1881), "that I have not been able to answer your first letter, and I am also late in thanking you for your second. I thank you from the bottom of my heart for the affectionate letter you wrote to me when you heard of my awful misfortune. I am thoroughly prostrated, and, alas! thoroughly alone; and I hardly know how to submit to the hard law which, however, spares none of us.

"Since I was born I had never ceased to live at the side of that tenderest, most devoted, and generous of mothers; and although I had lived for a very long time with my eyes fixed on this fearful predicted trial, I had not imagined so awful a void!

"I call up all my courage; but I confess to you I

PRÆTORIUM STUDY.

THE DEATH OF MADAME DORÉ.

find the old maxim which makes work the grand restorer but partly true.

"At the time when you wrote to me about Shakspeare, I was at my dying mother's bed-side, and it would have been impossible for me to string two ideas together. My reply on this subject, *cher ami*, is that I should be afraid, and should consider it rather unskilful, to show any part of my Shakspeare illustrations before I was prepared to enter into serious negociations. Since this exhibition* would be announced with some *éclat*, and much commentary in the press, the bloom would be taken off them, even if the general judgment were favourable; while, if the criticisms were unfavourable or mildly favourable, the consequences would be disastrous. All the charm of the unknown, the unpublished, would be broken. If this be not your opinion, I regret that I think in this way; but it is after mature reflection that I feel compelled to abstain.

"I am highly flattered at having been invited to take part in this exhibition,* and beg you to convey my thanks to these gentlemen.

"Thanks, thanks, *cher ami*, for your kind thoughts.—Yours devoted, G. DORÉ."

---

* An exhibition of paintings and drawings referring to Shakspeare, in the Shakspeare Memorial Theatre, Stratford-on-Avon.

To Canon Harford he wrote on the morning of his mother's funeral:—

"She is no more, dear friend: I am alone. She is dead—my tender and venerable mother—dead, after a long and cruel agony; and this morning, in a few hours, I shall follow her to her last resting-place. I am without strength, and I don't know how to submit to the hard law which, however, spares none of us. A black abyss seems to lie before me."

He never took heart, however, to cross the Channel that year; nor was he destined to cross it again.

I received the following note from him in June (24th):—

"I have just written to the Lord Mayor to excuse myself for to-morrow. I have explained to him that the very bad state of my health prevents my making the journey to accept his amiable invitation. I am really prostrated by the vicissitudes of my recent life, and the perplexing organization of my new condition—all solitude and mourning. As soon as I am delivered from the sickness which keeps me here, I will go and pass a few days in London, and chat a little with you. I hope that it will be by the end of the month: I even look forward to it. Have the

PRÆTORIUM STUDY.

THE DEATH OF MADAME DORÉ.

goodness to reiterate *vivâ voce* to the Lord Mayor my regrets. Until yesterday I thought I might be able to come, but my neuralgia has returned with redoubled force, and I must not think of it."

On the New Year's Day of 1882 he wrote to me as usual:—

"Let me address to you in my turn, *cher ami*, all my affectionate wishes for you and yours in the new year, and thank you for your kind remembrances. I hope that before half the year is over you will see disappear the last traces of the disease which has tired you so long, and that you will live even to forget it.

"For myself, I say good-bye, without regret, to a year in which the cruellest of trials has been inflicted on me, without counting many others—for misfortunes, like certain sinister animals, come in troops. I try, however, to be hopeful. You know that I am not wanting in courage. I have always loved a battle (*le combat*), and I shall love it to the end. —Cordially yours, G. Doré."

Miss Amelia B. Edwards said to Doré that his mother was like one of the sybils of the Sistine Chapel. "Or like a Hebrew prophetess," he sharply answered. "*Elle a la tête juive.*" Doré was right.

LIFE OF GUSTAVE DORÉ.

After his mother's death he wrote (May 1881) to the same lady: "You truly sketch in words the noble features and the sweet sympathetic smile of her for whom I weep. And, indeed, there was in her face a simple dignity and an attractive affability which commanded the homage of all who knew her."

I had sent him a copy of my life of George Cruikshank, which I had dedicated to him; and he had heard of a heavy bereavement I had suffered. On the 5th of April (1882) he wrote to me:—

"Your parcel, *mon cher ami*, has reached me almost at the same time as your letter; but before all thanks let me express to you the sincere and affectionate sympathy I feel for you at the cruel loss you have just suffered. You had not yet, if my memory serves me, paid your tribute to that painful experience in life—the loss of a child—the only drawback, to my mind, of the married condition; and that which stands to so many men as an excuse for hardening into celibates. It is bad enough to lose little creatures who have been able only to lisp a few words; but that which must shatter our strength, and make our heart revolt, is to see the child who has become our friend, and reciprocated the care and affection we have lavished on him, pass from us, at the moment when the book of youth and hope was opening upon his

PRÆTORIUM STUDY.

sight. I beg you to convey to Madame Jerrold my affectionate condolence, and my exhortations to take courage in the days of mourning.

"I have just been looking over, with keen interest, your two volumes on Cruikshank. It is admirably done, and got up, and it cannot fail to command success. There is in Cruikshank an inspiration so essentially English, and he has so charmed three or four generations that this work appears to be one which had the best *raison d'être*. It appears in good, well-measured time after his death.

"I need not tell you how touched and flattered I am by your dedication. I thank you once again. I have read the preface and what you say of our old recollections (in this I am always English) of Boulogne, and of our gambols with Ingram on the sands *O nos vingt-ans! O les beaux vingt-ans!* Neither you nor I thought, in those days, of days of mourning, of failures, of sorrows. Only many years later did we reflect that we must learn a little philosophy; and we were ignorant of the maxim of the ancient sage of the East, 'To live is to see others die,' or of the other, 'Suffering is the end of all science.'

"Very affectionately yours,

"G. DORÉ."

I went across to Paris to see him shortly after the receipt of this letter. I found him perched on his scaffolding working at the "Vale of Tears." He ran down the steps, threw his arms about me, embraced me, and said, "*Cher ami*, how you must have suffered!"

In his New Year's letter to his friend Canon Harford, written in December 1882, only a few weeks before his death, we find him still desponding.

"As for myself, I say good-bye without regret to the most fatal of years in which I have known only disappointments and sorrows. Since the death of my mother it is always the same thick cloud that hangs over my existence; and in spite of much courage I have often despaired.

"I am finishing the picture, the 'Vale of Tears' ('Come unto Me'), which must reach London soon. I have been hindered by the execution of the monument of Alexandre Dumas, which has become, bit by bit, a considerable affair. It will doubtless be erected next spring. It is, assuredly, the greatest effort I have made in my life."

It was the greatest, and the last.

PRÆTORIUM STUDY.

CHAPTER XXII.

GUSTAVE DORÉ THE SCULPTOR.

It was in the back kitchen of the little house in Dean's Yard, Westminster (the residence of Canon Harford), that Gustave Doré first took clay in hand, and tried his skill in the plastic art. He endeavoured to realize a head of the Saviour, after a discussion he had been holding with his reverend friend. He produced a vigorous, but a rough and harsh work, that was left to crumble in the back garden; but it had served to open to the artist a fresh field for his imagination. It rejoiced his spirit as it had been rejoiced when he first played with the etching needle; and when he went back to Paris he parted off a corner of the studio in the Rue Bayard, and applied himself to the mastery of the sculptor's material and

technique. For a long time he kept the door of his sanctum for sculpture closed. His patient hand was labouring to acquire skill over the clay. It came slowly. The subjects for sculpture crowded upon him. He must have an original idea to embody before he could work with fervour. The ideas were formed only too plentifully, creating that haste to realize which marred many of his works.

But just as, in his later day, Doré proved by constant progress in manipulative skill, and the refinements of light and shade and colour, that there was the stuff of a perfect painter in him, both in oil and aquarelle, he gave promise, even in the brief years of his labours with clay, of rare excellence as a sculptor. His mastery of drapery—conspicuous in his lightest and earliest work—was a potent help to the sculptor, as was made manifest in his group of "Glory," his "Night," and "Atropos and Love." It was in 1877, when he first exhibited some of his water-colour sketches, that he appeared at the Salon as a sculptor; and in 1878 his second group was allotted the place of honour in the gardens of the Palais de l'Industrie.

In the boarded-off corner of his studio he had wrought his group of Love—pressed upon the bosom of that fate Atropos (one of the Paicæ) who cut the

DORÉ THE SCULPTOR.

thread of life. The critics who had scoffed at the painter could not but bow to the genius of the sculptor. The piece was a striking success, and it remains famous. M. Claretie said of it that the two figures are superbly modelled, and are arranged with infinite art. Atropos is a figure, noble and mysterious, it is difficult to forget. In the same corner from which this work had proceeded Doré designed and elaborated, among minor works, his monster vase for the Universal Exhibition of the following year (1878). His group of Glory pressing Ambition to her breast, her hand covered with palm-leaves, and a dagger under them, his beautiful design for a chandelier, his "Ecce Homo" (hung in the *salon carré* of the National Exhibition), and his "Orlando Furioso," made 1878 a year of prodigious toil, but also of great reward to the artist. He appeared at once as painter, aquarelliste, sculptor, and illustrator, and in each department with some of his best work. His Vase—the form of "the big-bellied bottle" or wine-flask of Italy—called the "Vine," was an extraordinary *tour de force*. It is the poem of the grape, expressed in the most marvellous varieties of Cupids and Bacchanalian processions, fauns and satyrs, and Hebes and wantons, intertwined with the tortuous vine, and graced with its delicate leaves and fruit; from the base, where Cupids chase the spiders from the roots, or raise themselves ladder-fashion to steal the ripe bunches, to the "beaded brim," at which the voluptuaries of the cup are grouped. Here

> A Hebe of celestial shape
> Pours the rich droppings of the grape;

and there Silenus tipples and ogles. The movement, the life, the infinite variety of it, and, above all, the charm, the grace, and the vigour of the treatment of these tumbled hosts of figures, compose a monumental piece of sculpture that is absolutely original in conception, and of masterly force throughout as regards the execution. The Municipality of Paris proposed to buy it, but did not. It cannot fail, however, to find a national site. Had Strasburg remained in the hands of France, Doré's native town would have undoubtedly secured it. To him, however, it brought only a very heavy outlay, and a year's unrequited labour, and in the end a heart-burning that lasted long; for, at the close of the Universal Exhibition, his friends saw, with disgust, that he was not in the list of those to whom honours had been awarded. The omission was repaired, through the energetic intercession of M. Paul Dalloz and other influential friends; but the remembrance of the slight he had suffered remained and rankled at the

LIFE OF GUSTAVE DORÉ.

heart of the man of genius, the latter half of whose life was, as the reader has remarked, embittered by the treatment he received in his own country, which he nevertheless continued to love passionately. In 1879 he exhibited his group of "Maternal Love"—a negress holding her child away from a serpent. The idea is touching, and it is embodied with skill and vigour. The young negress's forgetfulness of self while the serpent creeps up from her feet, and the devotion with which she holds her babe aloft as far as she can stretch, tell the story with force.

In 1880 Doré exhibited "Madone," in 1881 a group symbolising Christianity, and in 1882 his statue ("La Danse") produced for the Monte Carlo theatre.

These, with his fine conception of "Ganymede," and his fantastic "Nymph and Fauns," constitute the plastic work that preceded his *magnum opus*, which, with his "Vale of Tears," brought the work of his life to a close.

Doré wrought some fantastic groups in clay. His acrobats making a human ladder; his Gulliver with the Lilliputians running over him; his owls, are dainty plays of his fancy and his humour, which, cast in bronze, he was pleased to show. They were the toys of his idle moments, representing playful rest from the severer work always in progress around

LIFE OF GUSTAVE DORÉ.

him. Taken together with the few important and successful pieces of sculpture he had given to the world, they helped to show the world, over the heads of his grudging critics—usually more anxious to exhibit their own *esprit* than to do justice to the many-sided creative artist—that in the illustrator of *Dante* and *Don Quixote*, and the *Bible*, the painter of the "Neophyte" and "Francesca," and the powerful etcher, there was the making of an original and powerful sculptor.

This general conviction, confirmed by the group that held the place of honour in the Salon, led to the incident in Doré's life which was destined to mark and dignify its close.

CHAPTER XXIII.

DEATH.

It is difficult to speak even now of Gustave Doré as of one whose light is quenched and whose hand is cold and rigid. He was my oldest and my closest friend. I was identified with most of the work of his last twenty-seven years, for I discussed his ideas, his plans, and his speculations with him, and watched every step of the progress made throughout this the better part of his working life. I was in close contact and sympathy with him, and I knew him to be one of the noblest, most generous, and devoted servants of art of whom we have any record. As a boy, as I have endeavoured in these pages to show, he lived in it. It possessed him like his blood. It was the master-passion of his whole life; and never was he so engrossed in it as when, on a chill November morning of 1882, we talked about the new studio he was to build by the Parc Monceau, over our breakfast at Ledoyen's, whither he had migrated, after the final closing of the Moulin Rouge. He was sad, and complained, as usual, that since his mother's death he had led a lonely life. He talked about marriage, and then, with one of his swift transitions from shadow to sunlight, he sketched, in rapid and vigorous phrases, full of observation and humour, the disadvantages of a man of fifty entering upon matrimony with a young girl. He was even more energetic when he came to the picture of a reasonable marriage with a person of suitable age. That would not suit him. "En attendant," he broke off, "let us smoke." And he smoked, and, while his dreaming eyes wandered over Ledoyen's shrubs, he talked about his statue of the elder Dumas, which we had been examining in his studio; his autumn travels in the Pyrenees and the sketches he had made; and then of an exhibition of his Highland, Alpine, and Pyrenean landscapes which I had suggested to him. The idea, as our neighbours have it, "smiled upon him." But how and where should it be? He would not trust the Parisians; they were always unjust to him. At that moment crowds were gathered all day before Goupil's window in the Avenue de l'Opera, gazing at an Alpine scene by him, and I reminded him of this; but he shook his head, and then cast the subject away with—"What do they think of French politics in London?" He listened carelessly and absently while I told him in a few words. Then he said, "An artist should keep to his art, and have no political opinions. I hold myself aloof. I am neither Republican, nor Orleanist, nor Bonapartist. What do these gentlemen who do us the honour of governing us care about art?"

Not once in the course of our morning did he laugh, or sing a snatch from an opera, as his wont was when in fair health and spirits. He was not the Doré of happy times, when in the studio he would throw down his palette and stand before his work, while he trifled with his violin, or played with his dogs, or the pair of superb eagles which were in a vast cage in a corner. There was dejection in his mien. Jean, his old servant, who could stretch a picture or reduce it, put everything to his hand, compel frame-makers and packers to be punctual, roll up a picture, and watch his master's moods from his rising till bed-time—Jean was dead. He had died in the previous summer. Doré had nursed him as he lay sick in the little

DEATH.

concièrgerie at the entrance of the studio, and when he died had buried him, ordering every detail of the simple ceremony himself. It was a great trouble to him, and he went away to the Pyrenees last autumn for rest and change directly it was all over, leaving Jean's widow and her children in their little dwelling, and having arranged for the future of the eldest boy in the navy.*

We were to have met on our autumn holiday, in Switzerland; and I called at the studio to make arrangements. Madame Jean, in black, opened the door and followed me, as I went to see what Doré had left upon his easels. Where was Jean? was my first question—was he with his master? The poor woman burst into tears, and told me her Jean was gone. She was astonished Monsieur Doré had not written to tell me. And then, between her bursts of sobbing, she gave me a description of Doré's goodness to her husband that was a noble, unaffected tribute of most respectful love to the great man she and Jean had served throughout their married life.

There has been already criticism, more than enough, of Doré's work. There has been much ignorant and unhandsome commentary on this conscientious and most

* In his will he had amply provided for his old servant, and for Madame Jean.

gifted worker. We have been told that he covered his broad canvases with the help of many pupils; he, who never had a pupil in his life. I saw his great canvases begun. I sat with him at frequent intervals while he worked at them, at every stage. I never saw a helper in his studio half a dozen times, and on these occasions he was merely filling in the masses of the merest architectural back-ground. But I forbear from pursuing the controversy into which false or erroneous statements about Doré's place as an artist might lead me. I prefer, in conclusion of this labour of love, rather to dwell on the gifted friend and courageous worker who, when I wondered at his unfailing strength, answered, "I live like an Arab." Poor Jean knew that, and so did Madame Jean. We have seen him at five o'clock on summer mornings at the workshop he kept in the St. Dominique, apart from his studio in the Rue Bayard. At an hour when fashionable Paris was still sleeping he would stroll from his mother's house across the Pont de la Concorde, with a cigar in his hand and a song on his lip—possibly recalling some of the music of his salon of the previous night; and ring the studio bell, which would be answered by Jean, a couple of his children, and three or four dogs. The master was ever welcome to servants, to the children, and to his

DEATH.

dogs. His neighbours smiled on all sides as he passed along. It was the pride and pleasure of his barber's life that he shaved Monsieur Gustave Doré. While the tears were streaming from her eyes, the widowed Madame Jean assured me that no angry word had ever passed between her husband and his master from the day when he entered his service to his death. "Not a word," she repeated; "and we came to Monsieur straight when we were married, and all our children have been born here. *Il est si bon.* And now I must leave him; for I cannot do Jean's work with the picture-moving, the colours—in short, poor Jean's business. He must find somebody else; but, he says, he will never find another Jean." Doré looked very grave when I mentioned his old servant's death to him. "The excellent man!" he said; "I had no trouble when he was with me."

Doré's love of home, and his disdain for what he called the *vie de cabaret*, were delightful traits in his frank and simple character. When I first went to see him, and our friendship began—it was in 1854—he was in an upper room in his mother's house in the Rue Dominique St. Germain, the house in which he breathed his last. He had the manners and appearance of a bright and handsome boy. The fair complexion of a girl; large and lustrous eyes that had

LIFE OF GUSTAVE DORÉ.

generally an upward cast; regular features, but weak for a man as regards nose and mouth; a broad and solid brow, over which the long straight hair fell here and there, uncombed; made up a presence fair and pleasant to see. When he laughed there was malice in the lines of the mouth, but the eyes were of the merriest. He was in an artist's blouse, and seated at a long sloping bench upon which some twenty wood-blocks were ranged. He worked while he talked, moving from one block to another, apparently to refresh himself with a change of subject. He was illustrating for his first patron Philippon, and was already famous as the illustrator of *Rabelais* and the *Contes Drôlatiques*. But even then he was preparing to soar beyond the illustrator, and had determined to win laurels as a painter. Under the maternal roof was his studio also in those days, and he was engaged upon several battle-pieces, drawn with vigour, but crude in colour and coarse in execution. In this resolve, of which he talked to me afterwards so often, so long, and so earnestly, he never faltered, albeit he was buffeted by the classical mediocrities, and assailed by their scribes. It was as strong as ever in him as he talked about the new studio he was about to build at our November breakfast at Ledoyen's. We have discussed enough whether he had in him the stuff of a great painter. I am anxious only, in this place, to speak finally of the intrepid spirit which ruled his life, and the lofty aspirations which made it an incessant battle against unsparing enemies. Only in November, over that saddest of our breakfasts together, his mind was disturbed by the rough usage he had encountered. His death has in some quarters rekindled the spiteful spirit it should have allayed, at all events till the earth had been laid upon the generous heart of one of the most thorough artists who ever lived. Even when he lay on his death-bed, some malignant wretch forwarded him an insulting extract from an article on his painting and sculpture. He was thorough in the devotion of every waking hour to art for art's sake, and not for its garlands and its money rewards. Doré was grateful for the generous reception he experienced in England. He said that his gallery in Bond Street was his comfort when his own countrymen mocked and scoffed. But he never stooped, the fever of his boyhood once past, to pot-boiling. When a subject stirred him, he worked it out with all his soul and with all his strength. He lost large sums of money in carrying out his own ideas. He refused uncongenial themes that were pressed, with handsome terms, upon him. He painted, not for the market,

DEATH.

but for himself. The money he amassed was treasured only because it would enable him to work out his own ideals in his own way.

While we sat at Ledoyen's he told me in a few words what his intentions were in regard to the land he had bought for his new *atelier*. He said he had been pestered by applications from architects who supposed he was going to build a palace; whereas all he wanted was a spacious studio (with a better light than he had in the Rue Bayard), and a bedroom. There he would paint for himself, keep his work about him, and leave the world now and hereafter to judge between him and his critics. To say that Doré had a thirst for the applause of the uncultivated many, is to do his memory a base injustice. His *Dante*, his *Rabelais*, his *Don Quixote*, his *Bible*, his *Orlando Furioso*, are his answers to the charge. He toiled with his pencil that he might be independent with his brush. For this end he lived a quiet home-life, in the midst of temptations, and never even afforded himself the luxury of a *coupé*. He, indeed, scorned delights and lived laborious days. He was no ascetic. He was not straight-laced. His conversation, which was rich and racy, was well-flavoured often with Gallic salt. But there is not a spot upon his life. The art of Gustave Doré is open to criticism; but the artist must remain a model of all that a student's life should be.

From Ledoyen's that November afternoon we turned towards the Faubourg St. Honoré, Doré talking in a subdued manner that was unusual with him, and we halted at the corner opposite the Elysée. I was going to turn back towards the studio with him, for we often strolled to and fro thus, but he took my hand and said, "Don't fail me at breakfast when you come back. Adieu, *mon ami*." He disappeared in the shop of a book-seller opposite, slowly and quietly. I thought he had aged much of late, and I walked away somewhat sad to think that he should feel lonely and adrift, at fifty.

I never saw him afterwards, nor received more than our usual interchange of good wishes at the New Year. Within two months he lay dead in the house where he had passed his life of labour—the house which his maternal grandfather had built.

It is pleasant to bear in mind that the close of his life was cheered somewhat by the anticipation of the triumph he would gather when his statue to Alexandre Dumas should be unveiled in the great public thoroughfare by the Parc Monceau, where the romancist had lived and worked; and by his preparations for the crowning of his career as an illustrator

DEATH.

with his Shakspeare. Not that his forecast was limited to these achievements. He had yet to raise the *atelier* on the ground he had bought with the savings of the years that were no more, and then to people it with the creations with which his unresting mind was pregnant.

During his last day in his studio he appeared to be well, and was more than usually cheerful. He sat at his piano; he sang. He had lately been distressed, so that he could neither work nor eat, because his dog had bitten the hand of the son of his concièrge; but the wound had healed, and the anxiety was removed. So he had resumed his work. But as the day wore on he became restless and sad, and went to the concièrge's room to see the hour. He never carried a watch, nor wore the most trifling bit of jewellery. He remarked to poor Jean's successor that the day seemed very long. And still again and again he returned to look at the clock and remark on the lagging hours. To a lady who called he remarked that he had never known so long a day. Then he stood at the door, gazing dreamily up and down the street. His last request to his man was for a sunny little picture from Ariosto he had painted. He sat and gazed at the flood of light he had thrown upon the canvas. He planted it against the "Vale of

Tears," and turned, from a drawing he was making for the *Roi s'Amuse*, several times to it. His eyes were fixed upon it when, by the light of his lamp, he put on his overcoat that Friday afternoon, and went quietly out—never to return. He passed the evening at a soirée, among his friends. The little bit of sunlight still stood against the great picture when the seals were raised from the studio door after his death, and I entered with a little crowd of lawyers who were bent upon inventory making!

On the Saturday morning one of Doré's friends called at the studio, to tell his man to go at once to his master in the Rue St. Dominique. "He had had a fainting fit," said the messenger, "and he was in bed."

He had risen at his usual hour in the morning. He went into the billiard-room, and played a little alone; then returned to his bed-room to finish his dressing. He was expecting a call from a friend. Suddenly he called aloud that he was in great pain, fell forwards over a table, and finally backwards, over the barber's basin that was at hand, cutting his temple. He remained for some time unconscious, and was persuaded with difficulty by the doctors to go to bed. He lay prostrate and sad, even to tears. When his man from the Rue Bayard reached him he said: "Ah, mon ami, vous ne me reverrez plus, Rue Bayard. Je suis perdu.

J'ai trop travaillé." Then in a whisper he told him what to do with certain pictures; and was anxious about his water-colour drawings for the approaching fifth exhibition of the French Water-Colour Society.*

The news of Doré's sudden illness spread consternation among his intimate friends. His brother Émile hastened from the town in which he was quartered to his bed-side. M. Paul Dalloz wept when he saw him. M. Pisan heard of his illness only on the Monday, having missed his usual visit to the Rue St. Dominique. Dr. Michel and other men of science surrounded him with every possible care. He rallied on Sunday, and when his servant came to him from the *atelier* he talked cheerfully about the work in hand there, telling him the Dumas statue must be pushed forward, and to be careful about sending the *aquarelles* to the Rue de Sèze. He even became impatient to get up; and said he must lose no more time over his Shakspeare.

"My Shakspeare! My Shakspeare!" he exclaimed repeatedly. In order to give him sleep, the

---

* Doré took great interest in the new Society. He had prepared eight water-colour drawings for the Exhibition of 1883, including a fairy scene from the "Midsummer Night's Dream," a group of poor London children, a sketch of the docks, some Spanish beggars, and six fine drawings in black and white of the outskirts of Paris during the siege.

doctors injected morphia on Sunday night; and when M. Pisan stood at his bed-side on the Monday morning he found him drowsy with it; but he put out his arm and shook his old fellow-worker's hand, and looked kindly at him.

By Sunday evening Doré appeared to be so much better that the doctors who had remained in constant attendance on him went away, believing that all danger was over and that he would be well on the way to convalescence on the morrow. In the evening Pisan, who had remained near his friend, played a game of billiards with Colonel Émile Doré, and they were in good spirits at the happy turn of events. The Colonel was even preparing to return to duty. It was half-past eleven o'clock when Pisan left the house. At half-past twelve, after a spasm, Gustave Doré passed away.

When, in the morning, M. Pisan returned, he found him lying in the sweet peace of death, with the smiling calm of infancy upon his noble countenance. By his head was the portrait of his mother, entwined in the grey hair he had stroked and reverenced throughout his life; over his bed was the head of the Saviour, and by the foot of it, against the wall, the earliest water-colour drawing he had executed.*

* A soldier carrying flowers to his payse, dated 1849.

FIRST SKETCH OF THE ASCENSION.

DEATH.

In the course of the day his couch was covered with flowers, and the hands that had been busy so long were folded upon a cross.

Around, in indescribable disorder, lay the work of those fingers, become rigid and nerveless. Stacks of drawing-boards, piles of plate-proofs, hundreds of sheets of sketches, principally Shakspearian notes, extraordinary quantities of drawing and water-colour materials, testified, mutely eloquent, to the energy of the prodigious worker who, in three days, had been laid low in death. The walls were covered to the ceiling with his creations, and with the gifts of friends. Here was the immense water-colour portrait of his mother, the labour of the most dutiful of sons; there was Carolus Duran's portrait of the illustrator of Dante; a portrait of old Françoise; and on all sides were treasures of bronze, china, and marble, making up such an artist's home as we have not in England.

In the death-chamber friends appeared, burst into tears, and went sobbing away. M. Pisan sat by the bed-side and tried to make a faithful drawing of his friend in death. Another old friend, Nadar, came and photographed the features he had known so well.

Far and wide the news was spread in the course of the day, and expressions of regret were conveyed from all parts of the world to the Rue St. Dominique.

LIFE OF GUSTAVE DORÉ.

The universality of Doré's fame was shown by the world-wide sorrow caused by his death. Some of his detractors did not spare him, even at his open grave; but when the world's good opinion is conquered the fame of genius defies the shafts of envy, malice, and all uncharitableness. The too-sensitive heart of the man could be wounded no longer.

CHAPTER XXIV.

THE FUNERAL.

BETIMES on the morning of the 25th of January the body was carried from the death-chamber to the Chapelle Ardenti, which had been draped, under the gateway of the old house in the Rue Saint Dominique. It was a sad scene on that winter morning in Doré's room, where he had slept so many years, with treasured mementoes of his life about him. A sketch, made in his college days, of a soldier awkwardly offering flowers to a country wench; engravings "War Time," and "After the Peace"; a fine drawing of the head of the Saviour; and by the bed, where the dutiful and loving son would see it as he closed his eyes for the night, the portrait of his mother, with a medallion enclosing a lock of her hair. On the beloved face he had gazed as he turned to his long sleep.

In the Chapelle Ardenti the coffin rested, covered

with flowers from loving hands, and with wreaths from the Alexandre Dumas Statue Committee, the Society of Engravers, the French Water-Colour Society; and conspicuous in the mound of flowers was a yellow wreath, encircled with palm-leaves, from his old friends and comrades of the *Monde Illustré*. At the foot of the coffin, upon a craped cushion, the Orders which had been conferred upon Doré were arranged—the officer's cross of the Legion of Honour holding the principal place. Within the house there were many signs of the swiftness of the artist's death. Paintings, water-colour drawings, sketches, artists' materials of all descriptions, were massed in confusion about the spacious studio in which Doré had worked for many years; where he had held his lively soirées; where he had sang, played, and danced, and performed gymnastic feats—in the midst of the most distinguished intellectual company Paris could produce. The silent mourners wander in the littered and deserted rooms, glancing for the last time at well-known memorials upon the walls—as Rossini's portrait, inscribed by the maestro to the young violinist Gustave; and calling to mind, in whispers, the lively dinners, the improvised concerts, the frank gaiety, in short, which had never ceased to reign while Madame Doré lived, and her son, at the height of his revels,

THE FUNERAL.

could glance at her solemn and dignified figure and catch a loving look from her eyes.

At the Church of Sainte Clotilde, near at hand, the square of which was covered with snow, a crowd of notabilities in literature and science, and hosts of personal friends, even to Doré's humblest servitors, filled nave and aisles. He had been a popular neighbour, and the idol of all who served him, in any capacity. Among the artists who attended the mass were Detaille, de Neuville, Gérome, Puvis de Chavannes, and others of lesser note; letters were represented by Taine, Claretie, de Goncourt, Emmanuel Caro, Edmond About, Pierre Véron, Ernest Daudet, Ratisbonne, Eugène Plou, and Alexandre Dumas *fils*; science by the Baron Larrey, and many eminent medical men; and in the general company were Jules Ferry, Calmann-Lévy, young Théophile Gautier, Achille Comte, Saint-Germain, Jollivet, René Delorme, Nadar, the Baron de Rothschild, Colonel Lipmann, General Cambriels, Charles Ferry, Antonius Proust, and Froment-Meurice, Alfred and Louis Mame, the Baron Davilliers. There were many ladies among the mourners, including the Countess de Beaumont-Castries, the Countesses Marie and Hélène de Noé (Cham's daughters), and Madame Edmond About.

At Père la Chaise the wintry scene gave an inexpressible melancholy to the final rite. The hearse drew up by Pradier's tomb, and the remains of the most imaginative and industrious artist-sculptor of our epoch were borne past the grave of his distinguished fellow-countryman to his resting-place in the granite tomb he had lately erected for his mother. The two who had passed their entire lives under one roof, lie under one slab in their long sleep.

Alexandre Dumas was the first to advance to the edge of the open grave. He said, addressing the hushed crowd:—

"Gentlemen,—For some days past Death has been striking with redoubled strength. He has not, however, struck wildly, but has selected his victims with flagrant cruelty and perfidy. He must have the most valiant, the most robust, the most single-hearted, the youngest—for those were always young from whom much was expected. It would seem, as we look upon these successive sudden deaths, that the Supreme Power, to which so many names are now given, even to that of nothing (*le néant*), has conceived some strange design, and that it seeks to strike terror into the hearts of men, and to clear the ground to make way for something new. The most celebrated, the most beloved, the most necessary, or who appear so, dares not believe that he will see to-morrow. All that

THE FUNERAL.

lives trembles. At the present moment, he who builds up a project appears to be a madman who is calling down upon his head the anger of the mysterious and impassible Master, who disposes at His pleasure of human hopes.

"If there were a man who might consider himself justified in counting on the present, and even on the future, it was the prodigious artist whom we have just lost. Never did will, energy, grace, talent, life —that which appears to come from a God—show itself more radiant and confident in the human form. Who among us can forget the face of the young man with the broad forehead, the hair thrown back, the large limpid eyes, haughty and sweet, the cordial and tender voice, the hearty and catching laugh, the features delicate as those of a woman, which gave to him throughout his life, and even in death, the aspect of a handsome adolescent? The death of Doré alone could give us a new surprise in the midst of those which encompass us just now. These will pass away, but the labours of this *infatigable* will not.

"For those who, like ourselves, knew him when he was twenty—that is, when he had been already celebrated for ten years—Gustave Doré, with his slim figure, his active limbs, his pink and beardless face, full of high spirits and gaiety, his fine hand always armed with pencil, pen, brush, or crayon, had the air of the Angel of Work when he bounded, I was going to say when he flew, from the board where he composed thousands of drawings, to easel or ladder, where he formed his statues and groups. What rapidity, what originality in the conception, what inexhaustible and surprising imagination, what miraculous science in the order and the effect of his design! What grandiose, dramatic, confounding evolutions of the light, of darkness, of chaos, of the fantastic, of the invisible, of the dreams of this world and the next! What a world of gods and goddesses, of fairies and saints, of martyrs and apostles, of heroes, virgins, giants, spectres, archangels, of monstrous and celestial types, humorous and divine, took sudden shape, colour, movement, life, in that luminous brain, now shrouded for ever!

"But, also, what respectful intimacy, worthy of himself, with the great minds he interpreted and vivified with the point of his pencil, and which people who pretend to know everything would not know without him! Let us think, by way of consolation, of the enchantment an imagination like his must have felt when it entered into direct communication with Lafontaine, Milton, Chateaubriand, Balzac, Cervantes, Dante, Shakspeare, and the Bible.

THE FUNERAL.

Why should we be astonished at the wealth of his creative power and his faith when we see him, every day and at every hour, drinking at the eternal springs of the Beautiful, the Grand, and the True!

"Mark how the horizon of the illustrator was always widening, how his ideal took higher flights, how he aspired, and how he sought for the immensities, for the infinite, in material as in intellectual things. He was impelled even to multiply and enlarge the scenes of his labours, which never satisfied his creative fever. He added broad spaces, dense forests, lofty mountains. When he left his Paris or London studios, and people thought he was resting, he was traversing Switzerland, the Pyrenees, Scotland; he was descending precipices, wandering in solitudes, climbing to mountain summits; and from such magnificent repose he brought back his immense landscapes, now bathed in light, and now covered with gloom; with pine forests of sinister aspect, transparent lakes, sharp-edged rocks commanding the fathomless abyss; and with sapphire, opal, or golden skies, reddening the eternal snows of mountain ranges —while a grand eagle that, as the poet has it, travels a league by a movement of the wing, traverses the canvas and carries you with him.

"What a sum of work this mortal creator leaves

behind him. There will, in truth, not be too much calm and silence here at our feet to recover from so much labour. We have all heard, and, unfortunately, he heard it more than any other, that in this colossal work there was merely the indication of a powerful temperament, something like the conception and miscarriage of a vagabond genius, that had never known how to restrain nor correct itself.

"In France, and only in France, people passed with ironical smiles, or, worse still, with indifference before those great canvases, where the composition and the idea were always masterly.

"He suffered horribly because he was not understood. Who was wrong—he who suffered or he who did not understand? Both—the painter who craved the applause of the crowd, and the passer-by who refused it. Who among the contemporaries of a great artist can pronounce a final verdict on him? How many have left this world deceived by the plaudits of the mass, with the conviction that they had left an imperishable legacy behind them, the remembrance of which hardly survived a few years the recognition of work too easily understood by the crowd too ready to deceive! On the other hand, how many who have been misunderstood, who have despaired, who have even been maltreated, and have been long dead, do

THE FUNERAL.

we seek out here to make them enter into that glory that their contemporaries refused them.

"Our French Pantheon is paved with our repentances. Let us, then, not give our judgment hastily. Let us have patience. Leave something for posterity to say; and, above all, let us be respectful towards those who, like Doré, having lived but fifty years, have given forty of them, the noblest example which can be tendered to men, that of unceasing labour and passionate earnestness, in the pursuit of an ideal.

"It is not admiration only, it is not only friendship, which makes me speak at the grave of the great artist. With the enthusiasm and generosity which formed the basis of his nature, Doré, when others still hesitated, offered spontaneously and modestly, as a mark of his admiration for the father and of friendship for the son, the statue of the author of *Henri III.*, of *Ville de Belle-Isle*, of the *Trois Mousquetaires*, and of the *Impressions de Voyage*.

"He would accept nothing. He gave to this work all his time, all his talent; and it may be that he gave his life to it. Who knows whether this monument, which occupied him from morning till evening, and sometimes at night, which he executed in six months, did not quicken the disease—which was that of ardent and passionate workers—of which he died?

"For six months he lived face to face with that other great creator, whom he resembled in so many ways, by his fecundity, his invention, his variety, his power, his unselfishness, his kindness. This heart, which was to break suddenly on the completion of this work, throbbed filially in unison with mine for the consecration of the glory which is most sacred to me. The author and the artist were made to understand one another so thoroughly. Thus the whole soul of the artist passed into and shines in the image of the writer and the poetic figures with which he has surrounded him. They are thus before the world, and for ever united in the memory of men; for the statues of poets are not, happily, among those which are thrown down. Here the sculptor defies indifference and injustice, forcing the crowd at last to contemplate his work, and cast violently by death into that terrestrial immortality he has given to another. Here Doré and I become of the same family by the same love. It is as one of his brothers that I bring hither to his dear memory the homage of my sincere admiration and of my pious but useless gratitude, which I cannot, unfortunately, like him, cast in bronze."

Alexandre Dumas drew back, and an old friend stepped to the edge of the grave. It was M. Paul

THE FUNERAL.

Dalloz, of the *Moniteur Universel* and the *Monde Illustré*, whose trembling lips now bore witness to the personal character of Gustave Doré. Passing from his incomparable qualities as an infinitely various imaginative artist, M. Dalloz described him as a visionary, mingled with a Benedictine.

"How shall I find words," he said, "to praise adequately this waking dreamer, whom the sunrise found at work, and who, after dusk, was to be seen by the light of his lamp? What literary form can personify him, who gave form to the invisible and the vague, and with a firm hand forced the ideal to become a reality for all. I am not equal to the task. I appeal to the masters of all times and countries whose thoughts he has revivified, whose dreams he has condensed, to whose words he has given action, and whose visions he has crystallized. I invoke them at this grave.

"All! Dante, Cervantes, Rabelais, Ariosto, Chateaubriand, Balzac, La Fontaine, Perrault, Tennyson, Coleridge, all, not excepting Shakspeare, whom he carried in his powerful brain for many years, and whom he reserved to crown his work; nor our great Dumas, whose statue awaits in his studio the honours of a public site. All are here. Each bears a palm, and lays it upon the bier of him who was never contented with himself, but who contented them all. All thank their posthumous colleague. Fairies, priestesses of dreams, accompany this radiant areopagus. And while I seem to hear in these cypress alleys the irresistible footsteps of the Wandering Jew, sad as his lamentations, who approaches from the farthest corner of the world to salute the illustrator of his symbolical legend, I see a luminous hand trace the sign of the cross—which shines white on the black ground of this yawning grave. It is Christ as Doré made him appear to us in his *Bible*—the creation of his soul rather than of his genius. My voice can only trouble this concert. In the midst of this praise I can only raise the voice of friendship. To the man whom I have loved, and whom I shall love beyond this life, I address not a farewell, for my faith gives me hope, but an *au revoir* which is too deeply graven in my heart to be translated by my lips."

The light was failing in the winter sky when these words were spoken, and the crowd of friends began to withdraw slowly through the dark groves of Père la Chaise, leaving Gustave Doré to his last sleep by the side of the mother he had loved dutifully all the days of his life, and at whose grave it had been his pious custom to stand at the close of every week after

THE FUNERAL.

her death, until he was carried thither for his eternal sleep.

And in that grave sleep also, and for ever, the conceptions of his ripening intellect. What he did was great, what he would have done was greater still. Progress in all departments of his art was his conspicuous characteristic; and his restless brain continually urged him to produce better and still better work. He had projected labours beyond the capacity of one life to execute. During the later years of his life Doré's mind was deeply impressed with the scenery of Scotland. The bleakness, the grandeur, the atmosphere of the Highlands took possession of his imagination. They appealed with irresistible force to him; for they presented in infinite grand varieties the effects he loved. The misty valleys with rare sunlight piercing through them, the cloud-capped hills, the broad sweeps of brown bog and of rough-edged heath, the picturesque bridges thrown pell-mell across trout-streams, the ancient castles, grey with age and romantic in story, as well as in their broken outlines and solitary sites—these set him off into new dreams. He filled book after book with pictorial notes, and he realized effects of colour and light and shade with broad sweeps of water-colour—astonishing in their truth and audacity.

When he came from the North we discussed his experiences, and our conversation wandered naturally to Sir Walter Scott. I proposed to him that we should give two or three autumns to the lands of

Scott; and that we should publish the result of our holidays under the title of

THE FOOTSTEPS OF SIR WALTER.

The idea delighted him. It is true that a complete tour in the wake of Sir Walter would lead the

THE FUNERAL.

wanderer, as Sir James F. Hunnewell has pointed out,* to nearly all the shrines of Scotland, through much of England, a part of Wales, the Isle of Man, France, Spain, Belgium, the Valley of the Upper Rhine, Switzerland, and even the far East. But our design was not to go beyond the native heath of our hero—we were to follow him from the Edinburgh wynd where he was born to Lasswade, through the Midland Border of Scotland, to the scenes of the "Lay of the Last Minstrel," Newark Castle, and grand examples of the Border Hill, Branxholm in the pastoral dale of Teviot, Melrose Abbey, Norham Castle on the Tweed, and the Abbey of the Holy Island of Marmion. The description of the Abbess of St Hilda and her five fair nuns sailing along the coast

>Of mountainous Northumberland,

suggests many grand scenes that would have delighted such an imaginative and well-stored illustrator as Doré. As we read we see the pictures he would have drawn:

>In Saxon strength the Abbey frown'd,
>With massive arches broad and round,
> That rose alternate, row and row,
>On ponderous columns, short and low,
> Built ere the art was known,
>By pointed aisle, and shafted stalk,

* *The Lands of Scott*: Adam and Charles Black, 1871.

> The arcades of an alley'd walk
>   To emulate in stone.
> On the deep walls the heathen Dane
> Had poured his impious rage in vain;
> And needful was such strength to these,
> Exposed to the tempestuous seas,
> Scourged by the winds' eternal sway,
> Open to rovers fierce as they,
> Which could twelve hundred years withstand
> Winds, waves, and northern pirates' hand.

The fair nuns tossed upon the sea, the storm-beaten headlands, the ruined Abbey, the atmospheric effects of which he was master, the gloomy keep and the sun-smitten height, the splendid array of fighting-men, the figure of Lord Marmion,—how he would have revelled in all this, as in *Waverley, Rob Roy, The Fair Maid of Perth, The Lady of the Lake, The Bride of Lammermoor,* and *Kenilworth!*

But it was not to be. It must remain one of the many dreams of great things to be done, that Doré carried with him to the grave.

CHAPTER XXV.

THE CROWNING WORK.

HE had looked forward to this November morning, when his monument to Alexandre Dumas was to be uncovered, in a public place, to the gaze of his fellow-citizens, and was to stand thenceforth, the work of his hands freely given, as a tribute to the memory of the great romancist and as an offering to his countrymen. It was to be his answer to his hostile critics, who, as he wrote in 1877, when he was sending a group of sculpture to the Salon, were prepared to scourge Doré sculptor as they had scourged Doré painter.

When Municipal Councillor Villard initiated the movement for a public monument in honour of the author of *Monte Cristo* and *Trois Mousquetaires*, the Committee first applied to M. Dubois. But M. Dubois was engrossed by his Connétable for Chantilly. Not liking to lose the commission, however, he suggested that the work should be divided among several of his pupils. The idea was to erect an edifice in the style of the Scott monument in Edinburgh. Dumas was to be encompassed by sculptured embodiments of the principal characters in his works. Fortunately this suggestion of piecemeal work, or patchwork of various hands, wherein the unity of the idea would be lost, and the erection of which would require the supervision of a permanent committee while it was in progress, was put aside.

Something striking, original, something fresh and vigorous, was wanted. In their perplexity M. Villard and his colleagues turned to Gustave Doré.

"You have an imagination *du diable*," said one to the artist; "you ought to find us a plan, a design, a sketch at least."

"It's easy enough," Doré answered.

On the morrow he appeared with the sketch. It was at once accepted by acclamation as the solution of the difficulty. Dumas was seated in his arm-chair, thoughtful and smiling as he appeared in life. On the pedestal were two superb bas-reliefs. At the feet of the romancist, a group of his readers; behind a loyal mousquetaire, on duty, sword in hand, guarding his master. The effect was in all respects vivid and admirable. It fulfilled, in every particular, the vague conditions of the committee charged to do honour to the memory of the great and beloved Frenchman.

"Bravo!" the younger Dumas exclaimed when Doré carried the sketch to him one morning to consult him about it.

"It pleases you?" Doré asked modestly.

"It more than pleases me. It is a remarkable conception."

"Well, then, I have a favour to ask. It is that I shall execute, or realize it myself, and at my own cost. I have been charged with being a too prolific inventor, or originator. I want to pay my debt to the most extraordinary creative genius of this century."

Doré asked to be allowed to give time, models, material, all to his idea. He obtained permission to make this noble sacrifice to an illustrious contemporary. He came in time to relieve the committee from their embarrassment; for the public had not supported their appeal generously. The ardour with which, in 1882, he set to work, is known to all who were his familiar friends. He lived in his work. His day-dreams were about it. He spared neither pains nor means. He cast forth without counting the fruit of previous labour, that he might make this his crowning work, worthy of his subject and of himself.*

He calculated that in the spring of 1883 the statue would be unveiled on the square close to the Parc Monceau, where the elder Dumas had lived, and where the younger Dumas' hotel is situated. When he had sent the principal pieces of his design to be cast in bronze, he would say to his friends, with something of the old brightness:

"In a few days you will receive a word saying, on a certain day come and see it unveiled, I hope you will like it."

He felt that he had wrought something that would

---

* "Content, il l'était, lui, de cette dernière œuvre, ce travailleur infatigable à qui son énergie même, ses dons de nature, ses inventions rapides, étaient reprochés comme des défauts. Cette grande vertu, la santé dans le travail facile, et cette qualité rare, la fécondité, sont volontiers traitées de vices. Les paresseux et les impuissants—on ne saurait trop le redire—font généralement courir le bruit que la production chez un artiste est un malheur. . . . Producteur infatigable, dessinateur inventif, genial, pour dire le mot, peintre et sculpteur, capable de traduire par son crayon les rêves dorés de l'Ariosto, et les réalités noires des misères de Londres de sculpter un vase féerique comme celui qu'on vit à l'Exposition universelle, et de rendre des effets singuliers de couchers de soleil sur les monts d'Ecosse, aquarelliste, et architecte au besoin, Gustave Doré me fait penser à ces stupéfiants artistes de la Renaissance, qui étaient peintres tailleurs de pierres, constructeurs de dômes, poètes, et, s'il le fallait, soldats."—J. CLARETIE.

THE CROWNING WORK.

stand the verdict of generations; that he had made his visible footprint in the Paris he could not but love.

But before every piece was ready for casting Doré had taxed his strength to the utmost.

"When I went to the studio to see him," M. de Leuven, the president of the committee, related at the brief ceremony of inauguration, "rather to bid him spare himself than to urge him forward, he exclaimed: 'No, no; I'm in a hurry. I want to repair a flagrant injustice. Here, in this Paris of ours, where the names of celebrated authors have been given to main streets, to splendid arteries, they have thrust the illustrious name which is dear to all of us, in a wretched bye-street. I want to avenge such a baptism.'"

Another friend has described Doré as he found him on a May morning of 1882, perched upon scaffolding in his studio, modelling in clay the mouth and then the thumb of Dumas. He was surrounded with portraits of the romancist, painted at different stages of his life. These were aids to his memory, and to the elaboration of Dumas radiant in the freshness of his vigorous manhood. He was represented loosely attired, in an ample chair, light in his eye and a laugh on his lip—at work.

"I want," Doré said as he went on with his work, "to represent that which was beautiful in this giant, this lion—his kindness based upon his strength—the generosity which shone always in his genius. The attitude I have given him was familiar to his friends. He is accessible to all, ready to do a service. He has paused at his work to receive and, if necessary, to help a friend with gold from his purse or gold from his lips."

The conversation was interrupted by Jean, already stricken with his last illness, who ushered in a porter carrying a heavy load of books, which he deposited, and then fetched other loads, until a solid square *mètre* of literature was stacked upon the floor.

They were the complete works of Alexandre Dumas, sent as a present to the sculptor by his distinguished son. Presently the son himself dropped in, threw off his coat, bared his neck, and sat in the attitude in which he remembered his "prodigal father" best.

On Sunday, the 4th of November 1883, Gustave Doré's statue of Alexandre Dumas was unveiled on the Place Malesherbes, by the Avenue de Villiers, in the presence of M. Kaempfen, representing the Ministry of Fine Arts, of M. De Leuven, president of the Statue Committee, Camille Doucet, representing the Dramatic Author's Society, of M. Edmond About, president of the Society des Gens de Lettres, of M. Halanzier, representing the Society of Dramatic Artists and of Dumas the younger. An immense crowd surrounded the platform; but the proceedings were brief the Paris municipality having granted the stoppage of the tramways past the statue for only half an hour and within this limit of time five orators were to speak. MM. de Leuven and Camille Doucet spoke with fervour of the generosity as well as the genius of the sculptor, who had presented this " splendid resurrection " of a beloved Frenchman to his country. M. Edmond About, who read one of his brilliant written speeches, bristling with points but devoid of one generous thought for the creator of the statue before him, albeit Gustave Doré had been his chum at Charlemagne, characterised the subject of the statue in a few happy sentences:—

" This statue, which would have been of solid gold had all whom Dumas has instructed or fascinated contributed a centime each to it, is that of a great madman who in his deafening gaiety possessed more real wisdom than all of us put together. It represents an irregularity who refuted rules, a man of pleasure who could set an example to all men of labour, a lover of amorous, political, and military adventures who outshines alone more than three monasteries of Benedictines. It is the portrait of a prodigal who, after having wasted millions in every kind of generosity, left, without knowing it, a princely heritage. This smiling face is that of an egotist who devoted his whole life to his mother, his children, his friends, and his country; of a weak and easy-going father, who had the rare good fortune to see himself continued in one of the most illustrious and best of men ever applauded by Frenchmen. . . . His works will be read longer than his comedies and dramas will be acted. For a century and more these stories, whose plot never wearies, whose style is as limpid as spring water, and dialogue as sparkling as green wood in the fire, will be the delight of young people, the consolation of the sick, and the entertainment of the fireside. I have seen men of a certain age—myself, for instance—pass the whole night in the country reading the *Chevalier de Maison Rouge* or the *Mohicans de Paris*. I sometimes hear my children disputing with each other because the one has not yet finished the second volume of *Monte Cristo* when the other, who is awaiting his turn, has arrived at the end of the first."

The public were of warmer heart than this sparkling speaker of artfully-elaborated phrases. When the veil fell from the crowning work of Doré's life, they greeted it with resounding cheers. It made a striking effect. The figure of Dumas, in his loose attire in folds of happy lines, his pen in his hand, his radiant face and thatch of curly hair, struck the spectators with delight. The figure of an old friend was revealed to them. The reading group and the Mousquetaire d'Artaguan stood out in bold relief. It would have been a perfect success had not the architect meddled over-much with the sculptor. There was too much masonry, and it dwarfed the figures somewhat. Still, taken as it stands, it will remain a superb offering made, as his last work, by the generous and gifted spirit of Gustave Doré to the great romancist whom the French people will never cease to love and admire.

In bringing the inaugural ceremony to a close, M. Edmond About said:—

"Good-nature composed at least three-quarters of his boisterous, effervescing genius. Beneath the good writer, who will soon rank as a classic, thanks to the limpidity of his style, you find always the good man and good Frenchman. He loved his country above everything; he loved it in the present and in the past, without sacrificing aught to party spirit or falling into the deplorable prejudices of politics. Nobody ever spoke of Louis XIV. with greater respect, of Marie Antoinette with greater pity, of Bonaparte with greater admiration than this pronounced Republican. With both Michelet and Henri Martin, with the most ardent and the most austere, he was a popularizer of our history. He deserved the bitter favour of fate, which made him die at the end of the terrible year, severed him from France with Alsace-Lorraine, and wrapped him, like a conquered hero, in the national banner of mourning. His literary glory is above all a patriotic glory, and we therefore see his statue, the first obtained in France by a simple novelist, muster round it the *élite* of all parties. This Freethinker, who was, however, a staunch believer in a hereafter, religiously respected the faith of others. This epicure, this jovial companion, diffused nothing but good principles and preached nothing but sound morality. We therefore see adherents of all confessions, philosophers of all schools, unanimously absolve the venial deviations of his life and pen. This impetuous, powerful writer, as irresistible as a bursting torrent, never displayed hatred or vengeance. He was merciful and generous towards his worst enemies, and has therefore left nothing but friends. The field of the future is the patrimony of the good. Such is the moral of this ceremony."

M. About might have added, had he been in a

THE CROWNING WORK.

generous—nay, I had almost said in a just mood—that this was not only the first statue obtained in France by a simple novelist, but that it was the first offered, out of the savings of his labour, by a French artist to the French people.

The writer of this biography was the bearer of a message of congratulation from the Prince of Wales, on the unveiling of the Dumas statue, to Gustave Doré's brother and representative, Colonel Emile Doré. It was conveyed to him in the following letter:—

"Paris, November 4, 1883.

"Sir,

"In the name of the Prince of Wales and of the English Committee of the International Literary Association, I beg to congratulate you, the Parisians, and, indeed, the French people, on the unveiling of this noble work, offered by the illustrious artist, your brother (whose death cast a gloom over the opening days of the present year), to the brilliant, the kindly, the universal genius, who has already taken his place as one of the French classics. Kindred spirits will speak to posterity in this bronze of Alexandre Dumas, wrought by the master-hand of Gustave Doré. It has been my privilege to know both the author and the artist. They were both men whose creative power knew no bounds—they were both prodigious workers, and both had generous hearts, open hands, a welcome for the young and struggling, and that sweet leaven of the boy in the man, which is not the least attractive mark of the children of genius.

"Alexandre Dumas has long been a household presence in England, and the creations of Gustave Doré's hand are in English homes of every class—from Windsor Castle, where the Queen has placed one of his poetic landscapes, to the smallest and most secluded cottage of the poor. The English Committee of the International Literary Association, which I have the honour to represent, includes Tennyson, whom Doré illustrated with some of the daintiest outpourings of his apprehensive and responsive imagination. It includes also the Prince of Wales, Mr. Gladstone, and Mr. Froude. These personages and their colleagues offer, through the humble individual who addresses you, their hearty congratulations to Gustave Doré's family and to the French people on the completion of this splendid tribute offered by a French artist of world-wide fame as a contribution to the glory of an immortal French romancist and dramatic author.

"The Prince of Wales, who was a friend of Gustave Doré, as well as a hearty admirer of his genius, has commanded me to offer on his behalf to the living members of the Doré family 'The expression of the interest with which His Royal Highness has heard of the approaching ceremony of the unveiling of a statue (the production of their illustrious relative) of M. Alexandre Dumas.'

"I am to say that 'His Royal Highness is led to take a greater interest in the work from the fact that it is the last one which was executed by an artist for whom he had so high an admiration, both on account of his distinguished professional talents, and for the numerous virtues which he displayed in private life.'

"I beg to remain,

"Faithfully yours,

"BLANCHARD JERROLD.

"Chairman of the Executive Committee.

"To Colonel Emile Doré."

On the day of the ceremony the family of Alexandre Dumas the younger placed a wreath on Doré's grave in Père la Chaise. It was his protest against the neglect of the artist's name by the organisers of the fête. At the same time, the ladies of the Committee of the Orphelinat des Arts, to which Doré had bequeathed 45,000 francs, gave a crown of immortelles inscribed with his name. It was well done. I had visited his grave on the previous Jour des Morts, expecting to find it covered with flowers. Only one or two very modest wreaths had been laid upon it, and these by the pious hands of his old servants.

APPENDIX I.

ORIGINAL OUTLINE OF "LONDON; A PILGRIMAGE," by BLANCHARD JERROLD, Illustrated by GUSTAVE DORÉ.

CHAPITRE I.
Resumé du plan de l'œuvre.

CHAPITRE II.
Arrivée à Londres par la Tamise.

CHAPITRE III.
Le Commerce de Londres, statistique, etc.

CHAPITRE IV.
L'Arrivée au Travail.—Le matin; Chemins de fer; omnibus; cabs; les banquiers, agents de change, courriers, commissionnairs; decrotteurs; marché de Billingsgate—de Covent Garden.

CHAPITRES V., VI.
Une Journée de Travail dans la Cité de Londres.—Les marchés; le Lloyds; la Bourse; le Stock Exchange; Bourse des Blés, du Charbon, etc.; la cour du Lord Mayor; Guildhall; Jerusalem Coffee-House (rendezvous des capitaines de long cours); la Banque; la scene à la clôture de la Grande Poste, etc. Restaurants. La départ de toute la cité pour la Banlieue.

CHAPITRES VII., VIII.
Le Commerce du West End.— Grands magasins; le Burlington Arcade; la Société co-operative de l'Aristocratie anglaise dans le

Haymarket; les magasins et equipages de Regent Street; les brevettes fashionables.

CHAPITRES IX., X., XI. XII.

Les Hommes d'Etat.—Chambre du Parlement; le Barreau, Westminster Hall; les Clergé, Westminster Abbey; le "Service for the People"; la Presse (Printing House Square, Bureaux du *Times*); la Clôture du Parlement.

CHAPITRES XIII., XIV., XV., XVI., XVII., XVIII., XIX., XX.

Les Travailleurs de Londres; et les pauvres.

CHAPITRES XXI., XXII., XXIII., XXIV., XXV., XXVI., XXVII., XXVIII., XXIX., XXX.

La Saison à Londres; les amusements; les courses; les amusements des diverses classes de la société.

Le Dimanche à Londres.

CHAPITRES XXXI. à XL.

Comment vivent, et sont secouries ceux qui ne peuvent pas travailler. Les Charités de Londres: les Soup-kitchens, Refuges, Orphelinats, etc.

Ceux qui ne veulent pas travailler. Les mendicants, voleurs: leurs garnis, thieves' kitchens, etc.

CHAPITRES XLI., XLII., XLIII.

Voyage autour de Londres: la Banlieue, Highgate; Hampstead, etc.; et la fin *Richmond*.

APPENDIX II.

LIST OF OIL PAINTINGS, WATER-COLOUR DRAWINGS, PEN AND INK DRAWINGS, ETCHINGS, AND SCULPTURE EXECUTED BY GUSTAVE DORÉ.

Oil Painting of an Episode of a Shipwreck at Boulogne-sur-Mer. Presented to the Humane Society of that town. 1849.
Familles de Saltimbanques. (Salon, 1853.)
L'Enfant Rose et l'Enfant Chétif. (Salon, 1853.)
Alsatian Women. (Salon, 1854.)
The Death of Rizzio. Height 8 ft. 6 in.; width 10 ft. 6 in. 1855.
The Battle of the Alma. (Salon, '855.)
La Prairie. 1855.
Sunset—Evening. 1855.
The Battle of Inkermann. (Salon, 1857.) *Received " Honourable Mention."*
Dante and Virgil meeting Ugolino in the Frozen Circle. (Salon, 1861.)
The Via Mala. 1862.
The Gitana. 1864.
Jephthah's Daughter. 1865.
Vivien and Merlin: from the "Idylls of the King." 1865.
The Neophyte. Height 8 ft.; width 10 ft. 3 in. Painted 1866-7.
Paolo and Francesca da Rimini. Height 8 ft. 10 in.; width 6 ft. 4 in. 1866.
Evening in the Alps. Height 4 ft. 2 in.; width 6 ft. 4 in. 1866.

The Titans. 1867.

Christ Leaving the Prætorium. Height 20 ft.; width 30 ft. Begun 1867, finished 1872.

La Prairie. Height 4 ft. 2 in.; width 10 ft. 1867.

The Triumph of Christianity over Paganism. Height 9 ft. 10 in.; width 6 ft. 10 in. 1868.

Andromeda. Height 8 ft. 6 in.; width 5 ft. 6 in. 1868.

Famille des Saltimbanques. (Salon, 1868.)

The Massacre of the Innocents. Height 12 ft.; width 17 ft. Painted 1869-72.

Portrait of Rossini after Death. 1869.

Titania. 1869.

The Flight into Egypt. (Purchased by Lord Borthwick.) 1870-71.

PATRIOTIC DRAWINGS.—La Marseillaise, Le Chant du Départ, L'Aigle Noir, L'Alsace, L'Enigme, La Patrie en Danger, Le Rhin Allemand. 1870-71.

Sister of Charity bearing a Wounded Boy. Painted during the Siege. 1871. In the possession of F. Graham, Esq.

Christian Martyrs—Reign of Diocletian. Height 4 ft. 10 in.; width 7 ft. 6 in. (Salon, 1874.)

The Victor Angels (Milton). 1871.

The Night of the Crucifixion (Les Ténèbres). Height 4 ft. 3 in.; width 6 ft. 4 in. Painted 1872-3. (Salon, 1873.)

Alpine Forest Scene. In the possession of Blanchard Jerrold. 1872.

The Dream of Pilate's Wife. Height 6 ft. 4 in.; width 9 ft. 7 in. 1873.

Mont Blanc from the Brevent. Height 4 ft. 2 in.; width 6 ft. 4 in. 1873.

Torrent, near the Grimsel. Height 4 ft. 3 in.; width 6 ft. 4 in. 1873.

Titania ("Midsummer Night's Dream"). In the possession of James Duncan, Esq., Benmore, Kilmuir. 1873.

Loch Carron, with Deer. (Salon, 1880.) Purchased by General Whittier, Boston, U.S.A.

Torrent in the Engadine. 1873. Also purchased by General Whittier.

French soldier taking Leave of his Child. 1873. Purchased by John Arnott, Esq., of New York.

APPENDIX II.

Knitters of Alsace. } 1873. Purchased by Hilton Phillipson,
Elaine (Tennyson). }   Esq., Newcastle-on-Tyne.

Soldiers of the Cross. Height 3 ft. 9 in.; width 6 ft. 2 in. 1875.

The House of Caiaphas. Height 3 ft. 6 in.; width 5 ft. 9 in. 1875.

Dante et Virgile visitant la Septième Enciente. (Salon, 1875.)

Spanish Beggars, Arrival of the Diligence. 1875. Purchased by John Moffatt, Esq., of Ardrossan, N.B.

Alsace. 1875. Purchased by the Baroness Burdett-Coutts.

The Flower Sellers. 1875. Purchased by H. Thompson, Esq., of Liverpool, for presentation to the Walters Gallery.

Christ's Entry into Jerusalem. Height 20 ft.; width 30 ft. Finished in 1876.

Battle of Ascalon. Height 4 ft. 2 in.; width 6 ft. 4 in. 1875.

Snow Scene. Height 4 ft. 2 in.; width 6 ft. 4 in. 1875.

Le Psalterion (Spanish Page playing Guitar). 1875. Purchased by Her Majesty the Queen.

The Infant Moses in the Bulrushes. 1867. Purchased by T. A. Blencowe, Esq., Marston House, Banbury.

High Lake in the Alps. 1876. Purchased by Robert Tennant, Esq., M.P.

L'Ange et Tobie. 1876. Bought by the French Government for the Luxembourg Gallery.

Ecce Homo! Height 20 ft.; width 13 ft. 6 in. 1877.

La Parque et L'Amour (Sculpture). (Salon, 1877.)

Souvenir of Loch Leven. Height 3 ft. 8 in.; width 6 ft. 5 in. 1878.

Scotch Landscape. Height 3 ft. 7 in.; width 6 ft. 3 in. 1878.

Remembrance of Aberdeenshire. Height 3 ft. 11 in.; width 6 ft. 6 in. 1878.

Genius killed by Fame. A Group of Sculpture. Exhibited in Paris Salon of 1878.

La Vigne. A Vase of Colossal Proportions. Exhibited at the Universal Exhibition. 1878.

The Ascension. Height 20 ft.; width 13 ft. 6 in. 1879.

The Death of Orpheus. (Salon, 1879.)

Maternal Love. A Group of Sculpture. Exhibited at the Salon, 1879.

Falls of the Garry, Perthshire. Height 3 ft,; width 5 ft. 4 in. 1880.

LIFE OF GUSTAVE DORÉ.

Loch Carron. (Salon, 1880.) In the possession of General Whittier, Boston, U.S.A.

La Madone. Group of Sculpture, (Salon, 1880.)

Head of Christ (mocked by the Jews). Pen and Ink Drawing. Height 25 in.; width 19 in. 1881.

Christianity. A Group of Sculpture. 1881.

L'Enlèvement de Ganymède. A Group of Sculpture. 1881.

La Danse (Statue). For the Theatre at Monte Carlo.

The Vale of Tears. Height 14 ft.; width 21 ft. 1882.

Day Dream. Height 11 ft.; width 6 ft. 8 in. 1882.

Nymphe dénichant des Faunes. A Group of Sculpture. 1882.

Statue of Alexandre Dumas. Erected on the Place Monceau, and unveiled on the 4th of November, 1883.

The following appeared in the course of one year:—

1. Les Vésuviennes et autres folies	14	dessins.
2. Les alarmés et les alarmistes	5	,,
3. Orateurs des Clubs	10	,,
4. Encore les Clubs	7	,,
5. Le communiste et tableau	13	,,
6. Les aristocrates sans le savoir	12	,,
7. Les vacances approchent	7	,,
8. L'homeo-pathos	2	,,
9. La distribution des prix	9	,,
10. Les plaisirs des vacances	7	,,
11. Laison des vacances	7	,,
12. La rentrée des vacances	7	,,
13. Autres temps mêmes bêtises	9	,,
14. Les collégiens	12	,,
15. La vie dans une petite ville de province	13	,,
16. La vie en province	33	,,
17. Internes et externes	7	,,
18. Promenade au Tuileries	4	,,
19. Les Anglais à Paris	4	,,
20. Encore les collégiens	15	,,
21. Promenades dans Paris	4	,,
22. Grotesques	28	,,
23. Une soirée au marais	1	,,
24. La vie à la campagne	7	,,

APPENDIX II.

25. Une fête au village	1	dessin.
26. Scènes maritimes	1	,,
27. Un bal champêtre dans la banlieue de Paris	1	,,
28. Les Champs Elysées le dimanche	1	,,
29. Une salle de bal au village	1	,,
30. Les chevaux de louage aux environs de Paris le dimanche	1	,,
31. École de village	1	,,
32. L'homme aux cent mille écus	21	,,
33. Dessin de circonstance	1	,,
Total	266	dessins.

LIST OF GUSTAVE DORÉ'S ILLUSTRATED WORKS.

1848.

Les Travaux d'Hercule. Par G. Doré. Paris, chez Aubert et Cie., Place de la Bourse, 29.

Began to contribute a weekly page of illustrations to the *Journal pour Rire*.

1849.

Désagréments d'un voyage d'agrément. Par G. Doré. Arnaud de Vresse, N.D.

Trois artistes incompris, méconnus, et mécontents; leur voyage en province et ailleurs, leur faim dévorante, et leur déplorable fin. Par G. Doré. Paris: Arnaud de Vresse, N.D.

1849-53.

Contributed Pen and Ink Drawings to the Salon, viz., Les Plus Sauvages, Le Lendemain de l'Orage, La Prairie, Les Deux Héros, Le Soir, etc.

1854.

Histoire Dramatique, Pittoresque, et Caricaturale de la Sainte Russie. Commentée et illustrée de 500 magnifiques gravures par Gustave Doré. Paris: J. Bry, ainé, 1854.

Œuvres de François Rabelais, et précédées d'une notice historique sur la vie et les ouvrages de Rabelais, augmentée de nouveaux documents. Par P. L. Jacob, bibliophile, etc.; accompagnée de notes succinctes et d'un glossaire par Louis Barré, ancien professeur de philosophie. Illustrations par Gustave Doré. J. Bry, ainé, Libraire-éditeur, 27 Rue Guénégand, 1854.

1855.

Voyage aux Pyrénées. 1 vol. in 16°; avec 350 dessins de Gustave Doré. MM. Hachette et Cie., 1855.

The second edition appeared in 1857, and the eighth in 1880.

1856.

Founded, with M. Philippon, le Musée Anglo-Français, illustrated with a series of Crimean battle-pieces by Gustave Doré.

Fierabras d'Alexandrie, légende nationale, traduite par Mary Lafou. Paris: Librairie Nouvelle, 1856. In 8°.

Histoire du Chevalier Jaufre et de la belle Brunissende, légende nationale, traduite par Mary Lafou. Illustrations de Gustave Doré. Paris: Librairie Nouvelle, 1855, in 8°. Published in English under the title of Sir Geoffrey the Knight, a tale of Chivalry. London: Nelson & Sons, 1869, 8vo.

The same work reappeared, under the title of *Le Chevalier Noir*, in 1876.

La Légende du Juif Errant. Compositions et Dessins par Gustave Doré, gravés sur bois par F. Rouget, O. Jahrer, et J. Gauchard. Imprimés par J. Best. Poème avec prologue et épilogue par Paul Dupont. Préface et Notice bibliographique par Paul Lacroix (Bibliophile Jacob), avec Ballade de Béranger mise en musique par Ernest Doré. Paris: Michel Lévy Frères, Libraires-éditeurs, Rue Vivienne, 2 bis. Paris, 1856.

1857.

Voyage aux Pyrénées, par H. Taine. Illustré par Gustave Doré. L. Hachette et Cie., Rue Pierre-Sarrazin, 14. Edition in 8°.

Eighth edition appeared in 1880.

1858.

Les Contes Drôlatiques, colligez ez Abbayes de Touraine et mis en lumière par le Sieur de Balzac, pour l'esbattement des Pantagruélistes et non Aultres. Cinquième édition. Illustrée de 425 dessins par Gustave Doré. Paris: Garnier Frères, Libraires, 6 Rue des Saints-Pères, et Palais Royal, 215.

APPENDIX II.

1859.

Œuvres de Rabelais, précédées d'une Notice sur la Vie, et les Ouvrages de Rabelais, par Pierre Dupont; nouvelle édition, revue sur les meilleurs textes et particulièrement sur les travaux de J. Le Duchat, de S. de l'Annaye, du Bibliophile Jacob, et de Louis Barré. Illustrée par Gustave Doré. Paris: L'Ecrivain et Toulon, Libraires, 10 Rue Git le Cœur, 1859.

1860.

L'Histoire des Environs de Paris. In 8°. Paris, 1860.

1861.

L'Enfer de Dante Alighieri. Avec les Dessins de Gustave Doré. Traduction Française de Pier Angelo Florentino, accompagnée du Texte Italien. Paris: L. Hachette et Cie., Rue Pierre-Sarrazin, 14.

Les Contes de Perrault. Dessins par Gustave Doré, préface par P. J. Stahl. J. Hetzel, éditeur. Paris: 18 Rue Jacob.

A new and cheaper edition appeared in 1866; and another, in the original form, in 1881.

Les Figures du Temps, avec une notice biographique. Paris, 1861.

Les Chansons d'Autrefois, par C. Vincent et E. Plouvier. Paris: Coulon Pineau, in 12°, 1861.

Le Roi des Montagnes, par Edmond About. Cinquième édition. Illustrée par Gustave Doré. Paris: Librairie de L. Hachette et Cie., Rue Pierre-Sarrazin, 14.

1862.

La Légende de Croque Mitaine, recueillie par Ernest L'Epine, et illustrée de 177 gravures sur bois par Gustave Doré. L. Hachette et Cie., Boulevard St. Germain, 77. 2ème édition, 1874.

L'Espagne, Mœurs et Paysages, par L. Godard. Tours, 1862, in 8°.

Les États-Nuis et la Mexique, par Malte-Brun. Paris, 1862, in 4°.

Contes et Légendes. Paris, 1862, in 8°.

1863.

L'Ingenieux Hidalgo Don Quichotte de la Manche, par Miguel de Cervantes Saavedra. Traduction de Louis Viardot, avec les dessins de Gustave Doré, gravés par H. Pisan. L. Hachette et Cie., Boulevard St. Germain, 77.

A second edition appeared in 1869-70.

Chasses au Lion et à la Panthère, par Gastineau. Paris, 1863, in 8°.

Atala, par le Vte. de Chateaubriand. Avec les dessins de Gustave Doré. Paris: L. Hachette et Cie., Boulevard St. Germain, 77.

Histoire du Capitaine Castagnette, par L'Epine. 1 vol. in 4°. Illustré de 43 vignettes, par Gustave Doré. L. Hachette et Cie.

A fourth edition appeared in 1879.

1864.

Histoire d'une Minute, par A. Marx. Paris: Denton, 1864, un vol. in 12°.

1865.

De Paris en Afrique, par Gastineau. Paris, 1865, un vol. in 12°.

Cressy et Poictiers, by J. G. Edgar, London, 1865, in 8°.

L'Épicurien, par Th. Moore. Traduction française. Paris, 1865, in 8°.

The Fairy Realm. London, folio, 1865.

1866.

La Sainte Bible, selon la Vulgate. Maine, Tours, 1866. London, 1866, folio.

Paradise Lost. Edited by R. Vaughan, D.D. London, 1866, folio.

La Capitaine Fracasse. Illustré par Gustave Doré. Paris: Charpentier, 1866.

1867.

Fables de la Fontaine. 2 volumes in folio, avec 80 grandes compositions et 250 têtes de page, par Gustave Doré. 1866-67. L. Hachette et Cie.

Second edition in 1868.

La France et la Prusse, par La Bédollière. Paris, in 8°, 1867.

Les Pays Bas: La Belgique. Paris, 1867, in 8°.

1868.

Il Purgatorio e il Paradiso. Texte Italien. 1 vol. in folio, et 60 compositions, par Gustave Doré. L. Hachette et Cie., Paris, 1868,

APPENDIX II.

Historical Cartoons, from the 1st Century to the 19th, by G. Doré. London: J. Camden Hotten.

1869.

Les Idylles du Roi. Traduction de l'Anglais. 1 vol. in folio, 36 dessins sur acier, par Gustave Doré. L. Hachette et Cie., Boulevard St. Germain, 77. 1869.

1872.

London; a Pilgrimage. By Blanchard Jerrold. Illustrated by Gustave Doré. London: Unwin, Grant & Co.

1874.

L'Espagne par le Baron Ch. Davillier. Illustrée de 309 gravures dessinées sur bois, par Gustave Doré. Paris: L. Hachette et Cie., 1874.

1875.

Londres, par Louis Enault. 1 vol. in 4°, avec 150 gravures par Gustave Doré, 1875-76. L. Hachette et Cie., Boulevard St. Germain, 77.

1876.

La Chanson du Vieux Marin. (An Ancient Mariner. By T. Hood.) Traduction française. 40 dessins par Gustave Doré, 1876-77. L. Hachette et Cie., Boulevard St. Germain, 77.

1877.

Histoire des Croisades, par Michaud, avec dessins par Gustave Doré. Furne et Jouvet, 1877.

1878.

Roland Furieux. 1 vol. in folio. 80 grandes compositions, 550 dessins divers, par Gustave Doré, 1878-79. Paris: L. Hachette et Cie., Boulevard St. Germain, 77.

OTHER BOOKS FROM CGR PUBLISHING AT CGRPUBLISHING.COM

1939 New York World's Fair: The World of Tomorrow in Photographs

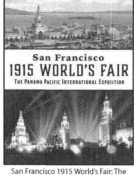
San Francisco 1915 World's Fair: The Panama-Pacific International Expo.

1904 St. Louis World's Fair: The Louisiana Purchase Exposition in Photographs

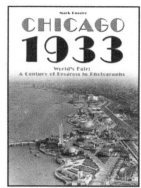
Chicago 1933 World's Fair: A Century of Progress in Photographs

19th Century New York: A Dramatic Collection of Images

The American Railway: The Trains, Railroads, and People Who Ran the Rails

The Aeroplane Speaks: Illustrated Historical Guide to Airplanes

The World's Fair of 1893 Ultra Massive Photographic Adventure Vol. 1

The World's Fair of 1893 Ultra Massive Photographic Adventure Vol. 2

The World's Fair of 1893 Ultra Massive Photographic Adventure Vol. 3

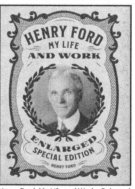
Henry Ford: My Life and Work - Enlarged Special Edition

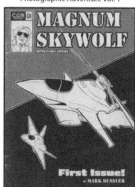
Magnum Skywolf #1

Ethel the Cyborg Ninja Book 1

The Complete Ford Model T Guide: Enlarged Illustrated Special Edition

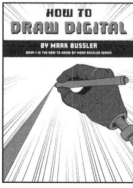
How To Draw Digital by Mark Bussler

Best of Gustave Doré Volume 1: Illustrations from History's Most Versatile...

OTHER BOOKS FROM CGR PUBLISHING AT CGRPUBLISHING.COM

Ultra Massive Video Game Console Guide Volume 1

Ultra Massive Video Game Console Guide Volume 2

Ultra Massive Video Game Console Guide Volume 3

Ultra Massive Sega Genesis Guide

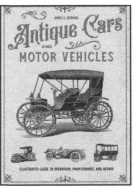
Antique Cars and Motor Vehicles: Illustrated Guide to Operation...

Chicago's White City Cookbook

The Clock Book: A Detailed Illustrated Collection of Classic Clocks

The Complete Book of Birds: Illustrated Enlarged Special Edition

1901 Buffalo World's Fair: The Pan-American Exposition in Photographs

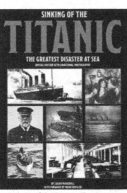
Sinking of the Titanic: The Greatest Disaster at Sea

Gustave Doré's London: A Pilgrimage: Retro Restored Special Edition

Milton's Paradise Lost: Gustave Doré Retro Restored Edition

The Art of World War 1

The Kaiser's Memoirs: Illustrated Enlarged Special Edition

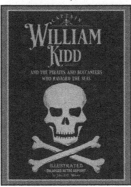
Captain William Kidd and the Pirates and Buccaneers Who Ravaged the Seas

The Complete Butterfly Book: Enlarged Illustrated Special Edition

- MAILING LIST -
JOIN FOR EXCLUSIVE OFFERS

www.CGRpublishing.com/subscribe

Made in the USA
Coppell, TX
29 September 2022